Appreciating Adults Learning

Appreciating Adults Learning:

From the Learners' Perspective

Edited by David Boud and
Virginia Griffin

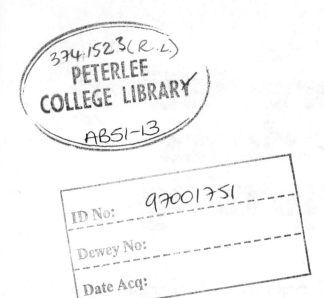

First published in Great Britain in 1987 by
Kogan Page Ltd, 120 Pentonville Road,
London N1 9JN
Reprinted 1994

British Library Cataloguing in Publication Data

Appreciating adults learning: from the
learner's perspective.
1. Learning, Psychology of
I. Boud, David II. Griffin, Virginia
153.1'5 BF318

ISBN 1-85091-275-0

Printed and bound in Great Britain
by Ipswich Book Co. Ltd., Ipswich, Suffolk

Contents

Introduction

David Boud and Virginia Griffin

Writing an introduction is like preparing an agenda for a meeting with a class: telling the learners what the purpose of the session is, what you hope they will learn, what activities you have planned, why you have planned these particular activities, and anything else you think they need to know in order to make the best use of the time. Some people appreciate a well-explained agenda; others do not pay any attention to it at all. No one really understands fully what the agenda means until they have experienced the session. However, it is useful to keep it before the group so that people can refer to it again whenever they become confused or uncertain or the direction of the path they have travelled – thus with this chapter. Our aim is to address three questions to provide a brief overview of what is to follow. Firstly, what is this book about? Secondly, how did we come to put it together? Finally, what does it include? In discussing these we will describe our own perspective on the topic and whom we think will benefit from the book.

What is this book about?

We have not called this book *Appreciating Adult Learning*, but *Appreciating Adults Learning*. The addition of one letter changes the theme from a thing to be studied to a dynamic process that people experience. This book is about what learning is like for those engaging in it. It represents primarily the viewpoints of learners rather than those who teach them. It portrays the experience of learning from the perspective of learners and aims to provide an insight into their process of learning. The plural *adults* is also intended to imply that we are not trying to separate adults from other learners – as if adult learning is somehow fundamentally different from the learning of younger human beings. Simply, we have focused on the group that interests us – namely, adults. We decided on *appreciating* rather than understanding adults learning in our title in order to suggest the importance we place on valuing the experience of learners and the need to develop a sensitive awareness of their perspectives.

In thinking about adults learning, we emphasize three perspectives: our view as a learner, our view as someone assisting others to learn and our view as someone trying to make sense of our fellow human beings. No matter what our job in the world, we find ourselves from time to time in these roles of learner, teacher and researcher. Much work on adult learning has derived from the perspective of teachers or researchers: they enter the world of learners with their own concerns and investigate matters which they believe to be important. This sometimes leads to important findings, but often these do not communicate well to those of us who are learners as well as teachers. It is not simply a matter of the way in which this research is expressed; it is the way in which it is conceived. If we wish to benefit from research then at least some of it must adopt the learners' frame of reference: it must address the concerns which they think are important and respect their felt experience. If, as teachers of adults, we wish to understand our role better we also need to become sensitive to what learners are experiencing and, perhaps, more aware of our own assumptions about learners and learning. We have all been learners, but it is important to know if our experience is the same as that of others. If it is, we are in a good position to help others in their learning; if it is not we can become more effective through developing an appreciation of the variety of learning processes that other people go through.

We hope that this book will be of interest to teachers of adults, researchers and adult learners alike. Learners will probably find that others have had experiences much like their own, and often the chapters will help them find ideas which will be useful in thinking about experiences or in communicating their experiences to others. One student told us that she was very excited because she had just read Marge Denis' thesis (*see* Chapter 2) and, in doing so, identified herself as an intuitive learner. She thought this explained why she had had frustrations and felt misunderstood throughout all her schooling. She now had a concept, a vocabulary, to use in understanding herself better and communicating with others about her needs in learning situations.

Although this book has been written by those who have researched adults learning, it does not aim to present the outcomes of their research in a traditional research style. We have asked our contributors to present what they discovered about how adults saw themselves as learners: what mattered to them and how they saw their own processes of learning. Each chapter derives from a substantial research investigation, but one using an approach which enabled the researcher to enter into the everyday, natural world of learners and to see their learning from the inside. The studies were concerned with the quality of the experience of learning. Because attention was given to a close understanding of the people who were being studied each one is based on work with a fairly small number of people. This means that the researcher has to be careful not to extend generalizations to all learners. However, as John Weiser points out in his chapter, it is amazing how the researcher who studies a topic close to his concerns, using these methods, often comes up with a report that 'speaks' to all of us or seems to address some basic aspect of the human condition. Although some of the contributors describe learning in groups with which we may not be familiar or in settings other than our own, each one of them communicates something important to our understanding of our learning process.

This book does not attempt to explain how to do the kinds of qualitative research on which it is based, but the chapters by John Weiser (Chapter 8), Peter Reason and Judi Marshall (Chapter 9), Heather Maclean (Chapter 10) and Lynn Davie (Chapter 15) give some useful ways to think about undertaking this kind of work. Many forms of qualitative research are referred to by the contributors, and it would require a separate book entirely to discuss the variations and different positions taken by proponents of these approaches. A useful starting point for those interested is the sourcebook edited by Peter Reason and John Rowan (1981), *Human Inquiry*, and the specific references made by each contributor. In the context of academic learning there are commonalities with the kinds of research described in, for example, *The Experience of Learning* (1984).

Qualitative research is not easy; it has its own standards of rigour, and not everyone is capable of doing it. It requires not only research skills, but also personal skills. Like any research approach, it is suitable for exploring only some kinds of questions – the meaning people attribute to their experiences, how people perceive themselves and their worlds and how they communicate their understandings to others. These are the questions which this book addresses and the qualitative approach is the one which we believe appropriate for an appreciation of learners' perspectives on the experience of learning.

We readily acknowledge that the conversations with learners and the observations, which were the basis on which these studies were built, were filtered through the biases or frameworks the researchers brought to their work. But each tells us something about those biases and has brought enough of the flavour of the conversations to allow us to make our own judgements about the findings. You may wonder whether they 'speak to' any experience you have had or whether the learners you work with ever had a similar experience. Further judgements we can make may include: Is the phenomenon studied here important enough for me to pay attention to it in my life and work? Is the context of the learner taken into account enough? Are my context and that of my learners sufficiently different that I would reasonably expect different outcomes? Whatever the answers you give to these questions, we will have accomplished our purpose in this book if you are more alert to the possibilities of the beauty, mystery and complexity of learning with adults. The studies aim not to persuade or convince, but to stimulate consideration of the issues they raise and to promote thinking about adults learning wherever they may be found.

How did we come to put it together?

In order to explain our agenda, we would like to explain our background – how the two of us from opposite sides of the globe came to be the editors of this book. Dave Boud had been a teacher of adults, a trainer of teachers of adults, as well as a researcher on teaching and learning in both the United Kingdom and Australia. He had long been dissatisfied with the paucity and incompleteness of research on adult learning. Although there was some research and development which he found useful in working with adult learners (for example, *see* Boud 1986), much of it was difficult to relate to as a teacher or learner, or even as a researcher. It often focused on questions which did not seem central to those involved in the education of adults. There was typically no sense of who the persons were as learners and what they aspired to, and little appreciation of the processes in which they were engaged. Rarely, if ever, were the learners' points of view taken into account – except for their response to the researcher's preset questions, based on a framework or 'theory' that the research was testing. Finding implications for how to teach or facilitate learning was difficult and arbitrary. The gap between researchers and practitioners was real, understandable and growing. With a few exceptions, research in adult education did not seem to have much impact on the field. Even researchers didn't find it very exciting to read the reports of their colleagues' work. Thoughtful practitioners had to turn to other sources for information that would inform their work.

In 1984, Dave was invited to teach two courses in Toronto at the Ontario Institute for Studies in Education, in the department of adult education. When he arrived, he found there — in addition to the work of Allen Tough (1979, 1982), which was world renowned — a rich reservoir of doctoral and masters' theses that had been completed since 1979. Most of this work had not been published, even though it was very exciting. Its impact was limited to those students and adult learners who had been directly involved.

He decided that something had to be done to get some of this work to a larger audience. He proposed the idea of co-editing a book to Virginia Griffin, who had supervised many of these theses, and who had long been working on understanding the processes of learning. Ginny had recognized that the literature in this field needed to be enriched by wider dissemination of the many valuable theses that had been produced, and had been searching for the best way to accomplish this. So, we agreed to co-edit this book to include some of the OISE work and that from elsewhere in the world. We invited people whose work we knew in Canada, the United Kingdom, Australia and the United States to contribute to a book on the learner's perspective on learning.

We did not predetermine a conceptual framework for the book; we told the prospective authors how we came to the idea and asked them what they wanted to write about. We developed a conceptual map for the work after we received their chapters and after they had been revised after feedback from other contributors.

Before we describe how the book is organized, there is one more thing which you should know. We asked our authors to include themselves in what they wrote — to tell us about their learning and how they reached their current understanding of learning, as well as how they see that others might benefit from their work. We did not want this book to be a set of dry, academic essays. We wanted readers to know the researchers, as well as the people they studied, as real, live, dynamic people engaged in learning. We take seriously this insight from the late Roby Kidd (1973):

> . . . Nothing is as transparent as the attitude of another to learning. And no one sets up such a block for others as he for whom learning seems so unimportant that he is not bothering with it himself, even though he claims it might be useful for others. (*p296*).

How is the book organized

There are many ways in which this book could have been structured, and some chapters could go in several places. In some ways putting them together is like analysing qualitative data. However, we have chosen four main groupings which we regard as important.

First are the chapters which deal with some of the aspects of learning that are overlooked in discussions of adult education. These include Lanie Melamed's discussion of play and playfulness (Chapter 1); Marge Denis and Ingrid Richter on intuition and intuitive learning and how to open oneself to it (Chapter 2); Lee Davies on the notion of human energy in learning (Chapter 3); and Gwyn Griffith on interdependence and how it is conceived, learned and lived (Chapter 4). Although these ideas are commonplace in our felt experience, very little has been written about them in the context of adult learning, and researchers have perhaps resisted grappling with what may seem to be very subjective phenomena. Yet despite their subjectivity, these ideas are sufficiently tangible and part of our common vocabulary of learning for them to be explored and considered as meaningful ways of describing experience.

In the second section are grouped the chapters which deal primarily with personal learning and growth: Stephen Brookfield discusses what he regards as significant personal learning (Chapter 5); Gill Robertson recounts how she struggled to learn how to help participants in a personal growth workshop uncover their hidden resistances to learning (Chapter 6); Ross Keane explores the growth that comes through facing doubts about oneself and working through a major learning project to resolve that doubt and arrive at a new level of personal integration (Chapter 7); and John Weiser, from his affiliation with psychosynthesis, examines two different kinds of growth of consciousness – the vertical and horizontal (Chapter 8). In Chapter 9 Peter Reason and Judi Marshall identify a phenomenon which we have long suspected occurs in research: researchers choosing a question that is of vital importance to themselves as the topic of research. They give examples to show how research can be a personal learning process, and how this can be helped to happen.

The third section is a little more diverse in content, but the common theme is that the settings for learning are in formal courses in which students have returned to study after often considerable experience in the workplace. It is likely that the ideas in these chapters are applicable to levels of education other than the postgraduate; intuitively this seems likely, but this has not been tested. Heather Maclean describes how she linked person-centred teaching to the training she provides for her students in qualitative research (Chapter 10). Jerry Apps reports results of a study of the perspectives of adults returning to college (Chapter 11). This is a companion piece to his major study *The Adult Learner on Campus* (1981) which took a teachers' perspective. Vivien Hodgson and Michael Reynolds describe some of the contradictions and conflicts between staff intentions and student experience in a course for managers (Chapter 12). They illustrate how complex social dynamics are if course tutors take seriously what students are experiencing as they learn in an interdependent design. Phil Candy's work is a masterful study of the literature to find assumptions that are commonly held about self-directed learning. He describes research which supports or refutes these often unexamined assumptions (Chapter 13). Marilyn Taylor proposes a model that represents the progression of learners in a course as they move as self-directed learners to interdependent learning

(Chapter 14). Finally, Lynn Davie reviews his evolving perspective on adult learning and assessment over the past 20 years (Chapter 15).

In the final section we examine some of the implications of work on adult learning from the two different perspectives of the editors: one with a focus on learning, the other focusing on how learning is *facilitated.* Ginny Griffin returns to some of the learning processes uncovered in the preceding chapters and adds others for completeness. She makes the point that learners being able to name in their own way the processes they are experiencing is an empowering skill (Chapter 16). To conclude the book Dave Boud looks at some of the questions which confront those who assist others in their learning. He draws implications from his own experience and notes issues from earlier chapters (Chapter 17).

In summary, we would like to restate the reasons why we think it is important to focus on the learners' perspective:

- Only learners can learn and whatever knowledge is generated about learning must, at some level, be accessible and have meaning for them.
- If learners read about other learners having experiences similar to their own, they will be able to understand themselves better and be able to learn more effectively. At least, they will be comforted to know they are not the only ones in the world who have their struggle.
- If we are to be effective teachers and facilitators of learning, it is helpful for us to see things from the point of view of the people we are helping. If, paraphrasing Ausubel (1978), the most important thing for teachers to do is to ascertain what the learner already knows and teach accordingly, it behoves us to find out not only what the learner knows, but what the world looks like from his or her perspective.

References

Apps, J W (1981). *The Adult Learner on Campus.* Chicago: Follett.

Ausubel, D P, Novak, J D and Hanesian, H (1978). *Educational Psychology: a Cognitive View.* New York: Holt, Rinehart and Winston.

Boud, D J (1986). Facilitating learning in continuing education: some important sources. *Studies in Higher Education.* 11, 3, 237-43.

Kidd, J R (1973). *How Adults Learn.* New York: Association Press.

Morton, F, Hounsell, D and Entwistle, N (eds) (1984) *The Experience of Learning.* Edinburgh: Scottish Academic Press.

Reason, P and Rowan, J (eds) (1981). *Human Inquiry: a Sourcebook of New Paradigm Research.* Chichester: John Wiley.

Tough, A (1979). *The Adult's Learning Projects: a Fresh Approach to Theory and Practice in Adult Learning.* (Second edition) Toronto: Ontario Institute for Studies in Education.

Tough, A (1982). *Intentional Changes.* Chicago: Follett.

Chapter 1

The Role of Play in Adult Learning

Lanie Melamed
Consultant in Educational Innovation, Montreal

Introduction

If play is a major vehicle for children's social and intellectual development (Christie and Johnsen, 1983), why is it so denigrated in traditional institutions of higher learning? Would it be sacrilegious to add some joy to what takes place in the classroom and what would that look like? Finding the connections between play and the way adults learn has engaged my energies in the past few years. Some of these learnings are outlined here.

Attempting to find words to express a concept as elusive as play is like asking an Eskimo to describe snow with one word. Nine and a half pages of definitions in the Oxford English Dictionary convinced me that the phenomenon would be impossible to pin down. Play is paradoxically frivolous and serious, spontaneous within prescribed limits, present-oriented and transcendant. Fundamentally radical in nature, it releases the individual from internal restrictions and demands freedom from conformity in intellectual as well as social settings. Although research suggests that a creative/playful lifestyle (one in which the individual remains open to growth, surprise, creativity and self-expression) results in improved mental health and happiness (Erikson, 1977; Vaillant, 1977), the subject has received little attention in adult educational and developmental contexts. The value-laden cloak of western puritanism has submerged most serious investigation of adult play, regarding it as inconsequential and wasteful, appropriate only to childhood and indolence.

Through play (the 'work' of children) the individual learns to concentrate, to exercise imagination, to solve problems, to try out new ideas and to develop a sense of control over his or her life. Discovery and intensity are combined with exhilaration and enjoyment, an integration which many adults envy. Are these attributes of playful learning forever to be denied to adults?

Twenty five years ago, it was assumed that childhood needs did not resurface once 'adulthood' was reached. Equipped with the rudiments of logical thinking and physical maturity, adults were supposed to remain developmentally quiescent for the remainder of their lives. Today, research in adult development is overturning notions of the 'ageing' adult and the 'developing' child. Instead, learning and development are viewed as a continuous process throughout life in a somewhat predictable manner (Kidd, 1973; Loevinger, 1970). Without a sharp demarcation between childhood and adulthood, it seems entirely possible that experiences which contribute to human growth and development will be more similar than disparate. If this is true, then play and adult learning need no longer remain antithetical.

The awareness that play facilitated my own learning occurred to me when my playful approach was noticed by fellow students. Upon reflection, I realized that the quality of my work improves when I can play at things, when I have time to try alternatives, when I can see, touch, laugh, and be physically involved in the learning process. My self-esteem soars when I am natural and spontaneous, following my own path and trusting that I will not be ill-regarded by others. In moments of play I am totally energized, involved and rarely bored. My richest playtimes are interacting with other people, experiencing affirmation and delight in myself and those around me. Basically a conscientious and intense person, I have come to view this playful 'gift' as enabling me to perform the serious work of life more effectively. Am I an abberation or do others share similar tendencies?

The research journey

The quest to understand the links between play and adult learning led me to nine women, mostly over the age of 40, white, and middle class, who considered themselves playful. Inspired by Maslow (1971), I decided to tap the wisdom of those who had successfully integrated play into the fullness of their lives. The women were professionally employed in jobs varying from artist to film-maker, therapist and adult educator. Semi-structured interviews were used to collect data, stimulated by guided fantasy and imagery in order to probe for deeper, less cliche-ridden meanings of play. The data were analysed according to principles of grounded theory and interpreted with the aid of hermeneutic and participatory research methods within an emancipatory or critical context. This eclectic approach borrows from the work of qualitative researchers who affirm play as a way of reaching understanding (Phillips, 1973; Schwartzman, 1978):

> Perhaps a playful approach to sociological inquiry would allow us to confront our own experience, to pay attention to what we have seen, heard, felt and wondered about, and to what we already know. By assuming a more playful stance we can perhaps free ourselves from the dogmatism of method. *(Phillips, p162)*

The opportunity to wonder (pose new questions), to allow for a truly emergent design (to colour outside the lines), and to move from *what is* to *what might be*, presented possibilities for both playfulness and rigour in the enquiry process.

Because the study emerged from a desire to understand my own experience, it seemed necessary to begin with women rather than a mixed gender population. So little is known about women's experience in a predominantly male-identified world, it seemed important to add to this growing body of knowledge. Recent findings support the relative invisibility of women's experience in academic research, as well as the distortion of that experience when measured against standards formulated from primarily male samples (Bernard, 1981; Gilligan, 1982).

My suspicions were well-founded. The interpretation of play which emerged differs notably from popular definitions. Clearly, play for the women I interviewed is an attitude or a way of being in the world rather than an activity. Unlike organized play which is instrumental and purposeful, the play they describe is intrinsically motivated and personally rewarding. It is more likely a 'happening' than something which is planned for, or takes place in our scant 'leisure' time. Fleeting and idiosyncratic, it comes and goes within the moment; what seems playful today may not be at all so tomorrow.

Part of an integrated lifestyle

The integration of play into the whole of one's psyche makes it difficult to separate from other intense emotions. Pain, seriousness and sadness are also intrinsic to our lives. Constantly I was reminded, 'But I am also a very serious person.' Corresponding to this sense of wholeness, play and learning are rooted in the same life source; *what makes play possible also makes learning possible.* One participant stated:

> There's something related to the stance of being a learner; one approaches one's experience, one's life work as a learner. It is the same as approaching it as a player.

Although the study did not intentionally search for 'non-playful' people, several turned up in the course of the investigation. Some were my own participants at a later point in time! Three interpretations seem to account for this occurrence. Firstly, some women felt constrained and fearful of loosening up or letting go. They said they needed to be 'taught' how to play. Growing up in authoritarian homes, frequently characterized by religious austerity, they had been taught that play was ungodly. Therapy may be one of the only ways to help unleash the natural joy and spontaneity of this group. Secondly, several women could not identify themselves as playful within the context of popular (male-defined) definitions. If being playful meant competing in sports or being a good joke-teller, then she was not playful! Reconstructing the meaning of play helped one woman to redefine herself on the playful/non-playful continuum. Thirdly, serious illness and depression appear to submerge one's ability to play. The fragility of a playful life stance was starkly illustrated when, six months later, I again met with the women I had interviewed. Three of them could no longer talk about or draw forth their previously avowed playfulness. One had suffered the loss of her husband, another was fighting cancer, and the third was deeply depressed. Because play comes from a feeling of well-being, both within the self and from the environment, it is as elusive as that very feeling.

Openness to learning

Most of the women were able to describe vividly not only how they learned, but the contributions of a playful stance to their learning. When a playful attitude is not present, learning is diminished and, for some, impossible. In describing the connection between play and the way they learned, there was nearly unanimous agreement that 'play opens me up to learning'. Variously stated, this metaphor depicted 'releasing the steel bands around my body of knowledge', 'opening doors', 'opening up possibilities', 'enabling me to see things in fresh new ways'. One woman described it thus:

> My image was that of a band around my body of knowledge, tightening, firming into a steel band so that my knowledge couldn't be dislodged, and therefore I couldn't be shaken, a defense . . . What play does for me is to loosen that band . . . Then it's possible for the blocks in the structure of my knowledge to be shifted around, or things taken out and replaced. When you replace something . . . then there's this shifting all through the system . . . I can see that loosening up the structure, making the structure of knowledge more fluid, is very much attached to letting go of the categories that define and therefore constrict things . . . [it] therefore opens me up to seeing things in different ways.

The risk and inherent vulnerability of a playful stance always seem preferable to what is predictable, routine or boring. The 'open' metaphors seem to describe a tripartite process: play opens me up, keeps me open and involved, and stretches the open boundaries themselves. The first of these dimensions is the easiest to comprehend.

Play opens me up

The preceding quotation suggests that there are resources within the psychological make-up of each of us that are not readily accessible, but which can be triggered by a playful attitude. In the literature of psychology and creativity these resources are variously called the unconscious, the pre-conscious, primitive cognition, or alternate realities. The concept of the functions of the 'right' brain suggests another image of under-used intellectual potential. According to Edwards (1979), the left hemispheric mode of thinking is hard-edged, sensible, forceful, and direct; the right mode is curvy, flexible, and 'more playful in its unexpected twists and turns'. The right hemisphere is in harmony, if not synonymous with playful learning – that which pertains to aesthetic understanding, to the unarticulated but powerful senses and passions.

One learner imagined her mind as a changing unfinished tapestry, rather than as a series of finite pieces:

> I think play is the lever. That's the image that I've come up with that makes the most sense to me. It's the great lever that allows all of my intelligence to interact. I use the word intelligence instead of selves or pieces because the process of becoming whole, to me, is not like a jigsaw puzzle, of putting my physical self, my emotional self, my spiritual, mental, intuitive (selves together) . . . It's a tapestry that is changing all the time, and because I accept that it's never going to be a static finished tapestry I'm more open for colours coming in, for different kinds of shapes – new information.

The mind as a multidimensional tapestry reflects current scientific assumptions about the nature of existence. The principles of linearity, stasis, and causation, once assumed to describe the universe, are being replaced by a vision which is circular, pulsating, stochastic (random) and interconnected (Bateson, 1972). Like other forces in the universe, human activity is also a playful blending of adventure, surprise, energy, circularity, trial and error, and interconnectedness. In order to know and understand, the many parts of the self must interact and bounce off each other randomly. Rather than ordered, sequential knowledge-building, most of 'follow our nose' in the quest to learn, filling and refilling shifting empty spaces within a lifetime. Despite the fact that most formal learning experiences emphasize deliberate and conscious processes, the vast bulk of learning takes place in the unconscious. Unfortunately, 'most adults learn to distrust this non-verbal, non-representational, and unconscious learning because it is difficult to verbalize and is often perceived as illogical and irrational' (Brundage and Mackeracher, 1980, pp.17, 18). A playful approach to learning helps us engage and connect with parts of ourselves which are usually dormant, inaccessible, or well-defended. In the process we shuffle, sort and arrange the various images and symbols which have been stored from life's experiences.

Play keeps me open and involved

On a pragmatic level, motivation is increased when we can play at learning. 'If it's not fun, it's not worth doing', says one learner. When behaviour is motivated by enjoyment, self-confidence, and contentment, feelings of solidarity with others are experienced (Csikszentmihalyi, 1975). As an antidote to boredom, play engages our energy, involvement and sense of curiosity. The pre-digested nature of learning, typical of so many learning environments, is dislodged by more personally relevant first-hand commitment.

Playing with ideas frequently results in better ideas. Surprise, adventure and discovery are key ingredients in expanding our potential and leading us to new thresholds of understanding. New things may be discovered and old ideas re-formed into new combinations. Similar to the process of creative thinking, we are unleashed from mediocre thinking and encouraged to think the unthinkable.

Play also contributes to the reduction of stress, frustration and the fear of failure. When an attitude of playfulness accompanies learning, the pressure to be 'correct' is removed; mistakes become vital parts of the process instead of tragedies. There is less defensiveness and more fun. In an experiment conducted by Bruner (in Samples, 1976), children were found to play at problems in equal proportion to the amount of time they spent in mental engagement or work. Beginnings were playful and explorative, with serious or rational thinking increased as they neared a solution. Unfortunately the teachers discounted (and, therefore, discouraged) the time spent in playful exploration, *eliminating this phase from their own research accounts.*

Play stretches the limits of our knowing

Part of staying open is the willingness to face the unknown. This involves risk as well as the potential for transcending our limits into the unknown. This stretching may occur as an accumulation of small steps, or as an explosive 'a-ha', toppling cherished belief systems. Both play and learning have the capacity to help us trigger new connections, surrender ourselves to an idea or an activity and lead us to the threshold of new understandings.

Because the social sciences have traditionally focused on the study of illness, alienation and social disintegration, there is little known about the healthy state of happiness and joy. Yet, it is the positive or participatory emotions which are self-transcending and which involve us in an expansion of consciousness (Assagioli, 1973; Koestler, 1964). Our emotions bring us to deeper insights and more profound ways of knowing; laughter and tears, awe and wonder, colour, sound and imagery are all vital parts of the learning experience. The ability to recognize and engage in the suspension of the ordinary, the taken-for-granted, and the conventional is what links play or the unserious to the deeper more radical questions of existence (Bologh, 1975).

In the process of accentuating the positive, we also need to consider the dangers. Closing down is also part of the open story, sensing how long to stay open and when to close down. With each of life's tasks we face anew the choice between opening up and retrenching, between regeneration and stagnation. Risks exist in both sets of choices. By releasing the controls to become more open we risk vulnerability and exposing our innermost selves. When we hold the reins too tightly, we may well cut ourselves off from many of life's joys. Because of the legacy of guilt surrounding pleasure and delight, playful people tend to be viewed as non-serious, carefree and irresponsible. Several of the women stated that they were distrusted by their peers and not taken very seriously on the job. Non-creative and 'predictable' workers seem better accommodated to an impersonal system than those who are not. Taking action toward *what could be* through spontaneous, uncontrolled and unpredictable playfulness is also threatening to those who would maintain the status quo.

The qualities of playful learning

The capacity for play belongs as much within the learning context as it does in other parts of our lives. Learning, in fact, may be one of the most joyful of all human experiences (Griffin, 1979). The type of learning I am referring to is an active, sometimes turbulent process rather than the passive absorption of immutable facts. Instead of learning that is instrumental or procedural or both, it is concerned with the creation of meaning in dialogue with others and through the process of self-reflection and personal transformation (Mezirow, 1985).

During the course of my study, five areas emerged as particularly compatible with a playful approach to living and learning. Although play is not an isolated phenomenon in these themes, its threads intertwine, enrich and humanize each of them. The areas are:

Relational – the capacity for cooperation and connectedness.
Experiential – validating and learning from experience.
Metaphoric – intuitive and right-brain thinking.
Integrative – valuing a holistic and organic connectedness to people and things.
Empowering – facilitating transformation in ourselves and the world(s) we inhabit.

Relational – the capacity for cooperation and connectedness

Both play and learning are enhanced by feeling connected to people and ideas rather than through distance and separation. According to the playful learners interviewed, interaction between learners, teachers and learners, and learners and the content to be learned, is basic to effective learning.

Learning is enhanced when situated in collaborative rather than competitive settings. When we play/learn with others a sense of community is created, fostering a special bond between members. When we give and take (play with) ideas, each person has a chance to articulate his or her personal meanings. This feeling of comfort makes it easier to try on new ideas and be willing to appear stupid while fumbling to understand. One woman expressed it this way:

> I learn best when I am relaxed and feeling good about myself. Play helps me to centre in. When I'm feeling playful I know I am feeling centred. That's when I am most open to learning.

The union of trust and playfulness often forms the basis for a group's cohesion and best work. Repeatedly, participants talked about competition and being judged by others as a major inhibitor to playful living and learning. Griffith (1982 and Chapter 4) finds a spirit of playfulness directly related to letting go of the need for control and the ability to express onself freely in mature interdependent relationships.

Unfortunately, the implications of relationship as a feature of cognitive development have not influenced the structure and content of formal learning environments. Climate-setting exercises, knowledge of small and large group process, values exercises, and person-centred learning are some of the ways to encourage individual comfort and group cohesion. Most important, there needs to be a change in the teacher's value orientation from competition to cooperation, from the fragmentation of ideas to interconnection and from hierarchical structures to collaborative ones.

Experiential – valuing and learning from experience

Experiential learning occurs on several levels: learning through direct experience, validating personal experience, situating ourselves within the experience of others, joining colleagues in a shared community of experience, and helping others develop insights into their own experience. Despite extensive research efforts supporting experience and action as a primary source of knowledge (Dewey, 1968; Kolb, 1984), learning from experience is still considered less rigorous and less credible than 'pure' thought in most colleges and universities. Kolb describes the learning cycle as beginning with experience, then moving through stages of reflective observation, abstract conceptualization, and finally active experimentation to begin a renewed cycle once again. Although learners may begin at any stage along the cycle, personal experience remains the starting point for most learners.

Continuous learning offers the possibility for fresh and deeper meanings to everyday activity, which in turn generates meaning and fulfilment to subsequent endeavours. Experiential learning invites the companionship of play and playfulness. It integrates not only energy, incentive and enthusiasm but also the gamut of emotions from pleasure to pain.

Experiential learning is one of the easier ways to incorporate play into the classroom and is widely used in informal educational settings. When students can begin with their own experiences, the questions they raise are more engaging and personally motivating. Popular education techniques based on the work of Freire (1972) and feminist pedagogy (Spender, 1981) both start from this premise. A variety of non-verbal hands-on techniques can be used to make exercises memorable such as drawings, photographs, films, song-writing, dramatic representations, music and dance (Arnold and Burke, 1983). It would be difficult to imagine dull classes when such methods are used to act as catalysts in learning.

Metaphoric – intuitive or right-brain thinking

Metaphoric thinking may be the closest we come to engaging in playful learning. We seem to learn best when we are allowed to follow hunches, play with ideas, draw on our emotions, value our insights, approach things from many different angles and treat learning as part of life's great adventure. Metaphoric or right-brain cognition is especially compatible with the sensory and emotional side of learning (Ornstein, 1972) and is frequently experienced as a sense of certainty which comes from a place deep inside the self. The women interviewed frequently reported understanding something which could not be translated into words. Engaging in a non-verbal exercise intended to represent her learning style, one participant described it this way:

> It was the most integrated sensation of understanding of how I learned, so precise that I could never have said in words, 'that's how I learn'. I really understood the power of learning without words . . . there was an articulation that happened at that level, in that instance. *Exquisite!* There is no other word for it. It's a wonderful balance between intensity, play, and seriousness . . .

This kind of knowing precedes proof and is precisely what the techniques of analysis and proof are designed to test (Bruner, 1966). Many great scientists admit that their 'a-ha's' came to them, not when they were at their desks, but during walks, in the bath, in dreams or when at play (Koestler, 1964).

Imagination, dreams and imagery are other important right-brain resources for learning. Through imagery we connect with memories of past and present happenings located in the complex tapestry of the mind. Inner, real or imagined experiences appear in thoughts, dreams and fantasies in fleeting moments as well as during intentioned day or night time hours. Archetypical symbols and personal images extend our attention from the concrete to an exploration of connections which would otherwise be unsuspected. In psychotherapy, healing, and learning, images are a credible source of personal information for growth and development (Williams, 1983).

A fluid sense of time and space enhances both play and learning, with images moving in and about, creating new connections and enabling tired ideas to be reconstructed in fresh new ways. Disorder and confusion as well as linearity and neatness contribute to playful creation; the former may even be a sign of vibrant health and a condition of the mind's fertility (Koestler, 1964).

Exercises such as brainstorming can be used to unfreeze tedious thinking and develop creative alternatives to individual or group problems. Playing with ideas, colouring outside the lines and creating bizarre scenarios within a context of postponed evaluation helps to move us away from left-brain or rational modes of thinking. The further out we go, the more likely we are to come up with unusual and creative solutions (Gordon, 1961).

Expanding the concept of the intellect to include the equally important functions of the right brain is one way for teachers to initiate playful learning. Conditions need to be constantly created which release the 'steel bands' constricting such a large part of human potential.

Integrative – valuing a holistic and organic relation to life

Integration and wholeness are essential underpinnings of the playful life/learning stance. Repeatedly, the learners stated that they saw things as 'both/and' rather than 'either/or'. Information about themselves and the world was constantly being connected and re-connected into regenerative frameworks. No contradiction exists between being playful and serious at the same time, the ideal mental condition according to Dewey (cited in Shibles, 1979). Instead of mechanistic sequences of cause and effect, human systems are interactive and mutually causal. For Bateson (1979), perspectives of reality can no longer be explained in dualistic Cartesian terms in which the world is viewed as measurable, predictable, and ultimately controllable. Conversely, mind and body, subject and object, are seen as complementary parts of a holistic process.

Freezing concepts into oppositional categories negates what in reality is a continuum and an essential unity. The tendency to overemphasize one end of a polarity at the expense of the other, results in an unnatural splitting of human potential or the creation of a situation where one end must win over another, or both. When play and work, feeling and intellect are viewed as oppositional, then the removal of pleasure and play from educational, business and technocratic institutions is a logical consequence.

Organic metaphors were used by most of the women interviewed. The need to live harmoniously within the cycles of nature, as contrasted with the exploitive, linear mentality of forward progress, seems to be integral to their worldview. In place of technological order which is controlling and mechanical, the patterns which seem to shape their lives are cyclical, ecological and relational. Flow, flexibility, the complex and the unresolved are preferred to precision, predictability, control and order.

Honouring the integrated (and interdisciplinary) mode of teaching requires incorporating dialectics or the concept of opposing tendencies in our work. The choice is not between poles, but an ecology of 'both/and'. Hopping back and forth between the whole and the parts can be both a playful and a rigorous way of reaching understanding.

Empowering – the possibility of transforming ourselves and the world(s) we inhabit

Both play and learning have the potential to empower and liberate. Both can be equalizers, enabling people to break out of constraining moulds toward greater freedom. Through learning we develop information and understanding which helps us live more coherently within ourselves and the larger world.

In play we are permitted, or rather take the right, to affirm ourselves, to wonder and to question, to extend boundaries and to say 'yes' to life. Combining the two makes it possible for the best in ourselves to be expressed.

Both play and learning are essentially empowering, radical (leading us to our roots), and may even be subversive. More fundamental than fun, play is what links instinct and imagination with politics and reconstruction (Cox, 1973), enabling us to move from *what is* to *what can be.* A radical refusal of the logic of the adult world is implied, a state in which we can be neither commanded nor controlled.

To empower learners we need to become actively engaged in the process of creating knowledge so that we as well as our students become actors upon the world instead of passive reactors. This means creating opportunities for collaboration instead of control, being willing to adventure beyond ordinary thinking and engaging in the liberating act of imagination and action toward social change.

Conclusion

My intention has not been to reify play or to pretend that it is a panacea which alone can combat the lack of excitement in most educational environments. Nor is it to negate the hard, painful and serious (left brain) parts of learning. Rather, it has been to resurrect the subject from scorn and to incorporate it within the viable parameters of adult learning theory.

The findings of this study strongly support the presence of play in andragogy (teaching adults) just as it is firmly situated in theories of pedagogy (teaching children). More experimentation with these ideas is required. The learners in this study did not articulate, nor did I probe, which phases of the learning cycle were most conducive to playful behaviour. I tried to monitor those times in my own research process. Instead of one large undertaking, the journey was conceived as several cycles within cycles. In each there was a place for adventure and discovery, particularly at 'beginnings' where I collected materials, shared ideas with people and bounced in and out of readings and conceptual analyses. A favourite time was collecting, sorting and cross-referencing ideas which were noted on colourful cards. Coming to understand writing as part of the process of 'meaning-making' increased the possibility for play even at this stage (Elbow, 1973). Distinctly unplayful were the periods of closing down, having to make final decisions about what could or could not be included, and saying good-bye to paths which would remain untrodden. The periods of loneliness experienced during the 'hard thinking' phases as well as the long periods of solitary work were also joyless.

Is play necessary or useful to all learners? I think it is. If the development of intelligence is a matter of having wonderful ideas (Duckworth, 1972) then the quality of playfulness so vital in the creative process is crucial. It is thrilling to learn to think and to begin to understand oneself in the context of a socially complex world. Ideas can be freeing, joyous experiences that give us a framework for action and participation. To tap that pleasure and to liberate ourselves from teaching and learning methods which are boring, mundane and joyless, is a goal worthy of us all.

References

Arnold, R and Burke, B (1983). *A Popular Education Handbook.* Toronto: OISE Press.

Assagioli, M (1973). *The Act of Will.* New York: Viking Press.

Bateson, G (1972). *Steps to an Ecology of Mind.* New York: Ballantine Books.

Bateson, G (1979). *Mind and Nature.* New York: Bantam Books.

Bernard J (1981). *The Female World.* New York: The Free Press.

Bologh, R W (1975). On fooling around: a phenomenological analysis of playfulness. Paper prepared for the 70th annual meeting of the American Sociological Association, 25-29 August.

Brundage, D and Mackeracher, D (1980). *Adult Learning Principles and their Application to Program Planning.* Toronto: OISE Press.

Bruner, J (1966). *On Knowing: Essays for the Left Hand.* New York: Atheneum.

Christie, J F and Johnsen, E P (1983) The role of play in social-intellectual development. *Review of Educational Research*, 53, 1, 93-115.

Cox, H (1973). *The Seduction of the Spirit: the Use and Misuse of People's Religion.* New York: Simon and Schuster.

Csikszentmihalyi, M (1975). *Beyond Boredom and Anxiety: the Experience of Play in Work and Games.* San Francisco: Jossey-Bass.

Dewey, J (1968). *Experience and Education.* The Kappa Delta Pi Lecture Series. (First published 1938.) New York: Collier-Macmillan.

Edwards, B (1979). *Drawing on the Right Side of the Brain.* Los Angeles, California: J P Tarcher.

Elbow, P (1973). *Writing Without Teachers.* London: Oxford University Press.

Erikson, E H (1977) *Toys and Reason.* New York: W W Norton.

Freire, P (1972). *Pedagogy of the Oppressed.* New York: Seabury Press.

Gilligan, C (1982). *In a Different Voice.* Cambridge, Massachusetts: Harvard University Press.

Gordon, W G (1961). *Synectics.* New York: Harper and Row.

Griffin, V (1979) Self-directed adult learners and learning. In: *Learning*, 2, Nos. 1 and 2. Toronto: Canadian Association of Adult Learning.

Griffith, G (1982). Images of interdependence: meaning and movement in learning/teaching. Unpublished doctoral dissertation. Department of Adult Education, Ontario Institute for Studies in Education.

Kidd, J R (1973). *How Adults Learn.* New York: Association Press.

Koestler, A (1964). *The Act of Creation.* New York: Macmillan.

Kolb, D A (1984). *Experiential Learning: Experience as the Source of Learning and Development.* Englewood Cliffs, New Jersey: Prentice-Hall.

Loevinger, J and Wessler, R (1970). *Measuring Ego Development 1.* San Francisco: Jossey-Bass.

Maslow, A H (1971). *The Farther Reaches of Human Nature.* New York: Viking Press.

Mezirow, J (1985). A critical theory of self-directed learning. In: S Brookfield (ed.) *Self-Directed Learning: From Theory to Practice.* San Francisco: Jossey-Bass, 17-30.

Ornstein, R E (1972). *The Psychology of Human Consciousness.* San Francisco: W H Freeman.

Phillips, D L (1973). *Abandoning Method: Studies in Methodology.* San Francisco: Jossey-Bass.

Samples, B (1976). *The Metaphoric Mind: a Celebration of Creative Consciousness.* Reading, Massachusetts: Addison-Wesley.

Schwartzman, H B (1978). *Transformations: the Anthropology of Children's Play.* New York and London: Plenum Press.

Shibles, W (1979). How to teach creativity through humor and metaphor: a philosopher looks at creativity. *Creative Child and Adult Quarterly.* 4, 4, 243-51.

Spender, D (1981). *Men's Studies Modified: the Impact of Feminism on the Academic Disciplines.* Oxford: Pergamon Press.

Vaillant, G E (1977) How the best and the brightest come of age. *Psychology Today.* 34-9.

Williams, M M (1983). Images: toward an understanding of the links between adult learning and image learning. Master of Arts thesis, Department of Adult Education, Ontario Institute for Studies in Education, University of Toronto.

Chapter 2

Learning about Intuitive Learning: Moose-Hunting Techniques

Margaret Denis and Ingrid Richter
Ontario Institute for Studies in Education

Introduction

> We think the way we hunt moose. Never in a straight line because then the moose knows where you are. You go around and around the moose, coming closer all the time until you finally close in on him.
>
> *Edward (Native hunting guide, 1969, Jasper, Alberta)*

Whenever I try to describe my views on intuitive learning, these words from my native friend come to mind. Such conversations and observations stemming from my work with native people in Canada over the years actually spawned my curiosity and subsequent exploration of paths for learning (and thinking) which are something other than linear. Through this exploration I have found that intuitive learning is best examined and described by using my friend's moose-hunting method, and, therefore, I hope both the content and the shape of this chapter will begin to illustrate some of what has been discovered about intuitive learning so far. In the next few pages, a more recent traveller and fellow intuitive learner, Ingrid Richter, and I will both describe (in conversation) some of the intuitive learning processes identified by my research. Some of these processes will be illustrated by examples from our experiences as intuitive learners, as well as through quotes from other sources.

What is intuitive learning?

> Like intuition, intuitive learning is best described by negation. Webster defines intuition as 'knowledge obtained without recourse to inference or reason'. Intuitive learning is that process of acquiring knowledge, skills, habits or actions without recourse to objectives, goals or consciously planned steps. As with intuition, so too with intuitive learning; we do not know how people perceive it to work in themselves. Intuitive learning, as a mode of learning, differs from intuition in that the former is a process extending more or less over time; intuition is a sudden insight, instantaneous in occurrence. *(Denis, 1979)*

Marge: It is a misnomer to categorize intuitive learning as a kind or variety of learning and to compare or contrast it with other kinds of learning such as rational or experiential learning (although it is linked with them). Instead, I prefer to describe it as a *modality* which operates like a single thread in a weaving. (As a matter of fact, I expressed my ideas on intuitive learning through a tapestry, which also became part of my thesis on intuitive learning.) As a thread by itself then, intuitive learning is not nearly as strong or as useful as it is when woven with other learning modalities. And yet to ignore intuitive learning as one of the threads of the weaving of learning is to miss an essential aspect of the cloth's potential beauty and function. Therefore, in my view, understanding the properties of intuitive learning as a unique thread will also enable us to understand how to weave and combine our learning modalities to greater durability, usefulness and overall effect.

Ingrid: For me, because intuitive learning is so diffuse and global, the best way of describing it is by way of metaphor: an intuitively-oriented learner is someone who walks a beach for no specific purpose except to go for a walk. During the walk, all the senses are open, receiving information, both concrete and intangible – the water conditions, the clouds, the sand, the walker's feelings, etc. Objects washed up by the waves come to attention, are picked up, examined, discarded or pocketed, depending upon prevailing conditions and individual preferences.

Where intuitive learners differ from other learners in walking this metaphorical beach is in the *processes* they use to choose, collect and organize the material they learn. This orderly, but unsequential approach to learning is described in your research in terms of a distinct set of processes. Each process has its own dynamics and influences on learning. Some, or all of them are going on (with greater or lesser awareness of them on the learner's part) throughout all learning activities. In your research you identified 18 processes, although you have written that these are not a definitive statement of all the possible dynamics of intuitive learning.

The processes

(1) Knowing with unwavering certitude that learning will occur.
(2) Trusting in one's own intuitions and in the intuitive process.
(3) Remaining open to the expected, but more especially to the unexpected.
(4) Being absolutely honest in action and in reflection.
(5) Delineating generic boundaries for the area of learning.
(6) Reflecting upon and drawing new insight from one's own experience.
(7) Developing a sense of multiple realities.
(8) Focusing attention on the ground rather than on the relevant figure in learning; attacking learning obliquely.
(9) Embarking on a pilgrimage of learning.
(10) Developing a sensitive awareness of the proper timing of processes and events.
(11) Suspending or minimizing deliberate, conscious rational processes.
(12) Being aware of and responding to energies outside oneself.
(13) Dialoguing with the materials.
(14) Allowing oneself to be led or drawn in a certain direction; surrendering to the intuitive.
(15) Being aware of and following one's feelings in the learning process.
(16) Being in touch with the influences and the dynamics of the unconscious.

(17) Appreciating meaning in synchronicity.
(18) Recognizing the gift of revelation in the learning process.

Although the heart of intuitive learning, namely, the insight or illumination, cannot be produced at will or consciously controlled, the dynamics of intuitive learning can be initiated by attending to the basic processes. These processes are not steps or even progressive stages, but are interacting dynamics which enable one to learn intuitively. *(Denis, 1979)*

Following the moose-hunter

Dialoguing with the materials (13)

Ingrid: Out of the list of 18 processes the one I have most difficulty interpreting is *dialoguing with the materials.* What do you mean?

Marge: An interchange takes place between the (intuitive) learner and the content, object or substance of the learning activity. For example, as I mentioned before, I wove a tapestry to illustrate my thesis on intuitive learning. In creating the tapestry I practised the processes listed, *dialoguing* with what was there: getting in touch with the colours, the texture of the wool and so on, letting what was there reach out to me, giving me direction about how to go on with the design, what colours to use next and so on. I was letting *it* tell *me* what it wanted to become.

Ingrid: Do you mean listening or perceiving on many levels simultaneously?

Marge: Yes, and more than that: *dialoguing* is really the right word for it – the materials themselves speak to you about how they are to be treated, or learned about.

Ingrid: It's the way sculptors say the form of the sculpture is already present in the marble, waiting to come out.

Marge: Right. If you miss the dialogue with the materials you are using in learning, then I think you've really missed one of the most important processes in intuitive learning.

Ingrid: It seems to me it's not just *dialogue* in the verbal sense then; it's perceiving, appreciating the materials with all your senses, including your feelings, your unconscious – almost becoming one with them.

Marge: In some ways it's like holding a tuning fork and being aware of its response when the vibrations from the materials hit it.

Ingrid: Feeling the *vibrations* as you say, is an ongoing thing, isn't it? You don't just hold up the tuning fork when you think you might need it – you have to be attuned to it all the time, and ready to respond.

Developing a sense of multiple realities (7) and appreciating meaning in synchronicity (17)

Marge: In fact, *dialoguing* links closely with the process of *synchronicity* in learning. When many things and events are happening simultaneously in time and space, we need to look more closely, and reflect upon them. Gradually, we begin to see relationships where we previously hadn't noticed them or initially thought there were none present.

Ingrid. It seems as though experiencing synchronicity in learning is like becoming a detective. When you are intently looking for clues to the case or subject, everyday events or objects are looked at with a new eye, a new curiosity – you're searching for connections which could lead to what you're seeking and you're noticing things that are linked by timing.

Marge: Right. It's another way of looking at reality. The reality of day-to-day life consists of those perceptual interpretations which we, as individuals, have learned to make similarly. The intuitive learner constantly shifts perceptual gears and renders the familiar unfamiliar. Casteneda (1972) describes this as *seeing* rather than looking, 'responding to the perceptual solicitations of a world outside the description we have learned to call reality'. (p.14)

Ingrid: It's also like looking at things with a child's eyes, emptying your mind so that you can see, appreciate and make use of what's right in front of you. Sometimes things are so obvious they're *not* obvious, especially when our heads are so full of other preoccupations that we get distracted.

Focusing attention on the ground rather than the relevant figure in learning; attacking learning obliquely

Ingrid: When we began our discussion we had the list of 18 processes in front of us; before I asked my initial question, you chose *dialoguing* as the point of departure. Why did you choose that item to begin with?

Marge: Two reasons, Partly because, as I mentioned, I see *dialoguing* as one of the really central processes, but secondly, I made an *oblique attack* on the list. I deliberately let my mind go blurry, out of focus, and that item came up first.

Ingrid: On the list you describe *oblique attack* as *focusing attention on the ground rather than the relevant figure in learning.*

Marge: Yes, this takes us back to my friend Edward's method of moose hunting. To attack intuition directly is to lose it. Intuitive learning involves going over the hidden ground, leaving behind for a moment the obvious figure, which could be described as what you already *know.*

Ingrid: In effect then, you are exploring the context of the figure, scanning the horizon which provides information about the relative significance or insignificance of the figure.

Suspending or minimizing deliberate, conscious rational processes (11)

Marge: That's right. You're getting a very diffuse, blurry view of things and allowing the important characteristics to come to you.

Ingrid: It's like sitting at a control panel of a television set and scanning all the channels very rapidly and allowing yourself to decide where to stop and look more deeply, deciding on subliminal information.

Marge: Another way of saying it would be to call it a shift from rational activities to intuitive activities, or as psychologists term it, moving from *convergent* thinking to *divergent* thinking, from analytic logical processes to synthetic holistic gestalt processes, from being active to being receptive.

Delineating generic boundaries for the area of learning (5)

Ingrid: And yet, while you are suspending rational activity, you are also careful to make choices about the boundaries of your scan – the area of search, so to speak. I often have trouble defining the boundaries of my learning activities. Some subjects become too huge, too all-encompassing; it becomes hard to get a specific angle in the search.

Marge: Ah, the key word here is *generic* not *specific.* I don't allow myself to go in all directions at once; I delineate an area of interest and begin searching within it. For example, I was looking at the list of intuitive learning processes for the purposes of this discussion; I chose not to find a list of all possible learning processes or all learning theory for that matter. My boundaries were within the generic field of intuitive learning.

Ingrid: 'Columbus didn't just set sail, he sailed West.' (Strunk and White). This fits with some of my thoughts on what I called learning *subjectives* rather than learning *objectives.* To me, learning objectives are the planned stops, places to visit or attainments on a learning journey toward larger goals. Those who have travelled before us have left signposts which we identify in order to measure our progress and movement. The person who learns by objectives works very hard at moving toward the signposts – he or she tends to be *goal-oriented.* In contrast, I have discovered that my own learning style combines experience and reflection in a less orderly, but still movement-oriented fashion. Rather than a map or itinerary, I use an internal compass. I choose directions in which to travel or learn, frequently without clear goals, endpoints or signposts I'm searching for. The directions I choose I call *learning subjectives* – they are personal and subjective in nature. I tried to describe it in a poem once:

> It's like an old watch your granddad gave you,
> a fancy silver thing.
> Still keeps perfect time, if you wind it.
> And even though you don't use it,
> it's there.
> In the drawer with your handkerchiefs
> and scarves. It's a part of you,
> Your past, your now.
>
> Well, that's the way my compass is.
> Only it's not silver, and it doesn't tick,
> I don't keep it in a drawer,
> I wish I could, so I know where it is.
>
> Sometimes I'm afraid I've lost it.
> And just when I'm in a real panic,

Worried, doubtful about what to do next
Or what turn to take,
I feel that little twitch
that itch,
And there it is,
Pointing out the direction
I needed.
Reassuring.
My past. My now.

Allowing oneself to be led or drawn in a certain direction; surrendering to the intuitive (14) and embarking on a pilgrimage of learning (9)

Marge: Your compass is a useful tool for embarking on what is a pilgrimage of learning. You're never quite sure precisely where you're going, but you have a direction and you *do* know that eventually you'll arrive. The intuitive learner is comfortable with this journeying into and across new landscapes. In this respect the intuitive process strongly resembles the stages in the creative process as described by various writers: MacKinnon (1970), Zahn (1966), and Koestler (1964). Part of the decision to embark on the pilgrimage comes from the process of allowing oneself to be led or drawn in a certain direction – surrendering to the intuitive. It has strong links to the teachings of Zen as well.

Being aware of and responding to energies outside oneself (12)

Ingrid: In reading your thesis I found it intriguing that several of the people you interviewed spoke about energies in a very psychic way.

> Intuition is a connection with the magnetic field of energy, the cosmic field of forces. *(Paul)*

> I'm intuitive in my work with people. That means that I let myself perceive on a number of levels what is going on without processing it first. I stay open. The word I use for myself is picking up the vibes. *(Adam)*

Marge: The *energies* described to me by the people I interviewed for the thesis occurred on various levels depending, I suppose, on the individual's most sensitive area of reception. Sometimes energy is experienced as physical sensation, as a magnetic force or even as visual images – such as seeing an aura around someone or expressing it through drawing. To me, learning is alive, and, like life, has energy – is energy. Both physical and non-physical learning create an energy between the learner and the object of attention or learning.

Ingrid: And this energy, like electricity flowing between poles, is a type of power. Its properties are dynamic and powerful. But how does the learner harness this energy, putting it to its best use?

Marge: As with any other process of learning, intuitive learning requires discipline. The energy you are experiencing, no matter how or from what source, must be focused by the learner. This means using physical boundaries sometimes. For example, I often get a lot of work done on aeroplanes, as I travel between workshops, because I'm restricted to a small space with a limited field of view. I'm forced to focus my energy on the desk in front of me.

Ingrid: That reminds me of what I call *cornering myself into work.* I tend to have all kinds of work-study avoidance tactics, and often successfully distract myself until the last possible moment when I have to settle into my place and get at it before it's too late.

Marge: Your words 'my place' are significant. I find that part of my intuitive process involves finding a place in my apartment to settle down and work in. It's not always the same place and the choice of place has a lot to do with responding to energies – my tapestry shows this process as well. There's a section with a lot of activity, movement, colours and action. Suddenly there is a stillness and a quiet explosion takes place; there is movement and force in the space, colour and texture of the weaving there. Sometimes using your energies to create that explosion is extremely powerful. It's like watching images of a nuclear explosion with the sound off – there's this tense pause and then that mushroom cloud growing and expanding out of that immense, intense, focused energy.

Recognizing the gift of revelation in the learning process (18)

Ingrid: Is the *explosion* that you describe what some would refer to as the moment of insight, the 'aha!' which leads to connecting a number of pieces of information into a solid, completely new piece?

Marge: Very much so. The processes – the dialoguing, the generic boundaries and so on – are gradual, but insight is sudden. Isaac Newton's famous insight about gravity came about after a lot of thought and study had taken place before his encounter with the apple. The apple falling was like the final thrust for his thoughts. But he had already created a place for that meaning to fit. Intuitive learners, like any learner, still must develop a place for the insight or discovery to rest in. Otherwise the insight or discovery has no link to reality at all. It is an insight without grounding in reality.

Ingrid: In this respect, it seems to me that several of the processes you have identified, particularly *knowing, trusting, being open and honest (processes 1-4)* and *being aware of feelings, influences of the unconscious (processes 15 and 16)*, are all attitudes or predispositions within the learner rather than approaches the intuitive learner uses to learn. You have to be in tune with these processes in order to make the important connections.

Marge: That's true. Being in tune with your intuition means being in tune with your life generally. Especially with *being absolutely honest in action and reflection (process 4).* One of the more serious barriers to the intuitive process is self-deception. In this context, honesty refers to the ability to distinguish the differences between wishful thinking, fantasy and reality. The honest person resists the temptation to manipulate or force the process and is clear about which processes arise from rational efforts and which processes are intuitive. Because intuitive processes are highly subjective, scrupulous honesty is of paramount importance. Otherwise you'd find yourself down a lot of dead-end streets in terms of learning.

Ingrid: Honesty and the conscience work like warning bells for me as I float and flit and sometimes crash through the jungles of my learning process. Exercising honesty is being able to say to oneself, 'Oh, oh, I've chosen the wrong thing to pursue this time. I'd better stop now before I go too much further or waste my energy longer.' It takes a great deal of courage to admit honestly that your ideas or actions are on the wrong track or that they were too *unrealistic* to work. In this respect, I think this particular process is a painful but most necessary one to use.

Marge: And it takes a great deal of maturity to act on it as well. This is why reflection on past experience is so important to an intuitive learner. Intuition does not occur in isolation from experience, it is strengthened by experience, by one's personal history. Taking stock of the past, going over it with honesty is very fruitful.

> Intuition is a silent traveller. It travels from our own conscious questions of today to our inner storage room which contains forgotten or dormant memories and drives. It picks them up, renders them and travels silently back to our present, consciousness delivering the answers we have been looking for in a sudden flash. Valid intuition uses preconscious roads and sensory, logical and emotional vehicles to connect conscious with unconscious psychological data and organizes them. It then presents us with 'obvious' solutions. *(Cohn, 1968)*

Knowing with unwavering certitude that learning will occur (1). Trusting in one's own intuitions and in the intuitive process (2). Remaining open to the expected, but more especially to the unexpected (3).

Ingrid: There is really not much I need to ask you about these three processes, Marge, because they are so familiar to me. I don't think I've ever entered a classroom, for instance, and felt I wouldn't learn anything. Sometimes I didn't get what I expected, but I've always felt certain, open and trustful that something would be delivered. These processes remind me of a conversation I read as quoted in the *Tao of Pooh* (Hoff, 1982):

> 'When you wake up in the morning, Pooh,' said Piglet at last, 'what's the first thing you say to yourself?'
>
> 'What's for breakfast?' said Pooh. 'What do *you* say, Piglet?'
>
> 'I say, I wonder what's going to happen exciting *today*?' said Piglet.
>
> Pooh nodded thoughtfully. 'It's the same things,' he said. *(p xi)*

Marge: These kinds of straightforward knowing, trusting, openness and honesty, as well as the awareness of one's feelings, as pointed out, seem to be predispositions in the intuitive learner, but I think it's important to point out quite firmly too, that this does not mean they are rare or that we are born either with or without them. Everyone has the capacity to use intuition in learning. Some people have fostered them in their development, exercised and practised them, therefore allowing their intuitive approach to be stronger than other approaches. In effect, some people end up holding these approaches as personal values and become unable to see any other way of doing things. Values, as you know, affect everything one does and, unfortunately, get in our way sometimes too.

Ingrid: These values turn into polarities, such as science versus religion.

Marge: That's true, although many scientists and scholars recognize and affirm the roles of leaps of faith, intuition or insight in their work. I like to think of it in terms of a continuum: with revelation or insight at one end and rational reasoning or logic at the other. It's not an either/or experience – one approach supports the other.

Ingrid: The difference would be in your point of entry: the intuitive person may begin learning through a leap of faith and then back it up with logic and reasoning; the logical learner begins with an objective and builds on it towards revelation. Either way, the learning must be grounded in reality and experience.

> If you have built castles in the air, your work need not be lost; that is where they should be. Now, put the foundations under them. *(Thoreau)*

This chapter, and your research, Marge, are like foundations being built under intuitive learning theory. What are some of the conclusions that form the foundations?

Marge: Firstly, intuitive learning is a distinct mode of learning which does not, by nature, follow the ordered progression or cycles of other learning modes. The processes described are the beginnings of a language or vocabulary which help us talk about it more clearly. Certainly, intuition itself has received much attention in other academic fields, such as psychology, philosophy and anthropology. It is important that education, especially adult education, gives it recognition as well.

Secondly, actual moments or flashes of insight cannot be consciously controlled, but by attending to the dynamics and processes of intuitive learning, we can move ourselves toward insight.

Thirdly, intuition, insight and intuitive learning are not rare, nor are they limited to gifted people or to those that are labelled as *creative* or *intuitive.* Intuitive learning seems rare because it is often not recognized or reflected upon as a distinct thread among all the threads of other learning modes or styles. Nevertheless, it is clear that some people have a greater facility or preference for intuitive learning rather than rational learning, just as others prefer rational learning over intuitive learning. Despite this preference, these modes must weave together to form the whole cloth.

Ingrid: And by the same token, these preferences mean an ability to switch from one mode to another, depending upon the subject focus or intent.

Marge: Yes, during my research, many intuitive learners expressed relief and pleasure about being asked to talk about the intuitive processes they use all the time, even though their studies were in extremely structured environments. To talk about their intuitive learning gave it legitimacy, which is very important to all adult learners.

> It (intuition) thrives on love for ourselves and others. It feeds on the world inside and outside of our body-mind borders. It needs awareness and seeks rest, quiet and trusting waitfulness. It seeks the company of people and the openness in which to understand them well. It dies with bias, prejudice and social amenities. It lives in

> freedom, playfulness, and love of surprises. It responds best when we work hardest, yet not often does it meet with us unless we are at leisure. We can train and enjoy it.
>
> *(Cohn, 1968)*

Ingrid: I realize you might not like me expressing your processes as qualities, but I have found it helpful to express them in key words; and these may add to a vocabulary for intuitive learning.

Ingrid's key words	**Marge's processes**
Qualities of the intuitive learners	
Certainty	
about learning	Knowing with unwavering certitude that learning will occur (1).
Trust	
in own intuition	Trusting in one's own intuitions and in the intuitive process (2).
Honesty	
in action in reflection	Being absolutely honest in action and in reflection (4).
Awareness	
of unconscious dynamics	Being in touch with the influences and the dynamics of the unconscious (16).
of energies outside self	Being aware of and responding to energies outside oneself (12).
of personal feelings	Being aware of and following one's feelings in the learning process (15).
of proper timing	Developing a sensitive awareness of the proper timing of processes and events (10).
Reflective	
drawing from experience	Reflecting upon and drawing new insight from one's own experience (6).
suspending rational processes	Suspending or minimizing deliberate, conscious rational processes (11).
Visionary	
openness to expected and unexpected	Remaining open to the expected, but more especially to the unexpected (3).
seeing multiple realities	Developing a sense of multiple realities (7).
appreciating meaning in synchronicity	Appreciating meaning in synchronicity (17).
Qualities of intuitive learning	
Directional	
within generic boundaries	Delineating generic boundaries for the area of learning (5).

Magnetic	
being drawn or led (surrendering)	Allowing oneself to be led or drawn in a certain direction; surrendering to the intuitive (14).
Indirect	
going obliquely (ground *v* figure)	Focusing attention on the ground rather than on the relevant figure in learning; attacking learning obliquely (8).
Devoted	
embarking on a pilgrimage	Embarking on a pilgrimage of learning (9).
Communing	
dialoguing with materials	Dialoguing with the materials (13).

Ingrid: The last item (dialoguing with the materials) still sounds a bit awkward to me. I thought of characterizing it as *merging*, but that didn't seem to fit either. The problem is that I still feel the word dialoguing implies speech, but from your explanation, dialoguing is much more than speech.

Marge: Yes it is. You and I have been struggling with this because to my mind dialoguing means interacting, but not *becoming* that with which you are interacting. In point of fact, it could be called *intercourse*, because two become one and yet still retain distinct identities.

Ingrid: So *communing*, or *communion*, isn't too far off the mark then, because it's an intimate form of sharing.

Marge: Exactly.

Ingrid: I think we've found the moose, Marge.

Marge: I think so too.

The
path
leads
toward the music of the loom
where
reality is interwoven
and reveals its secrets.

To learn what is,
is to engage
with the threads
of that reality.

Learning is a preposition
a pre-position
to
toward
between
in among
with
by

I am modified
by what I am not.

into
intuitive learning . . .

(Marge Denis, 1979)

References

Castenada, C (1972). *A Separate Reality: Further Conversations with Don Juan.* New York: Pocket Books.

Cohn, R (1968). Training intuition. In: H A Otto and J Mann (eds.) *Ways of Growth: Approaches to Expanding Awareness.* New York: Viking Press. 167-77.

Denis M (1979). Toward the development of a theory of intuitive learning in adults based on a descriptive analysis. Doctoral dissertation. University of Toronto.

Hoff, B (1982). *The Tao of Pooh.* New York: Penguin.

Koestler, A (1964). *The Art of Creation.* New York: MacMillan.

MacKinnon, D W (1978) Creativity: a multifaceted phenomenon. In: J D Roslansky. *Creativity.* New York: Fleet Academic. 17-32.

Strunk, W and White, E (1979). *The Elements of Style.* New York: MacMillan.

Zahn, J C (1966) *Creativity Research and its Implications for Adult Education.* Boston: Centre for the Study of Liberal Education for Adults.

Chapter 3

Charting Human Energy in Learning: a Path to Understanding

Leland Davies
Victoria Hospital, London, Ontario

Energy: what is it?

Energy in learning has a strange sound to it. We hear so much about the expenditure of energy in using non-renewable physical resources. Yet human energy is a resource which has been studied less. How true this is for the human energy put into learning.

Webster defines energy as 'the capacity for action, or performing work'. Menlo and Miller (1976) define it as 'a sense of vitality, arousal and activeness'. Human energy is an obvious but overlooked phenomenon. When it is absent we observe, as Ingalls (1976) did, 'the tired, lethargic and ill'.

Learning requires the capacity for action. Although using energy in relation to learning is unfamiliar, it does make sense. The cycle of learning based on Lewin's work has *action*, *reflection*, *conceptualization* and *experimentation* as the four components. To really learn there needs to be completion of the four stages.

After examining my own experience of energy in learning and reports of others' experiences, I studied the experience of energy in ten adult learners in a programme planning course in a graduate programme in adult education. The study and my own consideration of my work in education in organizations provide further insights as we chart a path to understanding human energy.

My experience

The variety of learning experiences I have had through my life intrigues me. Elementary grades were exciting. I was stimulated by teachers whose classes opened up the world around me and helped to show whether it was working well or not. Miss Dove, my grade 4 and 5 teacher, gently but firmly showed us the marvel of learning in the world. Two examples come to mind. Her love of flowers was transmitted to all of us as we were involved in the activity of making these beautiful plants grow and bloom. She also made stories come to life as she read them with a feeling which enthralled us. Then we were challenged to try the same with the stories of our choice. We tried to ensure class members were involved with our stories too. These learning experiences were exciting, filling me with energy. I sought to explore with fellow learners ideas and meanings. I acted; I learned.

I continued to be challenged through experiences in high school, although situations did vary. I was surrounded by other students in a special school who were filled with energy by new ideas and new learning challenges. The teachers varied. There were some who were worn out. They were just hanging in – waiting for the end of the class, of the day, of the year and of their careers. These learning experiences were dull and boring. Yet there were some teachers who were different. They were charged with the challenge of leading our bright young minds to new ideas. They introduced subjects and fields of study to us. They allowed us to interact with the ideas, to pursue them, to use the ideas. I recall Mr Harrison who taught English. He presented poems, stories and novels with a powerful analytic style. We were charged to react from our experience to his statements and those of fellow class members. If we fell short of clarity or honesty, he would argue for more from us. He did not let us be. We had to wrestle with our intellectual choices. We had to face the dreadful possibility of not choosing. We were not to let others act for us through our no-decision choice. The analogy of being the 'hollow men' was a threat for us at this boys' school.

Experiences in university classes were quite different. I remember myself in a biology class. I was one amongst hundreds battling to stay awake in a lecture delivered by a professor who could not bother to bring examples that related to us. The excitement of learning fled from that room. There was no energy left.

Several other university teachers presented information in their own way. They had no concern for me as a learner. I had not yet seen that learning occurs only when I choose it. I suffered. Finally, I found by my third year at university some courses which I could relate to my experience, to what I felt I needed. In genetics and physiology, I explored how the body worked according to a system or map; this made sense to me. I could relate to these ideas and use them to understand myself and interact with other learners on these ideas. I began to learn again.

I discovered that to learn well for me meant that I needed to explain what I knew to others. I became a teacher and with energy pursued this career. I found that I taught adults best. I liked to use their experiences, to challenge them to work together to understand their experiences within the frame of new theories and ideas. They could learn these theories or better create their own. Some learning experiences were especially significant and meaningful. A surge of energy would carry us forward to new personal discoveries.

My experiences convinced me that I should go further to understand this energy dimension of learning. It was a component important to my experience; was it so for others? I began a search for others' views on human energy and learning.

Perspectives on energy

I turned to the philosophies of the east. I read and wrestled with the meaning of the 'I Ching' (Dhiegh, 1973). There are two principles – yin (the receptive and docile represented by a broken line - -) and yang (the active and creative represented by a solid line —). The dynamic interacts with the passive. When in correct proportions, a creative surge or charge could take place. The yin principle and yang principle in interaction are what provides the vital source of energy for life (Banet, 1976). For instance, taken together yin and yang form trigrams (Pa Kua) which present elements of human experience. The trigram Ch'en (the creative) is represented by yang alone — an energy, strength and excitement. This contrasts with the trigram Ken, the keeping still, represented by two yins and one yang. Ken is associated with fidelity and waiting (see the figure below).

Trigrams (Pa Kua) of human experience

Ch'en: the creative

Ken: keeping still

Human experience requires a balance of these elements of high energy and low energy just as learning needs to include action and reflection.

Next I turned to physics. I had been a science student and was intrigued by the direction being taken in the study of quantum physics. I read Capra (1976) and Toben (1975) who helped in simplified terms to describe the understanding of energy in quantum physics. These scientists believe that there is no such thing as form. All that exists is energy particles that are perpetually moving in unique ways. The reality of structure is only so because we suspend the process when we try to examine for form. The energy is the process which is constantly changing. Research in the field of learning has rarely involved study of the process. Form and structure have received much more attention.

A further area where energy has been studied is psychology. Lowen (1979) showed the significance of the energy flow through the body and its role in ensuring health. Blocked flow signifies disease. Lowen's 'Bioenergetics' relates to the yin-yang principle and to the balance of energy in the principles of Tai Chi. I had experienced the phenomenon in a Tai Chi course which I enrolled in. Tai Chi is a structured approach to body movement and control based on an eastern martial art form. After each Tai Chi session, it is possible to feel the flow through the body. It recharges and renews. Maisel (1972) described this: 'If your energies are picked up, then there is no worry about being sluggish and heavy . . . this is accomplished by an interchange of empty and solid.' These flows of energy and the balance of active and passive were expanded as I came to understand acupuncture. The yin/yang flows along acupuncture channels indicate a similar phenomenon. The metaphoric was a key element in traditional

Chinese medicine. I have seen for myself practitioners using a variety of acupuncture entry points to affect body systems. The practitioners described how meridians (pathways) act as conduits to transmit Chi, which is defined as life force or vital energy (Steiner, 1983, p 73).

Csikszentmihalyi (1975) took the concept of energy flow and examined the peaks of experience felt by people. These creative moments where flow occurs are experienced as a holistic sensation of total involvement. Flow was described in playing chess, in rock climbing and in performing surgery. The capacity to act, to use energy, was at a peak. Learning was at a high for these people under these conditions.

For the general public, Miller (1977) counselled how to identify energy and vitality and described how to harness and use them. Ingalls (1976) and Ackerman (1984) extended the concept of human energy into organizational settings. Ackerman argued for a shift in attention in organizations 'to the experience of what is happening in the organization, what is assisting the fit and what is blocking the flow.'

After reflecting on my own experience and identifying insights from others on personal energy in learning and in organizations, I needed to study the experience of energy further.

The study

I chose to explore the experience of energy in learning with ten volunteers in two different sections of a graduate adult education course entitled *Programme Planning*. The learners were all adults who had returned to graduate school after work experience in business, service organizations and teaching. Six were full-time students while four were part-time. I contracted to hold an interview with each of the seven women and three men between each of the 15 classes, with one final interview a week after the course ended. The interview had an open-ended component in which learners described their experience of the learning situation and their awareness of energy in it. Learners were asked to complete a checklist to indicate their feelings in high and low energy situations.

The method of study chosen was based on the metaphysical view of man as developed by Wild (1959) who argued that 'existence, awareness and world are as indubitable as any . . . scientific data'. This method was a qualitative, discovery and participatory process. It was qualitative as the focus for analysis was on the descriptions of the experience of learning by learners. The research was a discovery process in much the same way Moustakas (1967) studied experiences of love. The process necessitated identifying the energy variations in learning experienced by the people in their course. In each case the reflective interviews with individual learners helped the investigator and the learners come to name and describe the experience. Its meaning was being more fully discovered. The research was participatory. As Mann (1974) said, 'the discovery can be a shared experience'. Investigator and learners were both participants. Meanings are drawn out and reflected together. The experience becomes a whole.

Through the study I sought to answer five questions. What was the personal meaning to adults of energy in learning? Did energy vary in some identifiable way over a learning experience? What factors did learners associate with any variations? How did the research process and the intensive interviews affect the learners? What are the learning and organizational implications of the phenomenon of human energy?

Research and experience results

The research I carried out provided a beginning to the answers to the questions, but my discovery process has not stopped with the study. I continued to make sense of energy in human experience. I have extended the answers on energy in learning into the experience of my own work as an adult educator in organizations. The results discussed here are related to the experience of learning and living in organizations. These discussions help to answer the 'so what?' question. The value of discovering more about human energy is shown.

Meaning of energy for learners

All the learners interviewed could describe their energy in the learning situation. The concept had a personal meaning for them. In this section many quotations from learners are presented which illustrate that energy existed in the awareness of the learners. For instance, a learner said, 'Energy is a flowing sensation that I can sense and it is often sustained by the group as a whole.'

Energy did vary. Learners identified high energy and low energy situations. In fact, two types of high energy experience were described. Active high energy was 'when everything was tearing along'. A learner found that 'when we were all working together on it . . . there was more active energy around that'. So this productive, free-flowing energy was like that described by a dancer, 'I am in control. I feel. I can radiate an energy into the atmosphere' (Csikszentmihalyi, 1975). This type of energy contrasted with a frustration high energy which is described as negative. One learner vividly described this form of energy,

> I see energy as being something that is expended and can be productive. I was expending a lot of energy but it was counterproductive. It was negative in the sense that it was holding me in position, like a helicopter hovering, but making no progress backward or forward – like a helicopter into a gale force wind just holding its position.

Finally, low energy was clear to all learners. Again, a learner picturesquely described this state, 'I am feeling a little muddy. My body is lethargic. My weight is in my feet, not up in my head or my lungs or my chest as when I am on a high energy cycle.' No clear description was given of a positive low energy, for instance a reflective state. It may be very difficult to identify this condition which is the balance to the active high energy time.

In essence, the interview provided the learners with opportunities to reflect on their learning experience. As a result new insights, new understanding and an ability to make sense of the experience developed. As one learner said, 'It is helpful to reflect back on the class and as you verbalize the experience, it becomes clearer.' The second main effect of the interview is on the learners' understanding of energy. A learner said, 'I'm more aware of the energy level and when I'm involved in something and when I'm not. This is not just in this class but in other classes too.' The third way in which the interview affects learners is to help with the learners' actions in the class. Being part of the interview is described as 'lucky for some of us. It helped deal with the frustration.'

Are there implications for these descriptions of learning and energy? My answer is, Yes. Awareness of energy can lead to discovering more meaning in the experience. Reflecting on learning energy helps to make sense of the experience. The ability to do so is useful. Progoff (1974) provides an approach to improving reflective skills.

There are implications for organizational life as well. Foy (1977) said that if we understand the situation in our organization, 'we release the forces of action (energy) inside the enterprise'. My own efforts at developing management skills in an organization suggest that a key is to see organizations as having dynamic energy where there is moving, changing, shifting, pushing and pulling. We should realize that there are many competing forces or polarities in our organizations. These forces create and stimulate energy from the tension that exists between the forces. Just as in our analysis of high active energy and frustration energy, if we understand these forces and use them we can have better organizational environments. Ingalls (1976) and Ackerman (1984) both have suggestions for using and transforming organizational energy.

Learning energy factors

A number of different factors were associated by the learners with their variations in energy. The commonly identified factors are summarized in the table on page 43. Each factor – personal, group, environment, task and communication issues – is described and the implications for each are developed below.

Personal factors

Personal factors were associated with variation in energy. When needs were being met or when something was felt to be happening, then active high energy seemed to follow. A learner said, 'When you think something is happening, it's creative, it sparks more and more energy.' When personal needs and feelings were kept to oneself, were trapped within the person, then frustration, high energy would build. 'It is like a spring in tension. It is just looking for an opportunity to break open. The emotions build like that in this kind of energy.' Low energy occurred when expectations were not met or they could not be met, 'the word impotent is running through my head, I have a feeling that has a lot to do with low energy' (a learner).

Time and pace were critical to personal energy variations. High active energy occurred when both were right for the individual learner. One person said, 'When I've got to perform in a certain time, my energy is high.' Good pacing

Energy variation and factors

Factor	High energy		Low energy
	Active type	**Frustration type**	
Personal	Personal needs met	Emotions kept in	Needs not met
	Sense of something happening		
	Sense of time/pace	Time pressure	Time/pace off
	Body state	Need interaction	Body overload
Group	Meeting others	Conformity	Not together
	Joint decisions	Circle decisions	No decision
	Synergy	Individual *v* group	Separate
	Energizers		De-energizers
	Optimal size		Too small/big
	Shared resources	Struggle	Work alone
Environment	Good set-up	Disagreement	Poor set-up
	Variety (limit)		No change
Task	Clarity	Effort but unclear	Not relevant
	Common direction	Not able to analyse	Not relevant
Communication	Confusion cleared	Unresolved	Dead end
	Sensitivity to others	Trying to see	Not sensitive
	Open communication	Open/confused	No openness

and timing allowed for flexibility which could spark high energy: '. . . the spontaneous discussion after class, that was high energy.'

Frustration energy developed when time was seen by the individual to be closing in from the outside, 'We had so much frustration, we felt time was running out for the class.' If no outlets emerge for frustration energy, the personal sense of it being too late can mean a transformation to low energy where, as a learner said, 'there is no willingness to invest energy in the situation'.

Body state had an obvious effect on energy. As a learner said, 'Things external to the learning situation had an inflating or deflating effect on you. It did for me. I was tired. My energy was dampened.'

The research showed that personal factors were significant in the expression of energy. People expressed energy in different ways. Of course, personal differences exist in other dimensions of the learning experience such as the variations identified by learning styles. As mentioned there is a need for more than one type of expression of energy – a balance. Only high energy may mean that the learner burns out. There is a need for that reflective, thinking, learning calm – that balance – described in eastern philosophy. As an analogy, Connelly (1985) described the two distinct styles of high performance of the Olympic runners in the film *Chariots of Fire.* The English runner's style of high energy using drive to prove himself was contrasted with the more balanced approach of the Scottish runner with his calm inner faith. The Scottish runner's style rejuvenates and feeds energy back to the spirit.

The ability to identify energy styles can be used to facilitate learning and improve performance in work settings. The expression of self-generated and balanced energy means better learning and working may be possible. The expression of this energy is affected by a number of personal factors. Resources exist to help use energy most appropriately in learning and organizational life.

Hendriks and Roberts (1976) are sensitive to the balance issue. They said, 'There is a time to let energy flow out, to be active and there is a time to let it flow in, to be receptive. We might think of energy as being like the ocean ebbing and flowing.' They provide methods to adjust pace and timing to be appropriate for energy expression. In dealing with blocked or misdirected energy expression a number of resources exist. Huxley (1960), Berge (1977) and Hammond (1975) described the phenomenon and provide exercises to help put energy to use. McKim (1972) offered ways to adjust body state for different learning conditions; Wlodowski (1985) and Miller (1977) described how to convert the disequilibrium caused by a frustration type of high energy into organizational involvement and change.

The challenge is to discover how to use the whole person in learning and working, to increase the range of possibility. Samples (1976) and Schindler, Rainman and Lippitt (1975) described ways of ensuring that a range of possibilities exists for people learning. Recently, writers have been identifying the same sorts of conditions for organizations. Yankelovich (1981) indicated the importance of personal value. Pasquale and Athos (1981) and Berlew (1974) described creating meaningful work so the individual's energy could be used. Jaffe and Scott (1984) provided a very useful set of strategies for rejuvenating individual contributions within organizations. Buckley and Perkins (1984) end on the positive note that said '. . . individuals in organizations have the opportunity to develop. If they are given the chance to be unique, to be recognized as something that is dynamic, and has integrity . . .' We can hope that the various efforts to involve employees more in organizations will prove the way to have the best expression of energy.

Group factors

Group interaction is a source of energy variation. Meeting others, sharing resources, making decisions, mixing of learners' energy to produce a synergy and certain individuals with an energizing effect were all found to be associated with high, active energy. One learner said, 'Interchange with others energizes me. We had chosen a direction so we knew where to put our energy.' An effect where total energy seemed greater than each individual's input was described. Frustration high energy was associated with pressure to conform: 'There was frustration . . . in his resistance but there was an awful lot of energy.' Poor decision making was associated with frustration energy, 'The discussion went around and around. It was so incredibly frustrating an energy.' When conflict between individual and group needs arose, then this type of energy could be present: 'We tried to respect people's needs. On the other hand, we wished that people would agree on something. The attempt to coordinate the two is often how frustration comes out.' Low energy was associated with an absence of the factors associated with high energy and with some people who drained energy from the group: 'When this person came in, he just had this manner so that we sat back.'

The group in learning situations has a powerful effect on energy expression. Learning is social, and interaction with others can energize learners. Participation in decision making, flexible control of the group, confronting task, dealing with differences, and taking responsibility are all issues to be worked out in the best way for each situation so that learning can be successful. Again, my own work in implementing group efforts in organizations adds a dimension to these issues. Work teams can create energy in the same way that Connelly described for the groups she called 'fusion teams' (1982). Task focus groups can be energy generating even without going beyond the task level: 'Partners in a collective structure share space, time and energy, but they need not share visions, aspirations or intentions . . .' (Weich, 1979).

On the other hand, groups that share deeper experiences can also generate real energy that improves conditions. Davies (1981) described the successful folk learning groups of Myles Horton in North Carolina, 'where meetings would begin with a singing game or the retelling of the beloved mountain tales'. Peruniak and Alexander (1985) described shared experiences which they feel build this type of work group within organizations. I agree with Nelson and Burns (1984) that the challenge for leaders, whether formal or informal in organizations, is to find the ways to manage the flow of energy in their team or organization. What needs to happen is for them to see the energy patterns and the human spirit these energy patterns release. Leaders should identify these indicators with a dedication that is equal to their dedication to the more ordinary indicators of performance such as profit.

Environmental factors

The environment of the learning situation affects the expression of energy. Thresholds for size exist. People find groups too big: 'In the large group of 18 there isn't as much energy as when we are in the smaller group.' On the other hand, they may be too small to share ideas and energy. Obvious physical problems such as inadequate heat and poor air flow make it difficult to generate energy in the situation. Variety itself was associated with active high energy. When different techniques, physical arrangements and different senses were used in the learning setting high energy was expressed. However, if the rate of change, the variety exceeded another personal threshold, high or low frustration energy resulted. More than three factors changing at one time resulted in frustration energy for most learners while variety in one or two dimensions encouraged high energy. For instance, in one class where the room, the format (the inclusion of a guest speaker) and the topic all varied from the expected, most felt there was too much change. Even a variety in the social dimension of the class, the food available at snack time, was described as assisting in the development of high energy for learning.

The implications of these environmental dimensions are significant. The study of threshold for size of optimal work and learning group could be continued. The same is true for the issue of variety. Someone needs to be sensitive to the need for variety but also aware of the thresholds for too much change. For it is the case that being in new situations provides stimulation but is also a source of stress. Bergevin, Morris and Smith (1963) provided ideas for structuring a variety of learning situations; alternatively, Sibson (1976) and Bennett (1983) offer approaches to creating variety in organizational work settings.

Task and communication factors

Task and communication factors affected how energy was expressed. Only the highlights for these two elements are briefly dealt with in this section. Clarity on tasks and a common direction meant high active energy might be expressed: 'When we were all working together on the project, there was more active energy around that.' If the task was unclear but there was a sense of value in it, frustration energy would build. If the task seemed irrelevant to the individual, low energy was likely to follow. 'It did not really seem to be my experience. I didn't really use it. I allowed it to happen. I was low energy.' If the content is inappropriate, again low energy followed. 'The presentation was so off the mark in terms of its position in the semester, in terms of where others were and in terms of its level of presentation, this was low energy.'

When there was a communication pattern that could deal with the inevitable confusion that arises, then active high energy was possible. A learner said, 'that a high energy moment was the point of talking to him personally to clear up the confusion about objectives.' Communication problems that are continuing but still being worked at can mean frustration energy is present: 'The high level of conflict or frustration energy would rise when we dealt with that issue.' When no resolution to communication issues seemed possible, then low energy would follow.

High active energy was associated with a sensitivity to others. A learner explained his feelings when the investigator described his work to the entire class. 'I know I was concerned about you and for you. As a result, my energy was high.' No openness in communication or no feedback resulted in a feeling of low energy.

What are the implications of these task and communication elements to learning and organizations? Firstly, responsibility for making tasks clear must be assumed by someone in our organizations and learning settings. Secondly, having choice and access to information means energy can be expressed, Wlodowski (1985) said, 'Whether it be the creation of an original product or the application of a new skill only if the learner truly wants to do it can the person actually benefit.' Employees also need to express their energy in organizations. 'The truth is that people want something active to do, something that tests them, that engages their mind and will, that involves not only effort but purposefulness . . .' (Gardner, 1978). In fact, Connelly (1985) described a phenomenon she called work spirit. Work spirit is manifested by those who have enormous energy and are often described as 'on a roll'. She noted that those who display work spirit 'generate from inside themselves a kind of doing and a quality of being that are pure energy: mental, emotional, physical and, some think, metaphysical energy'. She went further to argue a direct relation between work spirit and performance. In taking this one step further, achieving successful tasks and communicating them sparks energy. Miller (1977) said, 'A vital source is the psychological income and reinforcement, the amplification of energy we feel when we spend our energies successfully and gain a sense of growth.' So too for organizations as Neimann (1982) said, 'There is nothing like a success experience to generate confidence and momentum, the motivation to strike out for higher achievement.' Managers capable of producing real success and communicating these real success experiences in their organizations enhance the chances for valuable energy expression and likely improved performance.

The challenge

Underlying the study of adult learning and my recent efforts to help learning and development in organizations is the challenge to further understand energy and its manifestations.

First empowerment or energizing is possible for people who are learning and working. Educating creates power via sharing of information in a process which ensures interaction (Murrell, 1985). There are three levels to achieve empowerment goals for people and organizations (Vaill, 1982).

Firstly, individuals need self-knowledge of their energy and others' energy and the expression of it. We have described this phenomenon and provided some suggestions for developing and using energy in learning. Secondly, individuals need to have self-care. As noted, you cannot have high energy or the balance of the appropriate low energy unless your body is cared for. Resources such as Bertherat and Bernstein (1977) and Hayden (1976) can be used to develop this self-care principle. Thirdly, individuals need to absorb themselves in tasks, group interaction and in many different environments.

On the other hand, organizations need, firstly, shared, clear purpose. The power and energy that are released when individuals and organizations are in alignment in terms of their vision is just beginning to be understood. Maiden (1980) and Naisbett (1982) both describe the power of this in organizations such as NASA where the goal of getting a man on the moon provided startling examples of personal energy expression over a whole decade.

Secondly, organizations need to develop climates that allow for the expression of energy (Kilman, 1984). Buckley and Perkins (1984) suggest how this might happen: 'When the organization experiences personal power, individual energy becomes aligned rather than diffused . . . In integration, the individual experiences increased amounts of physical energy, emotional depth and mental concentration.' Work to develop this potential in organizations should continue.

Thirdly, organizations need to have a developmental approach for all. Learning empowers and energizes. A significance of the study of energy in learning is that it does transfer to working in organizations. As Kotter (1985) noted, we need to think about work in more relational terms. Power and interdependence are focal concerns. The AT&T corporation, for example, in trying to change to meet the deregulated environment to make a new internal interdependence did not do well. 'Manufacturing and marketing executives seemed to be locked in a major power struggle which drained energy away from the real tasks at hand.' The challenge is to deal with this kind of frustration energy at work and unlock it through creative approaches.

We need to have ways to understand and use energy in work as well as learning. We need to be able to see that 'Learning can be beautiful. Adults newly discovering a sense of themselves as learners in touch with their own flow, creative turns, power and strength are a joy to see . . .' (Griffin, 1977).

We have identified the challenge of human energy both for adult learning and for work in organizations. We have the path charted – let's take it for further exploration.

References

Ackerman, L S (1984). The flow state: a new view of organizations and meaning. In: John D Adams (ed) *Transforming Work.* Alexandria, Virginia: Miles River Press, 114-53.

Banet A G (1976). Yin/yang: a perspective on theories of group development. In: J W Pfeifper and J E Jones (eds). *The 1976 Annual Handbook of Group Facilitators.* La Jolla, California: University Associates, 169-85.

Bennett, A C (1983). *Productivity and Quality of Work Life in Hospitals.* Chicago: American Hospital Publishing Inc.

Berge, Y (1977). *Body Alive.* New York: St Martins Press.

Bergevin, P, Morris, D and Smith, R (1963). *Adult Education Procedures.* New York: Seabury Press.

Berlew, D (1974). Leadership and organization excitement. *California Management Review.* 17, 2, 21-30.

Bertherat, T and Bernstein, C (1977). *The Body Has its Reasons.* Toronto: Random House.

Buckley, K W and Perkins, D (1984). Managing the complexity of organizational transformation. In: J D Adams (ed) *Transforming Work.* Alexandria, Virginia: Miles River Press. 56-67.

Capra, F (1976). *The Tao of Physics.* Bungay, Suffolk: Clay.

Connelly, S (1985). Work spirit: channelling energy for high performance. *Training and Development.* 38, 5, 50-4.

Connelly, S (1982). The fusion team. An experimental group management technology. In: L L Franklin (ed). *An Army of Excellence: Visions of our Future Force.* Carlisle Barracks, Pennsylvania: Delta Force.

Csikszentmihalyi, M (1975). *Beyond Boredom and Anxiety.* San Francisco: Jossey Bass.

Davies, L J (1981). Adult learning: a lived experience approach to understanding the process. *Adult Education.* 31, 4, 227-34.

Dhiegh, K A (1973). *The Eleventh Wing: an Exposition of the Dynamics of the I Ching for Now.* Los Angeles: Nash.

Foy, N (1977). Action learning comes to industry. *Harvard Business Review.* 55, 5, 158-68.

Gardner, J W (1978). *Morale.* New York: W W Norton Co.

Gelb, F (1981). *Body Learning.* New York: Delilah Books.

Griffin, V (1977). Paper presented at the Wisconsin Adult Educator Lyceum, Pewaukee.

Hammond, D (1975). *The Search for Psychic Power.* Toronto: Bantam Books.

Hayden, N (1976). *Energy.* New York: Hawthorn Books Inc.

Hendriks, G and Roberts, T (1976). *The Second Centering Book.* Englewood Cliffs, New Jersey: Prentice Hall.

Huxley, L (1968) *You Are Not the Target.* New York: Avon Books.

Ingalls, J (1976). *Human Energy: the Critical Factor in Individuals and Organizations.* Reading, Massachusetts: Addison-Wesley.

Jaffe, D and Scott, C D (1984). *From Burnout to Balance.* New York: McGraw-Hill Co.

Kilman, R (1984). *Beyond the Quick Fix.* San Francisco: Jossey Bass.

Kotter, J P (1985). *Power and Influence.* New York: Free Press.

Lowen, A (1976). *Bioenergetics.* London: Penguin Books.

MacNamara, M (1985). Action learning and organization development. *Organization Development Journal.* 3, 2, 10-15.

Maiden, A H (1980). Resonance. *GAIA (Institute for Study of Conscious Evolution).* 3, 2, 1.

Maisel, E (1972). *Tai Chi for Health.* New York: Holt, Winston.

Mann, R D (1974). Identity of the group researcher. In: G S Gibbard, J Hartman and R D Mann (eds). *Analysis of Groups.* San Francisco: Jossey Bass, 13-41.

McKim, R H (1972). *Experiences in Visual Thinking.* Monterrey, California: Brooks Cole.

Menlo, A and Miller, E (1976). A theory for energizing adult students in the classroom. Paper presented at Ontario Institute for Studies in Education, Adult Education Department.

Miller, D B (1977). *Personal Vitality.* Menlo Park, California: Addison-Wesley.

Moustakas, C (1967). Heuristic research. In: J Bugental (ed) *Challenges of Humanistic Psychology.* New York: McGraw-Hill.

Murrell, K L (1985). The development of a theory of empowerment. *Organization Development Journal.* 3, 2, 34-8.

Naisbett, J (1982). *Megatrends.* New York: Warner Books.

Neimann, R A (1982). Strategies for managerial impact. *Management Review.* 53.

Nelson, L and Burns, F (1984). High performance programming. In: J D Adams (ed). *Transforming Work.* Alexandria, Virginia: Miles River Press, 226-42.

Pasquale, R and Athos, A (1981). *The Art of Japanese Management.* New York: Simon & Shuster.

Peruniak, W J and Alexander, W E (1985). From teamwork to community: II. *Organization Development Journal.* 3, 3, 16-19.

Progoff, I (1975). *At a Journal Workshop.* New York: Dialogue House.

Samples, B (1976) *The Metaphoric Mind.* Reading, Massachusetts: Addison-Wesley.

Schindler-Rainman, E and Lippitt, R (1978) Awareness learning and skill development. In: K D Benne (ed). *The Laboratory Method of Changing.* Palo Alto: Science and Behavior Books. 213-39.

Sibson, R E (1976) *Increasing Employee Productivity.* New York: Amacom.

Steiner, R P (1983). Acupuncture – cultural perspectives. *Postgraduate Medicine.* 74, 4, 60-78.

Tannebaum, R (1982). Development in an era of paradigm shifts. *Training and Development.* 36, 4, 32-42.

Toben, R (1975). *Space, Time and Beyond.* New York: Dutton.

Vaill, T (1982). The purposing of high performance systems. *Organizational Dynamics.* 11, 2, 23-9.

Weich, K (1979). *The Social Psychology of Organizations.* Reading, Massachusetts: Addison-Wesley.

Wild, J (1959). *The Challenge of Existentialism.* Bloomington, Indiana: Indiana University Press.

Wlodowski, R J (1985). Stimulation. *Training and Development.* 39, 6, 38-43.

Yankelovich, D (1981). *New Rules.* New York: Random House.

Chapter 4

Images of Interdependence: Authority and Power in Teaching/Learning

Gwyneth Griffith
Centre for Christian Studies, Toronto

The issue of authority in education, its source and its power, has always been a contentious one for teachers and learners alike. Webster's dictionary offers the prevailing meaning of authority: 'the power, because of rank or office, to give commands, enforce obedience, make decisions etc. (the authority of a teacher)'. Yet authority is related to the word 'author' which means originator, one who creates from within oneself. Understanding the nature of authority and power in teaching and learning has been the focus within my learning journey in recent years. What follows is my story as an adult learner, including my experience as a researcher/learner, teacher/learner and administrator/learner. The story incorporates some of the learnings from the journey, discoveries which have enriched both my work as an administrator/teacher and my life as a whole.

An adult learner's story

My story as an adult learner begins when, in my mid-forties, I left a position as executive director of a large metropolitan agency to become a full-time student at the Ontario Institute for Studies in Education in Toronto. Although I had been involved in informal adult education programmes for many years, I still understood learning as related to courses and workshops, with specifically defined structure and 'teacher', and with a functionally defined goal.

At OISE I discovered that I was responsible for my own learning, a revelation that challenged many of my old assumptions. I was free to determine my own learning goals and to pursue themes of special interest to me. The exploration into new understanding and self-reflection could be done individually or with small groups of learner colleagues with the teacher as a resource. The emphasis was on *self-directed learning.*

As part of that experience, I became part of a *Core* group at the Centre for Christian Studies in Toronto, a theological education institution where students prepare for educational, pastoral and social ministry. Participants in the Core group determined their own learning goals (within guidelines), planned the curriculum and facilitated sessions. We were encouraged to reflect on experience, individually and corporately, using both concepts and symbols or images. The emphasis was on *self-directed learning in community.*

From the beginning in the group, I was encouraged to write reflections on my experience. In the first week I wrote:

> I want to be able to experience a fresh breeze in my life and to be part of one too, to accept the joys of community and commitment, while retaining a sense of freedom . . . I'm worried that my old ways of behaving will not be acceptable – to others or to me – and I'm not sure I'll be able to 'perform' in the new way. Will I be able to trust enough to let go, to learn in new ways, and not try to dominate or manipulate? . . . I have a lot of feeling about my identity . . . Right now, I'm ambivalent about the whole process. *(Core reflection, 7 September, 1977)*

At OISE I focused on procedures which help in adult learning. An early gift from that course facilitator, Virginia Griffin, was an article by Paul Nash (1973) in which Nash delineated three basic authority modes, ways of exercising and responding to authority (one's own and the authority of others). He identified interdependence as a 'radical view of authority relationships in education', describing it within American historical, sociocultural, and educational contexts, and contrasting it to two other modes (dependence and independence).

Among many other learning experiences, a time of shared conversation with Paulo Freire led to learning in action and reflection, naming, and education for critical consciousness, which emphasized co-learning of the teacher/learner and learner/teachers (Freire, 1970, 1973). My learning opportunities in both settings (OISE and CCS) and the opportunity to read and write on such themes became focused into the developing topic for my research. This was an exploration of the meaning of interdependence and of movement towards interdependence, with implications for both learner and teacher (Griffith, 1982).

As I began the formal learning journey I was very aware of how my own background brought to bear on my mode of learning. Raised in the Depression, I feared scarcity, which showed itself in adult life in such areas as money, food, and programme planning. A sense of limited resources led to careful planning of the future and a practice of counting and measuring, judging myself and others in terms of quantity and production. Perfectionism, expressed in the maxim, 'If it's worth doing, it's worth doing well' was linked with 'If you want it done right, do it yourself.' Competitiveness and striving for achievement in school and work was linked with my dependence on external approval. Acceptance by others was perceived by me as a result of my performing well, and I feared breaking rules. In my professional and volunteer activities, I was at ease in my strong leadership and conceptual ability. My focus on function, part of the 'independent' mode, meant that I had confidence in my 'doing', but not in my 'being'.

There was readiness for interdependence in that I remained open to others. I shared my vulnerability easily, and my energy and enthusiasm engendered a similar response in others. The 'child' in me could never be subdued. My ideological stance developed to include a strong concern for integrity, community, and social justice, and a recognition that systems as well as individuals needed to be transformed. My convictions frequently came in conflict with my primary authority mode, and I was eager to learn more congruent ways of being and acting in all aspects of my life.

As I began as an adult learner, I espoused an interdependent educational philosophy, but found it difficult to act out a belief that the designated teacher would learn from me or that I had much to learn from other learners. I perceived teaching and learning as separate functions. In my written reflections, the resulting pain was evident: 'I'm suffering about being a student, though my stress on "I still know something though I'm a student" may show a lack of respect for students.' (Core reflection, 3 October, 1977). I recalled later during one of the research interviews about both OISE and Core:

> I used to get so mad when they would not make the decision, when we would have to say how we wanted the class to go . . . 'That's what they're paid to do; they're paid to teach me. I'm the one that's here to learn; tell me what to do.'

After several other reflections, I wrote:

> It's astonishing how often I wrote about power and control and performance . . . I have thought before that if I controlled something I would know how to respond and I haven't wanted to not know how to respond. Yet when I do let myself go and just let whatever will come out, I feel really great. *(21 October 1977)*

> What *does* help me let go? . . . Part of it is the sense of shared responsibility, that I am not responsible for everything that happens even if I could be . . . but it is a very difficult thing for me to learn. *(6 November 1977)*

As I became a designated facilitator in Core, my struggle about the nature of learning and teaching continued: 'I still have feelings about quantity of learning, dependent on visible things like content, resource people etc. I have a feeling we're not doing "enough"; they're not learning "enough".' (18 November 1978).

Yet I was catching a vision of a new mode of learning and teaching: 'Adult learning is enhanced when the learning climate fosters self-esteem and interdependence' (Griffin, 1977). In such a climate, Griffin stated, people feel they are respected, accepted and valued by the teacher and by other learners, openness of self and differences are encouraged, people are allowed to make mistakes, and people's experiences, attitudes, and knowledge are recognized and built on. At CCS a statement of the centre's educational stance was evolving.

> We are called to be co-creators with God, engaged in the struggle to bring wholeness, justice and peace to the world . . . Education at the Centre happens within a living community with each person as both learner and educator. Learning is a process and discipline . . . Learning happens when persons are actively involved in their own learning, taking responsibility for that learning and for enabling the learning of others . . . We are all learners and teachers interdependently.
> *(Centre for Christian Studies, 1981)*

As I entered the research process, I was committed to reflecting on my own experience as a participant, both in Core and in the study, and I perceived the participants as co-researchers. Those 22 people (20 women, one of whom was the Core co-ordinator, and two men) had all experienced the Core programme at CCS and were identified by Hélène Castel-Moussa, the Core co-ordinator, as having some understanding of and trying to practise interdependence. An average of six hours of conversation was held with each one. In the first interview, participants were asked to reflect, through response to my questions, on their experience and understanding, using the sub-language of authority modes, and to express verbal images of interdependence. A second interview with each was a dialogical exploration of issues and themes raised in the first interviews, at the end of which each participant was asked to create a symbol of the meaning of interdependence for them.

The methodology, therefore, was designed to be congruent with what was being researched. The response of the participants to sharing in the process was, for the most part, enthusiastic. They were eager to contribute to new understanding and to continue their own learning. Only one expressed ambivalence, but agreed to be interviewed. The potential for learning *can* be overshadowed by the pain created by isolation and risking being vulnerable. At the end of the first interview, she said:

> I still feel badly. There's part of me that's protecting myself . . . I get stuck with whatever I bring up . . . That may be opening some wounds and I'm not willing to be by myself . . . You leave tomorrow to go back to all those people and a place to work this stuff through and if what I've said is not useful, you can chuck it out, but I can't chuck it out. I'm stuck with it.

Others reflected on their learning after the first interview: 'It opened up some windows for me.' 'Some of the concepts have been renamed for me.' 'It was a good learning experience for me because I like reflecting back and you always get new things out.' Excitement about shared learning grew in the second interviews as we played with developing new understandings, and connections were made. The excitement continued through the analysis, both as I consulted further with participants and dialogued with the data alone.

As I worked on the analysis of the research data, I realized that the discoveries emerged as I interacted with many others. 'How could I ever claim it as mine even if I wanted to?' (Research journal, 27 August 1980). I was aware, however, that my old, primarily dependent mode affected my way of doing research, with my fear of scarcity, reliance on authorities and reluctance to trust the process. I wrote in my research journal:

> The whole way I went about it was based on my mode at the time . . . The things I struggled with and thought especially important came out of that mode – sense of self, play, perfectionism – and the way I proceeded, for example the number of participants (wanting to have more than anyone thought I needed) based on counting. My question of moving from articulated value to practice is a dependent mode question. The dependent are more likely to have the value and then want to do it. Ginny [Griffin] and Hélène [Castel-Moussa] practised it and I espoused what they did.
>
> *(24 June 1981)*

I searched for outside factors and structures to help people learn. 'Find the right box and process people through it and they'll come out interdependent.' (Research journal, 24 August 1980). Yet there was excitement in opening the imagination and letting the data 'speak to me', along with developing my independence, valuing being alone, dialoguing with my own thoughts, and having to be responsible for those thoughts. I learned through the research process that reflection on the effect of my past authority mode enabled me to free myself from it more easily.

Adult learners in an interdependent learning group

As participants reflected in the interviews on their life experience before becoming students at the CCS, as well as on their experience in the Core group, they were also asked to identify their primary authority modes as they began

Core. They were linked with five authority modes related to dependence and independence, a mix of these two modes, and readiness for interdependence. Five modes were necessary to incorporate both the participants' self-understanding of the relation of their experience to the modes and my own growing understanding of the meaning of the modes. The authority modes of participants related primarily to learning experiences within their families. The modes affected the meaning of the Core experience for them, as well as the way they responded to it, what they needed to 'unlearn' as well as learn.

Those who tended to the *dependent* mode came from families which valued status, security (fearing scarcity), family, serving others and social graces. They did well in previous school experiences and avoided conflict and expression of anger. They had difficulty with most Core processes, fearing feedback (both affirming and critical), unclear expectations and breaking rules. They needed to know, to be right and to plan ahead. They were in awe of the teacher, who was seen as set apart, and were passive learners. One recalled:

> I had always viewed the teacher as being someone set aside and that's what I saw [Hélène] to be – the teacher . . . I didn't know what I had to offer her . . . because maybe I didn't want to take responsibility in being part of her learning process . . . I had to unlearn that I was going to be spoon-fed . . . I had to take responsibility in that learning.

Those who tended to the *independent* mode came from families which valued objectivity, rationality and achievement, and who were comfortable with conflict. In Core they had no difficulty in stating their learning goals and they felt held back by others. Feedback was easier for them to give than receive, and they had difficulty expressing their vulnerability. They perceived learning as information assimilation. One described her experience as feeling that 'I was just trying to walk along dragging all these people like a ball and chain . . . I saw them as 'duds' that I had to get around in order to do what I wanted to do.' Two others referred to the focus of unlearning for them as 'the fear of asking dumb questions' and 'burying my hurt'.

Those in the *mixed dependent-independent* mode focused on providing *for* others and on understanding feelings. They struggled with perfectionism and they learned from modelling. They had difficulty in asking for feedback and in challenging the teacher, who threatened them. One gradually recognized that she had to unlearn:

> My impatience and my academic approach . . . I wanted to have everything nailed down in order . . . I'd get very frustrated when I didn't have all the pieces on hand . . . I'd always had the sense that I was totally responsible . . . and the sense of perfectionism, that it was possible to do things perfectly as long as I was in control . . . I had to learn that I could trust other people.

Some participants had been ready for interdependence when they began Core. The *independent-ready* had learned to analyse, to explain reasons and to be open to criticism. They could take responsibility for themselves but were aware of others' needs. They enjoyed challenging teachers and perceived learning as a solo activity. Feedback was highly valued and, although they shared thoughts easily, sharing of feelings was difficult for them. One, who said he 'was ready for an interdependent community' and 'knew vaguely what type of qualities

I was looking for' recognized 'the unlearning that had to take place was that I had to stop, to slow down my brain so that my stomach would start up . . . stop trusting so much in my head and put more trust in my feelings.'

The *mixed-ready* had been encouraged to be their own persons and to make their own decisions within concerns for others. Relationships with teachers, who were seen as models, were important. Wholeness and integration were valued, as well as the naming of feelings, concepts and skills. One remembered:

> I fell into the Centre and when I came into the Core programme . . . it was like putting a name to something that you always knew was there and suddenly here was a group of people and a place that had a name for it, and suddenly the whole world opened up for me.

For her, one of the most exciting aspects was that the Core facilitator 'could put names on things that at that point I couldn't . . . She could make connections.' Yet, she recalled, 'the big accomplishment at the end of my first year at the Centre was to say "these are the gifts I have and I can do this well" . . . You have to unlearn the humble bit.'

With reference to the traditional educational model, therefore, all had unlearning to do, but the nature of the unlearning differed. The dependent mode unlearning is related to a struggle with authority figures, importance of grades and awards and a future orientation with a specific end to learning outside of learning itself. The independent mode is focused on achievement on one's own and an attitude to information and language that stresses ideas and the rational. Many, in all modes, struggled with self-esteem as they were helped in a learning/teaching setting that emphasized action/reflection, affirmation and challenge, self-direction, and mutual learning.

Images

From conversations with participants, it became clear that one's image of interdependence is part of a vision of a different kind of world, a world of 'shalom', of wholeness, peace and justice. The images vary, influenced in part by one's authority mode, regardless of how interdependent one has become. This is illustrated by images expressed by two of the participants. A man, who had tended to the independent mode, had an image of interdependence as:

> Two trees growing up beside each other, where they both have a purpose. One may be an apple tree and the other may be an orange tree, but they're together . . . The purpose is to provide fruit. . . One protects the other from the wind . . . but one's not a parasite.

A woman, who was in a mixed dependent-independent mode, had an image of:

> An orchestra in comparison to one flute, because one flute is nice. It's pretty and it can be very effective at times, but the orchestra brings all the instruments together, and together the sounds and tones create more than one flute can ever do. It [interdependence] is coming together and co-creating.

Images and symbols, although inadequate in themselves, are essential to our grasping the meaning of interdependence. It is both possible and not possible to 'see' it. One participant said that interdependence 'is just under the surface all the time. You break through to it and then it's gone again. In a sense it's with you always.' Interdependence is part of a vision of community and justice in the world to which we not only 'break through' but which keeps breaking in on those who are open to seeing it.

> I see a circle of people dancing around a rug and there are tall people and short people dancing to different types of music . . . There are times they let go of hands and dance by themselves. There are times they gather the hands and move to the centre and then back out again. There are times to sit on the floor and watch other people dance . . . There are times for little people to get in the circle. *(Participant)*

Moving towards interdependence

I discovered that within both dependence and independence, there are characteristics which tend to close people off from moving towards interdependence and other characteristics which open people to learning this new mode of consciousness. Most of us are mixed in our authority modes, but tend more to one. Most of us have been educated in societies which espouse independence and practise dependence (the dominant world view) and there are few models of another mode.

Those who tend to be *dependent* are strongly affected by the judgement of others and are guided by criteria external to themselves. They value hierarchy and the 'feeling' component in life and fear scarcity. They perceive power to be *power over* and related to one's position in the hierarchy. Some need power over others to enhance their self-esteem and need to take responsibility for others in order to have security. Some need others to have power over them and fear taking responsibility for their own lives.

Those who tend to be *independent* are more inner directed and value equality and the 'thinking' or rational component of life. They also perceive power to be *power over* but relate this as having power over their own lives. They fear vulnerability and being controlled, and so seek to protect themselves from others. Those who have more confidence are able to be open to ideas and experiences in order to achieve more self-realization.

As these modes are mixed, those who find themselves blocked from interdependence struggle with perfectionism, strive for achievement and have a need to control. Those who are more able to move show qualities of openness, childlikeness, and playfulness. The dominant world view, however, does create blocks for those wishing to move towards a new mode of seeing and being in the world. The transformation is never complete. As one participant said, 'The thing about being interdependent is that you're never there.'

One is, however, able to be intentional about learning to live interdependently. It is important to strengthen one's sense of self (both self-awareness and self-acceptance) because of the need for risk, vulnerability, openness and the giving up of the need for control and accomplishment. Too often one's self-esteem is based primarily on what one does, on how one performs, as one looks to authority for validation of the self or fears sharing oneself. One participant said that what enabled her to act interdependently,

> relates to self-confidence, which ties in with feeling good about myself and recognizing my gifts . . . and when I don't feel confident and I don't feel I have anything to offer, interdependence is just out of the question.

Visioning is also essential in the movement towards interdependence. 'Before you have intentionality, you have an awareness that things could be different, should be different ' (Participant). The vision can be both exhilarating and painful. It brings both hope and empowerment as one recognizes that the movement towards a different kind of world is not all in one's hands and trusts shared responsibility.

There are other dynamics which enable the movement towards interdependence. They interact with each other within the dialectic of the personal and political, expressed in the sense of self and the vision. A strengthened sense of self enables trusting and being open to grace and the unexpected. As one lets go, one is able to play and imagine, opening oneself to the power of symbols, images and metaphors. Acting/reflecting and naming the reality that is in oneself, in society and in the vision of new possibilities enables one to move towards a new mode of learning and being (*see* Chapter 16). In a formal learning group, the facilitator may stimulate these dynamics and this requires skill and intuition.

> I don't know. There's what I call the magical moment when it clicks and it's usually a moment you've never thought of as a facilitator, never planned on, but suddenly [the learner] makes those connections, and there's where you just have to trust your intuition. There's no blueprint . . . fundamentally because we are different.
>
> *(Core co-ordinator)*

An image of interdependence – the open circle

In the open circle (*see* Fox, 1979) there is continuous change and learning, with openness to new possibilities both within and without the individual and the community. Here, apparent opposites, such as playing and working, symbolic and rational thinking, being with others and being on one's own, and learning and teaching are both present, but changed from being dualistic to being in dialectic. There is a synergy in the combining of 'open' characteristics of dependence and independence with the catalyst of grace and vision. This enables a new creation which, because of their dialectical relation, is more than both combined. From the dependent mode comes openness to other people, recognition of the need for others, the acceptance of responsibility in relation to others, and the appreciation of feeling, synthesizing and being involved in situations. From the independent mode comes openness to new experiences and ideas, focusing on choosing and on being responsible for oneself, and the appreciation of thinking, analysing and standing outside of situations. One is then able both to be and to act on one's own, and to need and be needed by others.

Another word for interdependence is mutuality, which differs from the independent mode word 'equality' in that differing needs and gifts are affirmed. One participant commented:

> I know it isn't a mathematical thing, but the curious thing about interdependence is that everybody feels equal. When interdependence is really happening, I feel like I'm

> being filled and the person with whom I'm interacting also feels filled. And there's something about the reality of shared pain . . . There are no levels of hierarchy. Nor is there equality – it's irrelevant.

In interpersonal relationships, one's needs can contribute to the growth of others, and giving and receiving are part of one reality. Mutuality also means affirming our solidarity with those who are oppressed, sharing both power and responsibility.

Interdependence is for the sake of the other and of the whole community as well as for oneself. Because of commitment to community, one's individual action is carried out in the light of its impact on others and, in any group, all participants share responsibility for enabling the growth and well-being of others. One experiences integration and wholeness, and acts with integrity.

This does not mean that interdependence is heavy. While there is struggle, there is also humour, celebration, ecstasy and fun. 'It's laughter and tears and they're together', one participant said. There is spontaneity and synergy, where one plus one equals three or more. There is story telling, so that one is rooted both in the story of one's own life experience and in the collective history of the 'people' of which one is a part. And basic to interdependence is the child in us all, full of wonder and creativity, opening one's arms wide to the world.

Risk is an essential component of interdependence as a new way of being-in-the-world is chosen; one risks not only making mistakes, but being mistaken. There is vulnerability in taking action in ambiguity, especially in a world that seeks certainty, security and perfection. Yet within interdependence is acceptance of ambiguity and difference. The dominant world view affirms smoothness and sameness, with difference meaning better or less than. But difference brings richness, expression of passion and often conflict. One participant reflected:

> You feel interdependence when you feel you have permission to be who you are, knowing that is going to create some waves. It's being able to have disagreements and to penetrate into them more, knowing you're not going to destroy anything, but rather that you're going to reveal something.

Authority and power

Authority and power are intimately connected. In the dominant world view, power is perceived as quantitative, usually negative, and as 'power over'. The independent see that as power over oneself or a situation – hence the importance of maintaining self-control – and the dependent see it as power of one person over another. In order to gain power, power must be taken from another. In order to share power, power must be given to another, thereby reducing one's own. Within the open circle, power is seen positively, as limitless, and is experienced as empowerment with all. Power is the *ability to do* and empowering of oneself is enabled by naming one's gifts and beginning to use them. This self-empowerment can enable empowerment in others as it is also empowered by others. There is a transformation from power *over* to power *with*.

Where there is a designated teacher/learner in an interdependent learning group there are power differences which need to be recognized. Reflecting on her experience as a facilitator, the Core co-ordinator said:

> To say you don't have power is being phony. It's disconcerting how to use your power and that's really touchy. It requires a lot of self-criticism, reflection, and checking on yourself, vulnerability, and looking at your own power and your integrity . . . The tension is between manipulating and enabling/facilitating, that you do not impose your values, but enable others to become.

She also reflected on the nature of her authority:

> You can't deny that you speak with authority, but it's not being authoritarian. It's suggesting, recommending out of your experience and your knowledge . . . I do have something to give and I do have that authority and therefore they respect it; they want to learn from it . . . but they also feel they have something to give me. I've found it's very important to let them know what it is, but very often I've found that's a threat to them.

Moving towards interdependence *is* a risk!

Learning and teaching in the interdependent mode

In dependent mode education, the focus is on transmission of knowledge (already 'owned' by the teacher) from the teacher to the learner, where learners are passive receivers and the teacher is the expert. What is learned can be measured by someone outside the learner. In independent mode education, the focus is on self-directed learning, where knowledge is seen as a commodity to be accumulated by and for the learner, and the teacher is a resource. In interdependent mode education, the focus is on self-directed learning in community, in which knowledge is being co-created, and the teacher is also learner. Learners are responsible for enabling their own learning and the learning of others with whom they are in community, including the learning of the teacher. This does not mean that learning must always take place in groups with a designated teacher, or that it must always take place in a group setting, but that learning is within the context of community at a wide variety of levels. When others *are* involved, all are committed to community with one another, as shared history and vision evolve.

The process of learning and teaching are transformed in interdependence and become one process. By being learner and teacher one is more than either and even more than both combined. Through our own learning we facilitate the learning of others and we learn through facilitating the learning of others.

Being self-directed means that one accepts responsibility for one's own learning. Being in community means declaring one's learning goals and contracting both to work on them and on enabling the goals of others. 'In this kind of learning, things don't just happen and work themselves out. Once you make a commitment, then that commitment goes beyond oneself' (Participant). Interdependent learning is integrated learning, both within the community and within the individual learner.

> In interdependence, it's really important to learn at more than a head level. That creative movement enables that learning to be at a different level and enables that freedom and unboxing of learning. It's a total body experience . . . It seems to me when I learn in an interdependent process then I learn it; I feel it; my 'a-has' are

> sensual experiences. They hit there and then spread and I get goose bumps . . . It's a physical reaction, but it's not physical separated from emotional or spiritual or anything else. It's just a congruent kind of experience, or the whole feeling of wholeness. (*Participant*)

An adult learner as teacher and administrator

My learning now is in the context of my work as teacher and administrator at the Centre for Christian Studies. Our academic staff is committed as a team to striving to act with integrity to live out the educational stance of the centre (CCS, 1981). We challenge one another to develop learning goals each year and share these with the team. These become part of our annual staff assessment in which we reflect on our own learning and functioning as a staff and give feedback to the others.

As a learner I recently participated in a summer session of a graduate institute where there was a stimulating mix of other auditors and of credit students. I experienced the joy of discovering new information and insights, and being in dialogue, contributing my experience and knowledge and being open to that of others. Since my own journey as an adult learner began, I have been thirsty for new learning and to integrate this into my living, without the stimulus of external credit (as common for the dependent mode). Yet the learning at summer session was not only for my sake (as in the independent mode), but also for the sake of the community. Our academic staff share new learnings and resources from such experiences and together discuss implications for our own learning and for our work with students.

As a teacher, I have shared with other members of academic staff in teaching a theoretical course, integrating conceptual understanding with experience and practice. Students also teach in this course as part of their learning. I found it stimulating to plan with another for specific sessions, developing processes and deciding on theory to be presented by each – sometimes related to our past work and sometimes related to new areas in which we wished to learn. We learn by facilitating and we facilitate by learning! A small group of students in the course joined me to form a reflection group which met at the end of each session. We shared our individual learning goals for the course, reviewed these at a mid-point and, at the conclusion of the course, each of us reflected on our learnings in light of our goals and received feedback from the others where they had observed learning and skill development. My learning was greatly enhanced by this process.

As an administrator, I am part of three staff teams where we work towards consensus decision-making with shared authority and power. This has been difficult with administrative and support staff who have been more accustomed to functioning in hierarchical structures. We all find such a mode of work more time-consuming and often less clear about who has offered to take responsibility for tasks. Volunteers on committees, and staff in related institutions, are sometimes frustrated in needing to know who is 'boss'; thus the title of 'principal' remains.

Students keep challenging us to act with integrity according to our educational stance as they struggle to shift their authority modes. As we strive to articulate more clearly our criteria for admission and for granting of diplomas so that agendas are not hidden, power issues are sharpened. The nature of the power of students and staff *is* different, but each works at mutuality in exercising power.

Much of our structure and mode of functioning is still part of the dominant world view, but there is excitement in working with others to discover a new mode of teaching and administration where authority and power are shared and all are learners. I often feel the same as one participant who said:

> On the down days [interdependence] feels frustrating because it would seem a lot simpler to go ahead and make your own decisions and do your own thing or to take orders handed down or to give orders . . . On the good days . . . almost a magical feeling, like when you're working in a group and learning together, it's almost like electricity that's flying between you all, so the feeling is one of satisfaction . . . It's a peacefulness, but not peace in the sense of passivity, but a peace like yes, everything's working and moving and growing.

An adult education institution – risks in moving towards interdependence

Adult educators trying to relate to other institutions take risks in being intentional about moving to a more interdependent mode. Our experience at the CCS has sharpened our awareness of what some of those risks might be, in the midst of excitement and affirmation about our educational philosophy and methodology. The same aspects of the methodology about which others express enthusiasm are those which threaten established structures and create the risks.

In our admission policy we affirm that other vocational preparation and work and life experience is as valid for admission as a bachelor's degree. We are therefore able to grant 'only' a diploma (although the church denomination for whose order of ministry many of our student are preparing considers it equivalent to a master's degree) and are ineligible for accreditation by the accrediting body in North American theological education. Courses taught by our academic staff (qualified to teach according to others' academic standards) are not credited within the university's theological education faculties because 'undergraduates' and 'graduates' are learning together. Because we do not give grades in major parts of our programme and focus on integrated learning of the whole person, and because students share in the assessment process, we have been perceived by some as not having standards and as making invalid decisions. Our graduates, whether or not they have graduate degrees, are seen by many as 'second class' within the Church and society. Fortunately they have learned an action/reflection mode and to name their gifts; their sense of self has been strengthened and they have a vision. With the other dynamics identified here as important in moving towards interdependence – trusting, imagining, playing, and becoming open to grace and the unexpected – they have learned what is most essential for their life and ministry, to be learners. One of them when asked in the study what interdependence meant to her, said:

> It's being open to learning. It's to do with having a sense of awe about life and about living and about learning, to realize that if you have that intuition inside, you set

aside what's important to you at that moment, not because anyone's dictating, but . . . you have a sort of expectancy . . . It's an attitude of learning.

References

Centre for Christian Studies (1981). *Educational Stance Statement.* Centre for Christian Studies, 77 Charles Street West, Toronto, Ontario M5S 1K5.

Fox, M (1979). *A Spirituality Named Compassion and the Healing of the Global Village, Humpty Dumpty, and Us.* Minneapolis, Minn: Winston Press.

Freire, P (1973). *Education for Critical Consciousness.* (M Bergman Ramos, Ed and Translator). New York: Seabury Press.

Freire, P (1970). *Pedagogy of the Oppressed.* (M Bergman Ramos, Translator). New York: Seabury Press.

Griffin, V R (1977). *Principles of Adult Learning.* Toronto: Adult Education Department, Ontario Institute for Studies in Education.

Griffith, G P (1982). Images of interdependence: meaning and movement in learning/teaching. Unpublished doctoral dissertation, Toronto: University of Toronto.

Nash, P (1973). Toward a radical view of authority relationships in education. In: Shimahara, N (Ed). *Education and Reconstruction: Promise and Challenge.* Columbus, Ohio: Charles E Merrill.

Chapter 5

Significant Personal Learning

Stephen Brookfield
Teachers' College Columbia University, New York

When I review the learning I have undertaken during my years on this planet I am struck by how much of that learning which I regard as the most important, profound and crucial has very little to do with my job or with my participation in formal courses of instruction. If I knew that universal extinction was due tomorrow, and I was asked to identify that learning which had been most important to me, I would probably think of the insights and understandings which had been developed in the course of my participation in intimate relationships.

My most significant personal learning has had to do with how to develop relationships with people who are important to me. I have had to learn how to fight my self-centredness, vanity, laziness and arrogance. I have had to learn how to accept change in relationships as inevitable and natural, and to try to make a virtue of necessity by embracing such change as a creative force. I have had to learn how to be more open about my feelings (both affectionate and hostile) and how best to communicate those to my intimates. I have had to learn how to accept that no one person (whether spouse, lover, parent, child or friend) can be the total centre of my universe, and that I cannot expect another person to meet all my needs. I have had to learn a set of very complicated skills needed for intimate relationships – how to listen, how to comfort, how to air doubts and criticisms while preserving another's self-respect, how to compromise, negotiate and communicate as fully and clearly as possible. Finally, I have had to learn how to enter others' frames of reference, so that I can see situations from their points of view.

All these learning efforts have been alternately difficult, rewarding, painful, joyful, frustrating and satisfying. None of them has been fully achieved, and I suspect that I will be engaged in such learning throughout my lifetime. Indeed, one of the most significant learnings for me has been that one never achieves a point of emotional stasis, when all aspects of one's personal zodiac are in a state of permanent harmony. Because of the ever-shifting configuration of intimate relationships, we are involved in a continuous process of reflection, action, further analysis, altered behaviour, further reflection and so on. Personal relationships are characterized by this dialectical dynamic (Cronen, Pearce and Tomm, 1985). To Basseches (1984) a participant in a dialectical relationship assumes that 'my traits are not fixed and that the relationships I enter will shape who I become as much as they are shaped by who I am and who my partner is' (p 26). Gould (1980) writes of the dialectic of growth and intimacy comprised of the 'transformational and developmental envy dynamics that make up the rhythm of joys and disturbances within an intimate relationship' (p 233).

I suspect that my feelings about the most important learning I have undertaken are not too untypical and that many people would select the insights they have gained about their intimate relationships as some of the most profound learning in their lives. Yet despite this apparent importance, very few psychologists, and even fewer educators, have paid much attention to the phenomenon of learning within relationships. There are exceptions, of course, such as the anthologies by Gergen and Davis (1985), Duck and Perlman (1985), Perlman and Duck (1986), Rogers (1984) and Smelser and Erikson (1980). One of Carl Rogers's most enduring pieces is *Significant Learning: In Therapy and Education* (1961). Considering the crucial importance of the topic, however, the attention granted to learning within relationships has been minimal. The need for intimacy may be recognized (Merriam, 1983), but its analysis from the perspective of learning and education has been neglected.

Significant personal learning

In analysing that learning which occurs within intimate relationships, we need a term to distinguish the processes and focuses under review from other forms of learning commonly considered. I propose the term *significant personal learning*, an adaptation of Rogers's (1961) significant learning. Significant personal learning is that learning within personal relationships which is distinguished by the following four characteristics:

(1) It is self-consciously perceived as profoundly important by the learners themselves. Hence, in studies of perspective transformation (Mezirow, 1977; Musgrove, 1977), the learners interviewed were quite explicit in recognizing the learning occurring as being of crucial significance in re-shaping their lives.

(2) It is frequently triggered by a major life crisis of some kind. In explorations of how women decided whether or not to have an abortion (Gilligan, 1982) and of marital dialogues (Gilligan, 1984), for example, it appears that the kind of self-reflection and appraisal characteristic of significant personal learning requires a prompt of considerable potency. Adults are not likely to engage in such potentially painful self-scrutiny without a powerful stimulus.

(3) It entails a re-definition of some aspect of the self. For example, in Musgrove's (1977) study of adults in positions of voluntary and involuntary marginality, his subjects were reported to have stored their 'real' selves until a crisis or changed set of circumstances allowed these to emerge. The artists, religious converts and homosexuals he interviewed had voluntarily assumed positions of marginality because of some sense of dissatisfaction with their previous identities. They came to re-define themselves in terms of newly assumed identities, some of which had previously been flirted with, some of which were wholly new.

(4) During this process those involved call into question some aspect of the

> assumptions underlying the way the 'proper' conduct of personal relationships has previously been conceived. They become more reflective concerning such things as criteria governing 'acceptable' conduct, appropriate roles and behaviours of participants in such relationships, false stereotypes which inhibit communication, and expectations which participants in intimate relationships place upon each other.

Intimate personal relationships constitute powerful crucibles for significant personal learning, yet this sphere of research has been left chiefly for psychoanalysts, psychotherapists, counsellors and developmental psychologists to explore. Educators, in particular, have fought shy of assisting adults to understand and negotiate the inevitable processes of change, decay and creation within their intimate relationships. It is as if they have felt their professional sphere to be restricted to understanding bodies of abstract empirical knowledge. The idea that educators might have something useful to contribute in promoting an understanding of personal relationships is, on the whole, regarded somewhat suspiciously. This is despite the fact that anyone who wishes to do so can advertise as a therapist, marriage counsellor or adviser on relationships, with no form of professional licensing or period of professional training being required. Educators' reticence to become involved in helping adults understand their relationships has meant that a void has existed in educational programmes for adults. Into this void has moved an army of therapists and advisers who have felt no such sense of timidity on these matters.

What is perhaps most surprising about this is that educators of adults are frequently forced to engage in precisely this activity. In many educational situations in which adults are trying to understand some aspect of the world this involves sacrificing time which would otherwise be spent with family, friends and lovers. Not only does this induce feelings of guilt on the part of learners, it also frequently creates actual resentment on the part of those who perceive themselves to be neglected. It is not uncommon for many members of adult learning groups, whether informal or for credit, to be experiencing massive changes in the fabric of their personal and occupational lives. Sometimes educational participation is a cause of discord between marital partners, lovers or friends, particularly if the learner is perceived by these significant people to be betraying shared values, allegiances and identity. Family and friends may feel 'jilted' by the learner in favour of unfamiliar intellectual terrains. When a participant in an intimate relationship suddenly appears to have jettisoned old likes, activities and ideas in favour of new ones, the other participant(s) may feel a distinct sense of threat that he or she is next on the list.

It is not surprising, then, that educators and trainers of adults are frequently faced with learners who turn to them for advice and assistance in managing the traumas and changes caused (in their eyes) by their educational participation. Many educators refuse to become what they feel are emotional accomplices of their learners, arguing that as educators they have no duties beyond the purely pedagogic. This attitude of emotional fastidiousness is hard to maintain, however, over a period of time in which case after case of marital disharmony is placed before educators by learners who see these disruptions as a consequence of their educational participation. When educators are advocating that learners draw upon their own experiences, and that they be forthcoming about these in discussions or assignments, it is contradictory (and practically impossible) to draw a line between educationally permissible and personally disallowable experiences.

Whether we like it or not, educators of adults are going to be drawn into exploring, with learners, the changes in relationships which these learners feel themselves to be experiencing. They may legitimately refuse to be drawn into marital disputes, or to serve as mediators in jealous friendships, but they should not draw back from helping adults try to understand the general processes of change within their relationships. These relationships are of three broad types: parent-child relationships, marital and love relationships, and friendships.

Learning within intimate relationships

Significant learning within personal relationships is, arguably, the most profound learning we experience. Unlike that learning which takes place under the aegis of formal educational institutions, the educators involved are people with whom we feel a powerful emotional affinity. Their actions and judgements are likely to be invested with a degree of significance far greater than that usually attributed to teachers' comments. When one's self-esteem is inextricably intertwined with the approval granted by another person, then offering challenges to that person, or receiving his or her critical comments on one's performance, are highly significant occurrences. One of the most difficult tasks to accomplish when attempting to learn from our experiences within relationships, is to be able to cultivate a genuine detachment from our own emotions and self-interest to be able objectively to understand another's criticisms, reservations and doubts.

Perhaps the most potent and traumatic of intimate relationships is that between child and parent. As Gould (1978, 1984) writes, we spend much of our adult lives negotiating how we are to detach ourselves from parental expectations concerning our values and behaviours, and then learning in turn how to manage the process of assisting our own children to negotiate such a detachment. There are many horror stories which readers will be able to locate in their own and others' experiences of how one or both aspects of this process of creative detachment has been mostly disturbing and painful for all concerned. What is often forgotten, however, is the tremendous potential for personal development which is realized when this process occurs with a degree of sensitivity on the part of parents. To realize that one's parents are regarding one as an equal, rather than a dependent, and that they are granting to one's own wishes, values, and behaviours an unconditional credibility, is a liberating experience for a son or daughter who also happens to be an adult. As a parent, it is also one of the most traumatic transitions, or developmental imperatives, to confront and negotiate.

To be aware of how one is (often unwittingly as well as deliberately) attempting to shape one's child in one's own self-image is to be possessed of an unusual degree of self-insight. To actively encourage and support one's own children in their attempts at experimentation with values, lifestyles and futures, and to be able to recognize when flirtations with ideas or unconventional behaviours are reflections of a child's desire for detachment, is to display exceptional wisdom. The most difficult aspect of a child-parent relationship for a parent to manage is when the child's attempts at detachment take the form of involvement with activities (such as drug abuse) which the parent regards objectively to be harmful to the child. For a parent to convince the child that advice and warnings regarding these activities are grounded in objective concern, and not possessive parental neurosis, is a complex and extremely problematic task.

For the child in a child-parent relationship who happens to be chronologically adult, the most difficult transition to negotiate is that of establishing a sense of separateness from a parent while retaining a bond of trust, affection and commitment with that parent. The onus in this transition is on the parent to attempt to create the conditions in which such a transition may take place. For the child, the traumatic aspect of this transition is that of risking parental censure which might result from efforts to establish a distance from the parent. Underlying this perception of risking parental disapproval is the fear, perhaps not brought fully into consciousness, of losing parental love. A major learning task for the parent in this situation is to create conditions in which the adult child can trust the parent's declarations that separation from the parent will not induce a withdrawal of parental love.

Within the sphere of intimate relationships, a second important relationship is that between marital partners or committed, long-term lovers. In terms of the first of the conditions of significant personal learning – that this learning is recognized as crucial and profound by the learner – it is this form of intimate relationship which may well be identified as more important than the child-parent relationship. This is quite simply because in the act of choosing partners in an intimate love relationship adults perceive themselves as having a degree of free choice. There is no volition in child-parent relationship in that the individuals concerned cannot be swapped for more congenial partners when the relationship becomes strained. In love affairs, however, adults perceive themselves to exercise a conscious measure of control over the choice of partner and the form the relationship should take.

It is precisely this awareness of self-conscious control and personal choice, however, which is one of the major sources of strain in a relationship. At the outset, each partner typically possesses idealized visions of the course the relationship is to take. Such visions will most probably be privatized, or at best shared only intermittently with the partner. This is just as well, since the essence of a developing relationship is a certain dynamism in which change and exploration are seen as integral to the relationship. When this vision is so finely honed and specific that any diversion from it is seen as an aberration, then it becomes a force inimical to, rather than nurturing of, a trusting relationship. When the vision is not realized in every detail, as it can never be, then the disappointed partner or partners inevitably begin to question the wisdom of their initial choice and commitment. It is at this point that partners can typically choose one of two courses of action; they can recognize the folly of adhering rigidly to previously idealized notions of how the relationship would develop, or they can begin to accuse the other of presenting a false self at the outset of the relationship. Such accusations typically centre on the other's apparently deliberate deception at the outset of the relationship. Charges such as 'you're not the same as you used to be', 'I never knew you were really like this', or 'you've changed' are common.

When the partner or partners recognize the folly of prescribing exactly idealized visions of the course the relationship should take, then real negotiation can begin. Endemic to this negotiation is a recognition that there can be no guarantees of the eventual success of the relationship (however that might be defined) and a willingness to consider scenarios of how it might develop which diverge markedly from those carefully imagined at the outset. It is this engagement in negotiation which is one of the most significant aspects of learning in relationships, a fact recognized by Gould (1984) in his discussion of development within relationships. As he points out, 'One person's developmental imperative can be the cause of both necessary and unnecessary problems in a relationship. Development and continuing a relationship are often at odds' (p 40). When development is sacrificed to the relationship, the developmental imperative is not killed. In Gould's words, 'It is only suffocated or sidetracked and is converted into either a high-tension centre or a dead spot in the person's psyche, continuing to provide the impetus to grow' (p 40). One of the most difficult transitions to make in relationships is to recognize this developmental imperative as inevitable, rather than as necessarily or wholly threatening to the stability of the relationship.

In her analysis of changing ideologies of love, Swindler (1980) notes the emergence of a 'love as heroic struggle' myth. According to this view, 'a love relationship that does not require painful change no longer performs its function. The value of love, and its challenge, is that it must stimulate and absorb perpetual change' (p 129). Thus, myth is certainly powerful and, like most myths, contains an element of truth. It is certainly true that a willingness to consider alternatives and to be prepared to negotiate on conflicting desires and aspirations is essential to a love relationship. However, if one slips into the 'love as heroic struggle' myth, the relationship is deemed wanting unless traumatic and painful struggle is perpetually present. For most relationships, such a continual warring, painful scrutiny of self, or constant reassessment of directions is likely to prove too stressful and to lead to the very dissolution of the relationship which it is intended to avoid. Although an openness and willingness to consider change is important, most partners will desire alternating periods of calm stability in between periods of intense negotiations regarding change.

Some of the most significant personal learning which takes place within the context of intimate relationships concerns the ability to reinterpret past actions in the light of a partner's view of these. The possibilities for self-deception in relationships is immense. We can convince ourselves that we are acting for the best of all possible motives in criticizing, belittling or punishing a partner when in fact our actions spring from selfish and self-absorbed motives. When one partner is able to place before another how the other's actions have been self-serving rather than altruistic, then that other is forced to reflect on the possibility of self-deception. This is, however, an intensely difficult and complex process to manage. It requires sensitivity on the part of the partner confronting the other with these critical interpretations to ensure that they are not made in such an injurious manner as to do further damage to the relationship, or to induce such a hostile reaction that the possibility that these criticisms might be accurate is never countenanced. The partner whose actions are being criticized also needs to be ready to make giant interpretative leaps to take on the other's perspective, and to see how apparently altruistic behaviour might indeed be less charitable than was previously supposed.

When this does happen, however, the learning which occurs exhibits all four of the conditions of significant personal learning previously identified. It is certainly generally regarded as important by the learners concerned. It is usually triggered by some kind of crisis, often in the other partner's reaching a point of frustration where the criticisms have to be voiced no matter what the consequences might be. It frequently results in changes in the person's self-concept, who now comes to view himself or herself in a much more careful and sceptical manner than was previously the case, and who comes to realize that he or she may be engaging in self-deception regarding the self-serving nature of apparently altruistic behaviour. Finally, it certainly entails an increase in the adult's critical capacities and inclinations, though these may be primarily of a self-critical nature, rather than occurring within the context of social or political action.

The final setting within which significant personal learning in the context of relationships take place, is that of friendships. Much more has been written on child-parent and marital/love relationships than on friendships, Yet for many in contemporary western societies characterized by high divorce rates, geographical mobility and occupational change, it is within friendships that their most intimate relationships might be located. The same strains induced by negotiated change are present in friendships as in the other two forms of relationship. What is generally absent from friendships, however, is the individuals involved holding tightly specified visions of an idealized future for the friendship. This certainly removes from this relationship a potential major cause of conflict and makes friendships more relaxed relationships, so much so, in fact, that they are often seen as an important refuge by those who are experiencing difficulties in their child-parent or marital/love relationships.

The major impetus for significant personal learning within friendships comes from the jealousy which often results from a friend's becoming intimate or close with a new person, group, or even interest. It is easy to invest friendships with a form of possessiveness very close to that sometimes evident in the other two forms of relationships discussed. The friend who is seen as a 'best' friend can become as significant an other as a spouse, lover or parent. When this best or specially intimate friend decides to form bonds with another person or group, or begins to explore ideas and activities not shared by the other, the relationship can suffer from the jealousy of the friend who feels neglected and harshly treated. For those who regard their friends as their most intimate companions, this can be a hard transition to manage; indeed, they may never be able to reconcile themselves to what they interpret as the friend's apparent betrayal and may decide simply to withdraw from the relationship in hurt, pique and feelings of rejection.

Logistically and legally it is much easier to effect this withdrawal in a friendship relationship than in either of the other two discussed. Emotionally, however, the consequences of withdrawal may be as traumatic and hurtful as any child-parent rift, divorce or break-up of a love affair. This will particularly be the case with a friendship within which the supposed 'real' self of the individual is invested. In a friendship in which an individual feels that his or her real self is revealed (in contrast to the artificial public face presented in, say, the workplace), dissolution of this friendship can be psychically devastating.

Friendship bonds seem to be particularly strong among individuals who feel themselves to be in a situation of collective oppression. Among resistance fighters, in women's consciousness raising groups, in political action groups, in gay rights advocacy groups or in support groups for, say, drug users or the recently bereaved, the friendship relationships which develop are intense in the extreme. The already mentioned study of Musgrove (1977) provides ample documentation of this intensity. It suggests that when such relationships founder the effect is likely to be equivalently devastating because the individual concerned feels that the psychological arena in which the real identity can be revealed and celebrated has suddenly been removed. Such devastations can result in the 'betrayed' friend engaging in swift and sometimes violent (psychological or physical) retribution.

Expressing and attempting to manage feelings of jealousy within a friendship is an effort in which the potential for a great deal of significant personal learning is certainly evident. In essence, the procedure and required sensitivities are similar to those within the other two relationships discussed. The individual who is the object of feelings of betrayal and jealousy has to be sufficiently sensitive to these not to react in a condemnatory manner when they are expressed. The friend who feels jealous and betrayed has to struggle to view his or her feelings and behaviours in as objective a fashion as is possible. In attempting to understand the psychological wellsprings of these feelings this individual is likely to be required to face some discomforting truths about the anxieties underlying perceptions of betrayal. Facing, attempting to understand, and living with a recognition of these anxieties is learning of a highly significant kind.

Change and reaffirmation

In discussing this concept of significant personal learning within relationships familiar questions asked refer to the implied necessity for constant change in relationships which this analysis might be thought to contain. 'Why', I am frequently asked, 'do we always stress change as necessary and positive?' 'Aren't there situations when people are happy with their lives, and don't need to change?' 'Why do accounts of significant personal learning always stress major traumas as the only triggers to change?' 'Why should we be made to feel guilty if we're not engaged in a constant and upsetting process of change?'.

These questions do not emanate from people who are evidently trying to avoid recognizing the need for change in their own lives and they make an excellent point. It is all too easy to accept uncritically a paradigm of personal relationships which sees these as characterized by continuous and traumatic change. Two points need to be made regarding how learning within intimate relationships might be studied.

The first of these concerns the nature of change within relationships. It cannot be emphasized too strongly that change within relationships does not always need to be constant, radical and traumatic. Were this so, we would be in a continuous position of ditching partners, seeking out new intimates, rejecting old contacts and creating new networks. There are many occasions when a process of prolonged reflection upon the assumptions undergirding one's relationships results in a reaffirmation of these assumptions. It may well be that in airing issues, raising doubts and offering criticisms the participants in a relationship will come to a more complete understanding of each other's viewpoints and decide that they are satisfied to continue with their present arrangements. Any changes they make may be small in terms of externally observable behaviours.

Nonetheless, those involved in this reflection will be in an altered state where their beliefs and assumptions regarding the conduct of relationships are involved. Instead of behaving in a reflexive manner (for example, unthinkingly following prescriptions derived from parents of appropriate marital conduct) they will have come to believe in the value of these prescriptions as a result of their own reflections. The end result of a period of reflection and scrutiny of assumptions and values may well be a reaffirmation of these same values and assumptions. The difference is that this commitment is informed, not unthinking. It has been reached after a process of critical reflection, not because of the insistence of some loved or feared external authority.

If one danger to be avoided is that of helping professionals coming to believe that major alterations in the fabrics of individual lives must always result from periods of reflection, another is that of presuming that the impetus for such change is always negative. In intimate relationships there are always positive triggers for participants to reappraise their involvements. For marital partners or lovers, the birth of a child will almost inevitably wreak major changes in their relationship, yet such alterations will be perceived as being caused by a joyful event. Falling in love is a process which causes those involved to question many aspects of their previous lives, most particularly their belief that their past relationships had been 'peak' emotional experiences. When the new intimate holds beliefs contrary to those held by previous partners, or when he or she is involved in activities which are unfamiliar to the other partner, these beliefs and activities are not perceived as threats to the relationship; rather, they are frequently viewed as engaging and positive areas for personal development. Participants in new relationships often speak of how the other's interests are broadening and developing them. They regard these areas for future involvement as tantalizing, not irrelevant. They are challenged and intrigued by the prospect of sharing their new partner's interests, and welcome the chance to explore these new arenas.

Conclusion

Learning within the forms of intimate relationships discussed so far can be seen to exhibit three conditions of critical reflectivity: the development of contextual awareness, reflective scepticism and imaginative speculation. Contextual awareness is evident in participants' realization that what they perceive to be the 'natural' order of things in a relationship is a reflection of social or subcultural prescriptions. Examples of this might be the following:

(1) Lovers who realize that their ideas on what are acceptable, appropriate sexual behaviours are derived from external sources (parental proscriptions, media characterizations, erotic novels) as well as from their own internal drives and desires.
(2) Parents who perceive that what they have been giving as apparently objective, considered advice on 'the best' career choice, partner or friendship network for their child, in fact represents a projection of their own unfulfilled hopes and dreams.
(3) Individuals who are aware that the expectations they have of their friends regarding these friends' obligations to them, reflect social norms assimilated from parents, teachers or the media.

Reflective scepticism – the questioning of beliefs, norms or advice which are supposed to carry universal truth and authority – can be seen in the following examples:

(1) A wife who rejects the various submissive role models of wifely behaviour laid down by her parents, religion or subculture.
(2) A husband who refuses to conform to notions of 'manliness' (domination, authority and even physical abuse) derived from his peer group, parents or the mass media.
(3) Gay and lesbian partners who do not accept that their liaisons are, by definition, wholly immoral, deviant and indicative of some serious emotional flaws in their personalities.

Imaginative speculation – the capacity to imagine ways of thinking and living alternative to those one currently accepts – can be seen in the following examples:

(1) Marital partners and lovers who re-negotiate central features of their relationships; for example, in regard to the distribution of household tasks, child-rearing, and the role of economic provider.
(2) Marital partners who decide to develop and sustain peer networks, even though their subcultural mores dictate that marriage commitments place friendship relations in a subservient position.
(3) Parents who make a deliberate and conscious effort to avoid replicating the kinds of domineering parent-child interactions they experienced in their own childhood.

The formal study of learning within intimate relationships is, as yet, relatively unexplored by educators. What exist are either popular psychological treatments of relationships written from a simplified psychotherapeutic viewpoint, or academic socio-psychological analyses which reduce human interactions to algebraic equations. Books such as Fromm's *The Art of Loving* (1956) or

Storr's *The Integrity of the Personality* (1966), both of which are intelligent yet very accessible, are rare. Given that forming and living within relationships is arguably the most important of all adult learning tasks, and the one to which we ascribe the greatest significance, it is surprising that this activity should have been ignored by educators. It is impossible to imagine adults traversing their lives without becoming entangled, by design or unwittingly, in an endless series of intimate relationships of the kinds described in this chapter. Assisting adults to become reflective learners within such relationships must be one of the most important functions which helping professionals can perform.

References

Basseches, M (1984). *Dialectical Thinking and Adult Development.* Norwood, New Jersey: Ablex Publishing Corporation.

Cronen, V E, Pearce, W B and Tomm, K (1985). A dialectical view of personal change. In: *The Social Construction of the Person.* K J Gergen and K E Davis (eds). New York: Springer-Verlag, 203-244.

Duck, S and Perlman, D (eds). (1985) *Understanding Personal Relationships.* Beverly Hills: Sage Publications.

Fromm, E (1956). *The Art of Loving.* New York: Harper and Row.

Gergen, K J and Davis, K E (eds) (1985). *The Social Construction of the Person.* New York: Springer-Verlag.

Gilligan, C (1982). *In a Different Voice: Psychological Theory and Women's Development.* Cambridge: Harvard University Press.

Gilligan, C (1984). Marital dialogues. In: *Adult Development Through Relationships.* V Rogers (ed). New York: Praeger Publishers, 28-39.

Gould, R L (1978). *Transformations: Growth and Change in Adult Life.* New York: Simon and Schuster.

Gould, R L (1980). Transformations during early and middle adult years. In: *Themes of Work and Love in Adulthood.* N J Smelser and E H Erikson (eds). Cambridge: Harvard University Press, 213-237.

Gould, R L (1984). Recovering from childhood: distortions of the past on the present. In: *Adult Development Through Relationships.* V Rogers (ed). New York: Praeger Publishers. 40-52.

Merriam, S (ed) (1983). *Themes of Adulthood Through Literature.* New York: Teachers' College Press.

Mezirow, J (1977). Perspective transformation. *Studies in Adult Education.* 9, 2, 153-64.

Musgrove, F (1977) *Margins of the Mind.* London: Methuen.

Perlman, D and Duck, S (1986) *Intimate Relationships: Development, Dynamics and Deterioration.* Beverly Hills: Sage.

Rogers, C (1961). *On Becoming a Person: a Therapist's View of Psychotherapy.* Boston: Houghton Mifflin.

Rogers, V (ed) (1984). *Adult Development Through Relationships.* New York: Praeger Publishers.

Smelser, N J and Erikson, E H (eds) (1980). *Themes of Work and Love in Adulthood.* Cambridge: Harvard University Press.

Storr, A (1965). *The Integrity of the Personality.* Harmondsworth: Penguin Books.

Swindler, A (1980). Love and adulthood in American culture. In: *Themes of Work and Love in Adulthood.* N J Smelser and E H Erikson (eds). Cambridge: Harvard University Press, 120-147.

Chapter 6

Learning and the Hidden Agenda

Gill Robertson
Wiltshire Area Management Centre, Swindon

Introduction

This chapter is about learning as self-directed personal development. It tells the story of my discoveries as a postgraduate researcher when I undertook a research enquiry which aimed to explore the nature of individuals' experiences and perceptions of personal change and development in their adult lives (Robertson, 1984). The particular methods of exploration incorporated into the enquiry were intended in themselves to further and develop the learning of those who took part in it, and the chapter focuses on the learning that took place in the process.

There were two major discoveries that emerged for me – one concerning the learning of the other participants and the other concerning my own. When I began the project, I had no precise model of personal development that I wanted to replicate in the enquiry – indeed, one of my purposes in the research was to develop new models based on the experiences and interpretations of the participants. But I accepted a general definition of learning as the experience of significant changes in self-perceptions and perceptions of others, and in actions and behaviours.

I was also influenced by the 'experiential' model of a learning cycle (Kolb and Fry, 1975) which implies that learning may be facilitated through the learner engaging in a continuing cycle of sequential activities, of experiencing, reflecting, conceptualizing and experimenting. What I was not fully prepared for was that the achievement of significant changes in perceptions and in actions was to be a long and difficult process. Seeing oneself in a new light turned out to be one thing, but knowing how to put these insights into action, and then to change the patterns of habitual actions and behaviours, was even more difficult. Learning turned out to be more of a painful process of each participant finding out why he or she had wanted to take part in the research project than of establishing clear personal objectives at the start and of working logically and systematically towards them, through action and reflection.

As far as my own learning was concerned I realized in retrospect that I had started out without any conscious intention of understanding or of learning about myself. I was interested in the experiences of others rather than my own. But as time went by, I found myself being drawn more and more into the learning process, through my interactions with the other participants, and through my role in the research.

Some time after the period in which the practical work took place (about 30 months in total) I could begin to make sense of it all. I could see that I too had learned from the research why I had wanted to undertake it, but that these reasons had not been clear to me at the start. I realized that learning, for me, as for some of the participants, had involved uncovering a 'hidden agenda'. Learning was all about rediscovering aspects of our experience that we were avoiding or that we were unaware of when we started out. It was all about discovering the very things that gave us a need and a will to learn – and also the uncertainty of how to go about it. As such, our learning turned out to have much more in common with theories from psychotherapy and psychoanalysis than I had anticipated. My lack of anticipation was itself a fundamental aspect of my own learning.

Some of the relevant assumptions derived from the therapeutic and psychoanalytic models of learning are as follows: that there is an inherent potential for conflict between aspects of the individual psyche, generally between the idealized, rational, order-loving part of ourselves and the part(s) that we associate with unacceptable and disruptive desires, needs, emotions and characteristics; and that the unacceptable parts of our selves may remain in or be consigned to the unconscious functioning of our psyche, through the mechanisms of repression and suppression.

Learning involves developing a conscious awareness and an acceptance of those aspects of which we are unaware and resist – as in Rogers's psychotherapy (1967) – in becoming a 'fully functioning person', or in 'gestalt therapy' (Perls, Hefferline and Goodman, 1974). Parallels may be found in Jung's theory of individuation, which involves assimilating the 'shadow'. Jung writes:

> The shadow personifies everything that the subject refuses to acknowledge about himself and yet is always thrusting itself upon him directly or indirectly – for instance, inferior traits of character and other incompatible tendencies.
>
> (1959, paras 512-3)

The general implication is that our needs for order and control, for social acceptance and for a 'distress-free' life prompt us to resort to defensive strategies in which we resist being aware of and acting in accordance with the parts of ourselves and our experiencing which conflict with this. Learning, development and change involve confronting these avoidances and blocks in our awareness, and accepting their contents – usually through the intervention of the therapist, analyst or counsellor.

This is how it happened through a research enquiry, through the discovery of the answer to the fundamental question, Why? – why it was that we all wanted to engage in an experience of learning in the first place. Our 'hidden agenda' held the key to discovering the resistances in our awareness that lay at the heart of our learning.

Setting the scene: combining learning and research

There were two key assumptions which underlay my initial design of a research methodology. One was the philosophy that action and experiencing are essential to knowing and understanding ourselves and our world (Merleau-Ponty, 1962; MacMurray, 1969). The other was that if I was attempting to describe and interpret the experiences of other people, then they should also take part in the reflection on and the making sense of their own experiences. I agreed with the arguments of practitioners such as Heron (1981, 1982), Rowan (1981) and Reason and Rowan (1981), that methods of the kind where the subjects engage only in the action or experiencing or both and the researcher only in the reflecting, are not adequate to develop an understanding of another's experience. I wanted to develop research that was not alienating the participants (Rowan, 1981) and that enabled the participants to learn through action (Torbert, 1972, 1978, 1981). I decided to develop a methodology that engaged the participants on as equal a footing as possible, as cooperative researchers exploring their own lives and experiences. The particular methods that I chose to do this were participative group workshops, followed by one-to-one in-depth interviews between each participant and myself. During the two and a half year period I held two separate workshop series, the first with 18 participants and the second with 7. Both workshop projects incorporated structured experiential exercises, which enabled participants to discover, explore and discuss aspects of their lives, past and present.

I advertised each project as a personal development workshop, which participants were invited to join voluntarily. In the initial contracting that took place it was made clear to the prospective participants that the workshops combined the opportunity for personal learning with contributing to a research thesis. Agreement was sought in principle that the information gathered would be included in the research thesis. I also explained at the start of each project that an essential element of the method would involve checking out, discussing, and seeking their agreement to the written interpretations that we would develop about their experiences.

The theme of the unconscious

In planning the first workshop series, I was aware that the defensive processes of the unconscious might well provide sources of inhibition and distortion in the accuracy and fullness of perception, the expression and the interpretation of personal experience.

Torbert (1972) identifies the 'mystery-mastery' syndrome as a major threat to learning and understanding, where a fear of looking foolish prompts the individual to resist and conceal information that challenges his or her self-image of mastery and control. Heron (1982) focuses on the resistance to noticing phenómena which threaten to open up unresolved conflicts and distress associated with childhood experiences. Other psychoanalytic theories of defensive processes, such as 'projection' (projecting our own characteristics and experiences on to others) and 'introjection' (taking on those that belong to others) also had implications for the experiential validity of our research findings. I accepted that I was no less vulnerable than the other participants. The methods would need to incorporate measures to confront and to counteract any such distortions in our perceptions of ourselves and in our perception of, and interactions with, each other.

Many ideas of how to go about this are given in the work of Heron (1981, 1982), Rowan (1981), Reason and Rowan (1981) and Torbert (1972, 1978,

1981). Methods include exploring all conflicts and contradictions experienced in the course of the enquiry; practising skills of attention and of noticing the full range of the phenomena of personal experience, particularly feelings and intuitions and thoughts and physical sensations, and the inner world of personal experience as well as the world perceived as exterior to self; and establishing systems for checking out the congruency of thoughts and experiences, intra-personally and interpersonally. The ideal setting is one in which researcher and participants assume equal, mutually supportive roles, contributing equally to the action and to the thinking, and working cooperatively in a climate of trust and commitment to the achievement of shared learning objectives.

I realized that the quality of the validity of the research findings would depend a great deal upon the quality of the learning achieved by the research participants. But when it came to putting these ideas into practice, in the first workshop project, I began to experience considerable conflict. The first signs of defensive resistances in myself, and in the other participants, started to appear.

The first project

In deciding what measures I needed to take to establish conditions in the workshops that would be conducive to the development of validity (that is, to the fullness and accuracy of the findings), I began to feel critical of the ideas outlined above. I decided that the feedback procedures for checking out the congruency of our feelings, their expression and interpretations, as proposed by Heron (1981), were too restrictive. I did not accept the implications (Heron, 1982) that the generation of valid information must involve a re-experiencing of unresolved childhood distress. I believed that learning also develops through enjoyment, and I was aware of the manipulative power held by the facilitator. I did not want to force the participants into anything that they did not want or choose to do themselves.

Yet was I trying to avoid and preclude any encounter with experiences hidden in our unconscious? Was I being over-protective? Were these rational criticisms grounded in my own defensiveness? I did not know, and the anxieties intensified in the course of the first project. Firstly, I found that the practical demands of running the workshops made it impossible to achieve all ideals. I did not attempt to introduce any means of enabling the participants to systematically monitor their own learning during the workshops. But the participants were encouraged to confront each other about the aspects of their accounts of their experiences that appeared to be contradictory or ambiguous. A session was devoted specifically to exploring significant conflicts in their lives. The following interviews provided further opportunities for me to confront the participants about aspects of their experiences and to facilitate their learning through simply feeding back to them my interpretations of them.

At the end, there was a general consensus that the project had proved useful and interesting, but at the time only one or two were able to identify more specifically what they had learned about themselves and what they might seek to change in the future. It also proved impossible to achieve parity in our roles. I found from the beginning that the organizational demands had prohibited my participation in the workshops and I took on the role of facilitator. As the initiator of the project, the tag of 'expert' was hard to lose and it was the participants' choice that I should undertake the main direction of the workshops and the writing up. But did the participants' readiness to agree to the proposed programme of activities and to the interpretations developed conceal their own resistances to exploring their experiences any further? Did the decisions of one or two of the participants not to engage in further detailed discussions after the workshops conceal a fear of venturing too far? These latter participants were those whose stories revealed much unhappiness, depression and unresolved conflict in their personal relationships – potentially those perhaps with a need for learning and change.

For my part, I became desperately worried about feeding back information that might re-stimulate strong feelings of anger or grief. I felt guilt that I was 'using' the participants for my own aims, although they had all volunteered to take part and were only too pleased to help. I began to experience extreme anxiety about how my own defensiveness might have contaminated and inhibited the learning of others – but it was too late now to be able to check this out any further. My confusion was so great that I was on the point of giving up the research altogether.

Fortunately, at this stage, I took heart from reading Devereux (1967), who argues that the fact of the 'partition' between observer and observed results in an experience of anxiety. Both attempt to compensate for the incompleteness of their communication with each other, through the fantasies of transference and counter-transference ('transference' referring to the observed's perception of the observer as if he or she were someone else of significance in the observed's life; and 'counter-transference' referring to the identical process in the observer's perceptions of the observed). Devereux's broad thesis is that recognizing and accepting our anxiety is actually the starting point for understanding our own experience and the experience of the other, and for exploring distortions and fantasies in our perceptions of the other.

I decided to undertake the second project and, as well as seeking to differentiate more clearly between my interpretations and those of the participants, to actively record my thoughts, feelings and anxieties in relation to the others, throughout the course of the workshops and interviews. I also decided to take deliberate action to counteract and to explore the empirical basis for my anxieties by doing the opposite of my inclinations, doing what I most feared.

As far as the other participants' learning was concerned, there were a number of innovations that could be made. It became evident during the course of the first project that at least half of the participants were in the process of making major decisions and changes in their lives: changing jobs, getting married, or ending a close personal relationship. In other cases, the need to expose and discuss with others an experience of extreme conflict in relationships at work appeared to be central to their participation in the project. In retrospect, I could surmise that these events in their life outside the project were associated with 'hidden agendas' underlying the choice to take part in the project, and were a potential focus for deeper learning and understanding.

In the second project I accordingly decided to introduce some innovations into the method in order to exploit more fully the potential for learning arising in the phenomena underlying each participant's choice to take part. I decided to ask participants to identify their learning objectives at the start and to monitor their learning more closely through the project. I chose to work with a smaller group (seven this time) over a longer period of time, to help develop closer relationships, and to try to participate on a more equal basis.

I also decided to try to begin each new workshop session with written feedback of material recorded on tape in discussions in the preceding session in order to achieve a greater integration of the active and reflective aspects of the research. With these developments in the method, I entered into the second project.

The second project

In the course of the second project, the interaction between my own learning and the learning of the participants intensified. Initially, the difficulty of knowing what one wants to learn before one has learned it once again became apparent. Although I spent more time discussing the project with the potential participants in the contracting stages, and more time clarifying the learning objectives of the research, the participants still experienced difficulty in establishing clear learning objectives for themselves. 'We are doing it to help you' or 'Perhaps we'll know at the end why we came' were typical responses. Only Sean had a clear idea of his learning objectives – which were to develop skills of communication which would help him in his work as a financial consultant.

In spite of the efforts that I made to clarify how I perceived learning would progress, the group as a whole initially appeared to hesitate in exploring aspects of their lives and experiences. Although as trust was established, some began to open up, to explore the conflicts in their lives, and to confront issues which were highly distressing to themselves, the degree of participation in this varied from person to person. Most showed an intermittent commitment to the project, throwing themselves into some activities but not into others. Then I began to accept that ambiguity and uncertainty are essential and central aspects of the learning process. I could also begin to accept that the potential pain and distress of challenging the resistances to our experiences may mean that 'learning' as such does not take place. I could begin to accept that it was in fact all right if people did not appear to learn. 'Resistance' may have its own positive function in the experience of the individual.

Realizing this, I began to question further the part played by my own perceptions in prejudging the learning of others. Were my perceptions of their resistance accurate? Were they indeed a function of my own defensiveness, rather than that of the participants? Or, worse still, could they be a function of my ineptitude in managing the project?

It was through the efforts that I made to differentiate carefully between my own interpretation of the participants' experiences and their own interpretations that the light began to dawn. I began to understand the relation between the apparent ability of each individual to learn through the workshop activities, and the patterns and dynamics of the individual's learning and change in his or her life as a whole. I could also identify more clearly the resistances and the hidden agenda that I had brought into the research.

The critical aspect of this was recording my own feelings, intuitions and conceptual interests. Relating these to my own theoretical interpretation of the participants' experiences, I began to understand something of the part played by my own fears and my own needs in undertaking the research. Doing what I most feared, confronting where I did not want to, I could establish whether my fears and anxieties were borne out in practice or whether they were simply manifestations of my own experience. Adopting an approach in which I could say, 'This is how I see you; is this how you see yourself?', I found that confrontation could be gentle and non-threatening, and that my fears of prompting unnecessary distress on the part of the participants were considerably diminished.

Then it was possible to ascertain the extent to which all the participants were open to new ideas, to exploring the conflicts and ambiguities in their experiences, and to taking action to make changes in their lives.

Three different groupings emerged. In one the participants preferred to accept their own initial accounts of their lives as they were, without enquiring further into them. The emphasis for them lay in looking to the future. Sean, for example, identified a major conflict between what he called his 'negative', 'frustrated', 'stagnating' side, prone to inertia and depression, and his 'positive', 'successful' side, associated with his capacities for achieving his material goals in life. His life was devoted to changing jobs in the pursuit of success and the gold watch that he wanted, so that the negative side could not surface for any length of time. Sean was unable to explore the negative feelings in any depth, and declared that it was vital for him to be able to develop a constant positive attitude. Failure was a word that he never used, and exploring his conflict ran contrary to his philosophy of life.

In a second group others showed excitement and interest in finding patterns of conflict that had persisted through their lives, but were unable to conceptualize how they might resolve them, accepting them as 'hang-ups' and not expecting any change. Mary, for example, identified a major conflict through her life in which she swung from dieting and working to the point of collapse, to over-eating and not caring about her work, and recognized that the conflict was exacerbated by her feelings of revulsion in sexual relationships. But she was unable to pinpoint what might have been cementing the conflict through her life or to explore these feelings in any great depth.

In a third group, the participants were the most open to looking at themselves, the most receptive to new ideas and to new interpretations. Typically both of the participants in this group identified a pattern of change in their lives in which each had persisted in a particular pattern of conflict, which resulted eventually in crisis in personal relationships and marital break-up, and was followed now by an awareness of what each had been resisting in self-awareness in the past. Don, for example, realized now in retrospect, after the experience of crisis, that he had been denying needs for love in himself and others in the past, and was aware of how much he had learned and changed in recent years, now stressing the importance of giving and caring for others.

For him, the conflict had been resolved and he was entering into a new phase where new conflicts were yet to be identified.

Paradoxically, the third group, who appeared to be the least resistant to the exploration of personal conflicts, who were aware that they had undergone a process of learning and change in their life to date, were in fact those who had the least to learn in the workshops in terms of the model that I had adopted. On the other hand the first group, who appeared to be the most resistant to learning in the course of the project, were those who had the most to learn. The paradox was that the latter group were never likely to perceive their learning in the terms that I was using.

It was in the second group, in the meeting ground of our interpretations, that there appeared to be the greatest scope for learning through resistance, for discovering their hidden agenda in the course of the project. Lorna, for example, identified a pattern of 'not learning' in her life in which she perceived that she habitually fell into relationships which tended to become vicious circles of dependence on the part of her partner, reinforced by her own lack of assertiveness and fear of hurting her partner's feelings. Some months after the project had finished, I learned from her that she was still applying the learning from the project to her life, and that she was now engaged in a relationship which was satisfying, and which did not conform to the pattern of the past. Yet at the time, she did not understand how she might actively resolve the underlying pattern of conflict in her life. Although the project may have helped to identify the nature of her resistances, and what it was that she wanted to resolve, the translation into action was not possible until some considerable time afterwards.

The findings give strength to the view that where learning involves uncovering and discovering aspects of our unconscious, the movement from unawareness to awareness must begin with contradiction and ambiguity in the attitude of the learner. Then the learner must confront or encounter a new perspective, and be able to reframe his or her past experience, be able to resolve the ambiguity and to accept that the ways of the past are no longer appropriate, and to look upon a resistance as a weakness rather than a strength. Learning through resistance may not happen if resistance is a way of life, or if learning through life has already aided discovery. In any case, the discovery takes time which may extend beyond the scope of an experiential enquiry, and learning is never finally completed.

My own learning

The discoveries about the participants' learning were accompanied by discoveries about myself. The exploration of my personal feelings played an important part in this, and I recognized a considerable change that had taken place in my own values during the course of the two projects.

In the second project I became aware of my feelings of empathy and respect for the two participants who had undergone crisis and divorce in their lives, but who had retained hope and a belief in the possibility of developing relationships of trust and love again. I learned that 'change', either in the sense of changing circumstances or of changing attitudes and behaviours, was not valued by any of the participants for its own sake, and that the preservation of values first developed in parental relationships and in childhood was a source of positive self-regard. I began to realize that I had begun my research and had undertaken the first project with the view that change and flexibility were 'good things', essential to the psychological health and well-being of both individuals and organizations. Now I found myself beginning to accept more readily the importance of stability and consistency, and more importantly, realized that I was actually seeking a conventional domestic life based upon traditional values inherited from my own parents.

This realization was strengthened by the experience of undertaking the research as a whole, and by the interaction between my work and my home life. Although I had set out with the attitude that what mattered most to me in my life was my work, I found that it was impossible to actually undertake the research and to invest in it the conceptual and emotional energy that it required, unless all was well in my personal life. But it was the deliberate relation of the theory emerging from the project to my own life, and particularly the review of my own interpretations, that helped to make sense of these experiences.

In the emerging theory of a life process of learning and development based upon the participants' interpretations, a central feature was the resistance through life to opening up and exploring bases of dissatisfaction and conflict in personal life. In some cases this eventually resulted in the experience of a 'life-crisis', which involved major decisions and changes in work and personal life; in some of these cases, crisis was followed by major change in attitudes and behaviours. But it was only those participants who had undergone the experiences of crisis who actually accepted the view that I put forward, that resistances were potentially negative. When Sean denied the view that suppressing his negative side could be construed as resisting learning, I realized that 'resistance' was my construct and not his. When I began to add to the participants' interpretations an interpretation which located all of their life patterns in a process of resistance and conflict since early childhood, I asked myself the questions: 'Where was my interest in "resistance" coming from? What was the pattern of resistance, conflict, crisis and change in my own life? Why my interest in the processes of unresolved childhood conflict?'

Then I understood. I too, like those participants who had experienced change in themselves, had undergone a domestic crisis in my life, shortly before undertaking the research. At the time I had tried to throw myself into a new way of life which demanded the denial of the unresolved distress that I still experienced, the denial of the importance of my personal life and a commitment to 'change'. I learned through the research that I could deny these things no longer, and that I did value relationships of constancy and stability, and still retained values developed in childhood. I learned from the two participants who had undergone divorce that there can be an integration of past and present, and that although conflict is never resolved absolutely, we may at least come to terms with it, and develop new attitudes and behaviours based on a synthesis of past and present beliefs.

Some conclusions

In this chapter I have been able to touch only briefly on one or two aspects of the complex process of personal learning, but whether we are learners or (especially if we are) facilitators, these findings emphasize that our understanding of any phenomenon is considerably enhanced by understanding the place of it in our own lives.

In understanding a phenomenon such as resistance to learning, a context of dialogue with as many people as possible is essential to facilitate the confrontation with whatever it is that we are each resisting. Through identifying the similarities and the differences in our perceptions of ourselves and of each other, we can encounter the boundaries of our own perceptions and reach the point where learning may begin.

The more certain we are of ourselves, the more we may have to learn, and the signposts to the latter are our niggling fears and anxieties, our intuitions that something needs pursuing. Critical activities which may help our discoveries are those of 'noticing' and of 'trying out' (as Reason and Rowan, 1981, point out in their discussion of validity in experiential research). More specifically, we need to notice and ideally to record what we are thinking, feeling, sensing and intuiting in our interactions with the other participants. The 'trying out' demands an attitude which welcomes challenge – not only challenging each other's self-perceptions but also welcoming being challenged in the passive sense. If we are unable to accept the disagreement and the challenge of others and to begin to challenge ourselves, then there is little likelihood of learning.

The findings also imply that a direct approach to discovering our resistances and to discovering what it is that we need to learn, such as that employed in the gestalt therapy described by Perls, Hefferline and Goodman (1974), may well be ineffective. Where a block in awareness is part of a pattern that has persisted for years, facing up to it and reconstruing as a negative avoidance what was experienced as a positive suppression, does not happen overnight. Concentrating initially on the achievement of a shared task involving reflection and action over a period of time may provide a less direct but more effective means of facilitating learning and change. A major issue which we need to consider is how we can monitor and develop the period of making sense and of taking action after our workshop learning, in the period of relation to the wider life patterns of individual learning. Nor is there any guarantee that there will be significant change, particularly when an individual has learned that the best way to survive in life is to resist and suppress any thoughts and feelings that challenge his or her positive self-image. It seems that learning is most likely when conflict within oneself is experienced and accepted as tenable no longer.

Finally, a further question which the research continues to pose for me is that of how we can best challenge and confront each other in workshop learning. Although my anxieties about stimulating undue and potentially destructive distress were proven to be unfounded, as far as I am aware, in the course of the projects, I believe that we should never take this for granted. We should always be aware of the need to combine confrontation with reassurance, and to ask for support if we find that we need it. Being able to help each other to take risks and to do what individually we cannot do, lies at the heart of the learning process.

References

Devereux, G (1967). *From Anxiety to Method in the Behavioural Sciences.* The Hague: Mouton.

Heron, J (1981). Experiential research methodology. In: P Reason and J Rowan (eds) *Human Inquiry.* 153-66. Chichester: John Wiley.

Heron, J (1982). *Empirical Validity in Experiential Research.* Guildford: Human Potential Research Project, University of Surrey, in association with London: British Postgraduate Medical Federation.

Jung, C G (1959). Conscious, unconscious and individuation. In: *Collected Works.* 9, 1, 275-89, paras 489-524. Translated from the German by Hull, R E C. London: Routledge and Kegan Paul (originally published in 1939).

Kolb, D A and Fry, F (1975). Towards an applied theory of experiential learning. In: C L Cooper (ed). *Theories of Group Processes.* 33-57. London: John Wiley.

MacMurray, J (1969). *The Self as Agent.* London: Faber.

Merleau-Ponty, M (1962). *Phenomenology of Perception.* (Translated by C Smith.) London: Routledge and Kegan Paul.

Perls, F S, Hefferline, R F and Goodman, P (1974) *Gestalt Therapy: Excitement and Growth in the Human Personality.* Harmondsworth, Middlesex: Pelican.

Reason, P and Rowan, J (1981) Issues of validity in new paradigm research. In: P Reason and J Rowan (eds). *Human Inquiry.* 239-50. Chichester: John Wiley.

Rogers, C R (1967). *On Becoming a Person.* London: Constable.

Robertson, G (1984). Experiences of learning. Doctoral thesis. Bath: University of Bath.

Rowan, J (1981). A dialectical paradigm for research. In: P Reason and J Rowan (eds). *Human Inquiry.* 93-112. Chichester: John Wiley.

Torbert, W (1972). *Learning from Experience: Toward Consciousness.* Columbia: Columbia University Press.

Torbert, W (1978). Educating toward shared purpose, self-direction, and quality: the theory and practice of liberating structure. *Journal of Higher Education.* 49, 2, 109-35.

Torbert, W (1981). Why educational research has been so uneducational: the case for a new model of social science based on collaborative inquiry. In: P Reason and J Rowan (eds). *Human Inquiry.* 141-51. Chichester: John Wiley.

Chapter 7

The Doubting Journey: a Learning Process of Self-Transformation

Ross Keane
Loyola University, Chicago

> The more faithfully you listen to the voice within you, the better you will hear what is sounding outside.
> *Dag Hammarskjold*

In this chapter I discuss the methodology and learnings of a qualitative heuristic enquiry into the phenomenon of doubting. This is the story of a research project in which I set out to understand doubting, not by defining and categorizing it but by experiencing it directly in my own life, by reflecting on that experience, and then dialoguing with other chosen people who were prepared to share their experiences. I entered the world of five men who, like myself, shared a common lifestyle within a church community by asking them to discuss their doubting experiences. I studied doubting in its essential form by entering my own experience and by listening to the experience of others with ears which tried to hear what the experience was like for them.

How I became interested in researching doubting and learning

My decision to research doubting and learning in this sample of adults came from the coincidence of two factors. The first was a decision to face and try to resolve an extended period of inner struggle in my life. The struggle involved a long standing sense of unease about self worth, competence, identity and life commitments and an inability to address it. This inner struggle had been surfacing in various somatic, spiritual and emotions tensions over two or three years. My self understandings no longer seemed adequate. Something was wrong yet I did not know what it was. I decided to use the space of a sabbatical period to come to terms with myself. I decided it was imperative to use the time away from normal roles, pressures, obligations and roots to look at what was on 'the back burner'.

Coincidentally with this decision I became aware that a search to understand self-doubt might be facilitated by a more formal study of learning processes in a course offered by Dr Virginia Griffin at the Ontario Institute for Studies in Education (OISE). She used a self-directed, interdependent, experiential and emergent design model of teaching which was totally foreign to my previous experience. She did not teach in a traditional way and this disoriented, disturbed and confused me for much of her course. This state lasted many weeks before I was able to let go of my 'shoulds' and culturally conditioned expectations of self, others, teachers and learning which had been gained in more traditional learning situations. I finally learned to accept my experience as a valid source of knowledge. I broke through the cultural conditioning which had me conceive of myself as a derivative learner. I perceived myself as a learner in a new way. This insight was an important shift which gave me the freedom to enter more fully into the class. This point of self-acceptance freed me, and my new perspective resulted in a much higher level of personal energy for learning within this course.

The focus of my course at OISE was 'learning processes' or inner happenings which occur over time within learners as they learn (*see* Chapter 16). I was challenged to name and describe my inner experience as I strove to find direction, motivation and resources for learning. I learned to reflect upon the reflection process. These insights into learning processes greatly facilitated my attempts to look at my inner struggles around identity, competence and commitments. I asked a learning partner to interview me on doubt in my life and wrote a paper which I entitled, *The experience of doubt in my development.*

In analysing my experiences I recognized that doubt had been a factor in many previous experiences which had produced new self-understandings. I identified characteristic patterns in past doubting experiences and compiled a list of questions and issues about doubting and learning which I wanted to study further. However, my inner struggles continued. Their outward manifestations took the form of bodily pain and tension, disturbed feelings, powerful dreams and general restlessness. I needed to learn more. It became important to find out to what extent such disturbing happenings were part of the experience of others who shared my commitments in life: At that point I decided to embark on a formal research project. I wanted to deepen my understanding of the painful experience of self-doubt, to find out what doubting experiences are like for others who endure them and to see how others cope with them. The adult educator in me wanted to go further and investigate the nature of learning associated with the doubting experience.

How I researched doubting to come to my understanding

Clark Moustakas (1967) believes that heuristic research is a discovery method which is particularly suitable for the study of significant problems, issues and processes relating to human experience. He explains his concept of heuristic research in an autobiographical story. Faced with a major decision about heart surgery for his daughter he felt utterly alone and cut off from human companionship. At first he searched into his own self and became aware that at the centre of his world was a deep and pervasive feeling of loneliness. This involved meditation and self-searching, intuitive and mystical reachings and hours of midnight walking. Then, in observing and being with children in hospital, he became aware of further dimensions of the phenomenon and set out to discover the meaning of loneliness in its simplest terms through a total involvement of himself in the experience. His study provided the methodological model for my enquiry.

My investigation of doubting which, like loneliness, is a non-measurable human experience, did not begin with a pre-set plan, hypothesis or method.

Rather, several years before I began a research project, I began a journey into self. From my own doubting experiences during this time I came to develop the form for my research. Later stages of the research grew out of earlier ones, and I often waited for moments of recognition and breakthrough as I moved forward within the general framework. I used a journal extensively in that period of my life and these records became important data. The autobiographical element was always integral to the enquiry.

An important aspect of the research was an exploration of different perspectives of doubting, to understand this reality more fully. I compared my frame of reference with that of others who shared my lifestyle through interviews with five men who had demonstrated an ability and willingness to talk freely about personal matters. I presented myself to these interviewees as an adult who shared their lifestyle and who experienced doubting feelings and experiences. Such sharing was helpful in creating a climate of trust and support, in reducing the level of anxiety, and in helping interviewees understand and express their own experience. I sought descriptive accounts of doubting experiences and used open-ended questions, questions of clarification, and probe questions which came from reflection on my experience and the experience of previous interviews.

This research involved a total immersion in the experience; a critical task was to unify comprehension, emotion, spirit and intuition in this self-exploration. There were challenges to be met at the rational level as I sought to identify the risks inherent in heuristic enquiry and to develop a strategy to minimize them. I needed the skills of reflecting, noticing and testing as well as learning partners who would provide the support and challenge necessary to reduce the dangers of isolation and self-delusion.

However, the most difficult challenges were at the non-rational level. Like Moustakas, I used myself as a primary research instrument while being immersed in the phenomenon being researched. I studied doubting, not in a detached way, but from the inside. Immersed in the pain and confusion of my own and others' doubts I tried to understand what was happening within myself while cognitively searching for patterns and relationships. Vague, confused and varied feelings, ranging from shame to anger, surfaced as I worked with the data. Loneliness was enormous. I often had to cease transcription because my emotions were stirred so strongly. The unconscious surfaced intensely in powerful dreams, spontaneous images and fantasies, and instinctual forces. I became a powerful learner in this non-rational world. Images, feelings, intuitions, dreams and bodily sensings led me to a knowing which went beyond a factual knowing and which I increasingly trusted and came to value.

What I discovered about the doubting journey as a learning process of self-transformation

My interviewees spoke of their deep doubting experiences as journeys into self. One interviewee, Tony, described it as 'facing up to myself and looking at the anomalies in my life'. Their experiences, like my own, usually extended over several years – years experienced as crisis periods. There was preoccupation with self and low self-esteem in these times of confusion, emotional turmoil, communication difficulty and often physical distress. Mick, another interviewee, spoke of a six-month preoccupation with a surfacing awareness that something was wrong within himself:

> It was just in there, all tied up. I was really het up, really troubled, crying inside. It became a whole constricting thing. You get to the stage where you are feeling so devastated that it is easier to cover yourself up and pretend you are not there. It is not only that, it is a total uncoping.

Two major patterns emerged as I analysed the doubting stories. Firstly, there were a number of moments within these stories where it seemed as if happy endings had been reached. I came to recognize these as moments of insight, experienced as breakthroughs or turning points, which resulted in inner peace and new understandings of self. Mick spoke of such a moment which came to him at prayer:

> Almost seeing for the first time that what I was being led to was freedom. I think the whole emotional experience has something to do with relief. I felt a lot more whole after that. That incident was a turning point.

Secondly, I noticed that these moments of insight and peace were often no more than a pause on the journey. They were usually followed by another movement which spiralled the doubter back into the journey and into deeper recesses of the self. Tony, with hindsight, spoke of the first of a series of insights about his pattern of relating with women. He recognized that this was followed by other more significant insights into himself: 'The insights of that are still very present but there were deeper things even than that. Even though that was a powerful spiritual experience, and the insight of it is still valid, it didn't really get to the heart of my suppressed affection'. This pattern repeated itself a number of times over the several years which it took for Tony's deeper doubting crises to be played out.

Closer analysis of the patterns of inner movement revealed further patterns within these experiences of learning from painful experience. I came to interpret doubting as a learning process which has four qualitatively different phases, each with its own dynamics. During any period of crisis the phases recur as a series of insights into self are experienced and more inclusive self-perspectives are achieved. I called the phases: the disorientation, search for meaning and peace, self-acceptance and integration phases.

The disorientation phase

Disorientation is a state of disequilibrium in which inconsistencies within the self start to surface in conscious awareness yet there is an inability to understand what is happening or to name it satisfactorily. Mick said this experience was like 'being sucked down into a giant whirlpool and yet there is very little you can do'. Tony spoke of 'inner things coming into the open', of 'getting in touch with myself', and 'facing unresolved issues within the self'. Evidence that something is wrong can accumulate gradually and then emerge into disorienting awareness. Interviewees became aware of disorientation in many different ways. Tony spoke of dreams and recurring memories of a girl he knew in his teenage years whom he did not feel free to bring home for fear of his father's ridicule. She became a symbol which he eventually recognized as a sign of the constrictions he felt in expressing feelings in friendships with women. Others spoke of comparable triggers to disorienting awareness being found in 'puzzling dreams', in behaviour which 'popped up' under the influence of alcohol, or in direct confrontation with perspectives which conflicted with their own.

Sometimes disorientation exploded into awareness and resulted in a distressing combination of symptoms. Tom, another participant in this study, spoke about such an experience which marked the beginning stage of a three-year doubting period in his life: 'I was starting to physically feel symptoms of depression: upset bowels, feelings of pain, nightmares, unable to sleep. This compounded my internal battle. I thought there must be something physically wrong with me, but that did not seem right.'

Tom made the negative evaluation of himself which was typical of the experience of others in this phase. He perceived himself as deficient. He felt shame, guilt and anxiety at the prospect of exposure of his inconsistencies to himself and to others. He expressed it this way: 'I feel I have let myself down and possibly reduced myself in the esteem of others.' Mick spoke of a fear of losing face, of feeling helpless, lonely and distressed. He spoke about his communication problem: 'The thing I cried about a few times was that I felt I couldn't make people understand. I was aware in the head it was my problem. People can't understand if you can't tell them what is happening. With all those things happening I just couldn't tell anyone. It was a real tearing apart.'

A range of strategies were employed to divert attention from these internal tensions and inconsistencies. Tony explained how he did this: 'I used to blame the job and pressures and past history – anything but me.' He further illustrated how people can come to recognize these inconsistencies when they experience a lessening of pressure in their lives: 'When I went to Uni this problem cropped up again and I was ashamed and disgusted. I wanted to find integrity. Now was the chance. It was the only space period in my life, nothing was going to be spared.' The beginnings of many extended periods of doubting in this study were related to similar easing of external pressures.

Search for meaning and peace phase

In this second phase there were attempts to restore inner equilibrium and emotional peace. One person called this the period of 'unravelling'. Tom spoke of a time of great self-preoccupation when: 'for the first half of the year particularly, "me" was the significant item in the study process'. For all the participants, distress provided the energy and motivation they needed to continue the process of unravelling. Tom spoke also of the importance of being able to name satisfactorily what he was experiencing:

> I read a book and discovered people who have this have depression. And I said: 'Good God! Wow! Other people have this as well.' There was enormous relief. Number one – the things I was experiencing were not unknown to mankind. Number two – it had been identified and (the book) would have some solutions about how to deal with it, how to cope with it. And number three – it really indicated I was not off the deep end of the world at all.

This enabled him to communicate his experience to others and gave him more control over his panic, fear, sense of helplessness and he lost his sense of being abnormal.

Fear of the unknown acted as a major deterrent to continuing the journey, and the temptation was for learners to protect themselves from unforeseen consequences. Tom, who was re-examining his commitment to his lifestyle, spoke of a previous attempt at such an examination:

> To not do this, with which I am at least somewhat comfortable, meant I had to change to something which was unknown and different to me. So, to opt out was to opt for the great big unknown. I was scared. I wasn't sure how I would face the consequences of doing something different from what I was doing. It was an easy way out, I suppose.

In researching this phase I became aware of the severe handicap it was for myself and others when we were unable to understand and cope with our feelings. In my paper on doubt in my development I noted: 'Part of my pattern has been a reluctance to accept the emotional aspects of issues and in so doing I seem condemned to struggle towards the resolution of these doubts for exceedingly long periods of time. I tend to use the rational mind to avoid looking at feeling messages which scare me.'

Tom revealed that abdication of personal authority and judgement in favour of that of others was a disabling factor in the doubting journey. He spoke of two occasions when he put aside doubts about his suitability to a religious lifestyle on the authority of another: 'On both occasions he told me, "Don't be silly. I will tell you if you are unsuitable for this life. Stop thinking such thoughts and go on with your work." Who was I to question such authority, so I progressed accordingly.'

Tony similarly revealed the disabling effect of allowing personal or group norms to inhibit any sharing of personal concerns. In hindsight he said he regretted how he had disadvantaged himself by adhering to a personal norm against disclosing weakness. In talking about this he said: '(I was) not confiding because within my eyes it was a taboo. I didn't feel at ease to talk about my weaknesses which were unacceptable things to talk about. I kept them to myself.'

I became aware of three learning processes which played a part in myself and the other study participants achieving understanding, peace and transformed self-perspectives. These learning processes were:

(1) developing autonomy in searching;
(2) trusting the harmony of the whole self;
(3) learning how to learn more effectively.

These can be illustrated by Tom's questioning about his suitability for the religious lifestyle. We have seen how fear and abdication of personal authority hindered his earlier attempts to resolve this question. He developed greater self-responsibility and self-direction as this search continued. In speaking of his later exploration of this question he said: 'While I was discussing it with the counsellor, in fairness I went to see someone of my own (from a religious community). And I thought it might make a bit of sense to go away and do a retreat as well.' In developing autonomy in searching he learned to seek assistance from a variety of sources, to be critical and selective in accepting advice, to view helpers as resources not rescuers, and to actively test limits and question assumed non-negotiable realities.

Tom found it more difficult to trust the harmony of the whole self because he had difficulty understanding his feelings. He recognized that: 'most of my communication has been purely cerebral – however, even within I did not acknowledge or express feelings I had.' This process involved learning to listen to the subconscious, dreams, fantasies, persistent symbols and images, intuition, emotions and the body as a way of learning about self. Tom learned from reflection on previous experience how to be in touch with inner agitation, physical stress and vague feelings:

> I wrote a letter saying I don't know what is going on, but it seems from the surface that I am unhappy. I am still feeling physically stressed. I feel agitated within myself. There is an area of doubt about my lifestyle which has arisen before.'

Tom also learned how to learn more effectively. He became empowered as he learned to look for patterns in his behaviour and as he came to recognize what type of help was helpful for him. As he had become autonomous as a searcher he sought help from doctors, priests, psychologists, psychiatrists, superiors, older friends and spiritual directors in his search for meaning and peace. Reflection on the extent of usefulness of this variety of resources led him to acknowledge the paramount importance, in his style of learning in this doubt, of interaction with peers:

> Only in the later stages of communication of doubt did it become apparent that an important way of resolving or examining these doubts was to confide in peer groups. There had been a dissatisfaction in talking about these doubts to alleged experts, older experts.

Tom developed new learning skills and used them to turn his experience more effectively into learnings. He was shy and conscious that this was a barrier and source of resistance in speaking with people. He revealed how he had learned to overcome this: 'When I talk about things I feel better about them. It isn't easy, though. Partly that is why I am talking to you about this topic. The more practice I get the more I get better at it.' He had learned how to face fears and risk new behaviour, to develop underdeveloped functions and to view avoidance behaviours as opportunities for self-knowledge.

The spiralling aspect of doubting experiences meant that each of the phases in the doubting cycle would be visited a number of times in any serious crisis period. Learning from this painful experience was possible and evident when interviewees variously spoke of the doubting journey as one of gradually 'putting self together', of 'making the whole fit together' and of 'seeking personal integration'. The spiralling journey eventually brought sufficient self-understanding and peace for the search to be set aside for a time. Tom was even confident that he had identified the criteria which would mark the completion of his journey:

> I have some sort of benchmark now. I think I will have arrived on this journey when I am a more peaceful person. That is my key word. And also when I am more confident about myself and of my dealings with others.

Self-acceptance

This third phase was at the heart of the movement to new perspectives on self. These were moments of insight when fear was finally penetrated and aspects of self, previously unacknowledged because they were thought to be unacceptable, were finally confronted and accepted.

Tony described in detail successive insight experiences which were important in his introspective journey and which related to struggles and inconsistencies between his espoused and actual behaviours towards women. He spoke of one insight in which he recognized: 'I would have to let go of things I had been trying to hang on to. The affections of that young circle.' He described the effects of that insight in these terms:

> When I recognized that, I remember a very strong sense of ease coming over me. Not until I admitted to myself that this was a big factor in my dissatisfaction did I feel at ease. I think it made me face up to reality a lot more.

This insight and emotional ease was merely a pause on the doubting journey. Within a year he was precipitated back into the cycle of doubting as a result of an incident with a woman friend:

> The confrontation, the challenge issued to me by this girl really sat me up. She took me on. I felt my cover had been blown, someone had found out the true side of me. Next day I was just so disappointed in myself and that all that had happened again. The old pattern. And that really sickened me, and I don't use that word lightly. I was really down for about two weeks. I wrote her a letter of apology.

A powerful self-acceptance experience occurred for Tony at the end of those two weeks:

> While in this fit of blues I picked up an article and read it. I became almost entranced by it. It was a major discovery to see that I had never really loved myself nor given myself the right to love. I felt I had hit something big, a major oil strike. And I just put the books away and said: 'That's the end, I think I have found it.' And I contentedly wandered around knowing no one could touch me. I was a free person. My head was full of this stuff. I would go for long walks and just think about it. Totally at peace with it.

There was a pattern to the dynamics of such self-acceptance experiences. Often they began with a black period of deep and disturbing feelings which stemmed from an experience which precipitated low self-esteem and left feelings of helplessness, depression or self-disgust. In these moments a breakthrough occurred as some truth about self, which was already known in a sub-conscious or non-rational way, was acknowledged. The insight was accompanied by an emotional catharsis which left feelings of peace, ease and hope. There was a new surety that the journey into self was 'on the right track'. The experience was one of 'facing reality' and was seen as a 'turning point'. It gave a sense of being more whole.

Self-acceptance experiences were often perceived as critical turning points in the doubting journey because they allowed for new perspectives which were based on different assumptions and which offered the possibility of new ways of being in the world. Constricting perspectives about self gave way to more inclusive ones. Tony spoke of the effect of his major insight in this way:

> It gave me a surge of hope that I could, if I wanted to, be in charge of my own life, of my decisions. And eventually be assertive. All the things I had written down and wasn't over the years. I began to see ways that were opening up to do those things.

Interestingly, in this sample of men these moments of breakthrough most often occurred within the context of their religious symbol system – in some connection with God, prayer, retreat or religious reflection.

Perhaps the most difficult task on the journey into self was the recognition and acceptance of those aspects of self which were hidden from conscious awareness as a result of the effects of earlier socialization and psychological adaptation. In reviewing the data of this study I identified five ways in which this sample of men were able to achieve emancipatory insights and thus free themselves from constricting personal assumptions. These were:

(1) finding and using a conceptual framework by which to gather and organize incoming data;
(2) identifying patterns of behaviour or habits of perception;
(3) re-visiting and re-interpreting past experiences;
(4) utilizing a range of personal learning capabilities in the search;
(5) identifying the types of help which were actually helpful to oneself.

Integration

In this phase new perspectives were held open to the confirmation of further experiences and there was a waiting for things to come clear again. There was a moratorium on decision-making until the new realizations settled. Tony described his experience of this waiting and integrating time which followed several successive, powerful self-acceptance insights in this way:

> I can just feel a major landslide, or glaciation. The whole valley has been scoured out and is awaiting fresh growth. They are the images I use. I feel I have scoured out my insides and I have to start re-planting and re-learning. I have hope though. It is good in that a whole new perspective is there for this new set of learning to take place. It will be a much stronger base I am building on, a new me.'

As Tony developed these perspectives in new learning opportunities he experienced new energy. 'It unlocked an energy within me to go out and act in a way that signified "I love you", talking to myself . . . I am going to make choices that you are going to be happy with.' He became excited as new choices opened up, as he discovered new depths of meaning in previous understandings of reality and as further experiences synthesized and confirmed his insights. Tony, myself and all the participants in this study experienced, at such decisive moments, surges of hope in the realization that answers to our search were within ourselves and were attainable. There was great relief in the realization that choked-off aspects of self, or previously denied longings, could at last be accepted and taken seriously.

The work of integration involved the re-organization of self. Mick compared this to the laborious but hopeful work of completing a jigsaw puzzle: 'You know how it is when you can see a jigsaw. At the start you have nothing, and then you get the edges . . . and gradually you get the key bits, and then it is only a matter of filling them in.' Ambiguity, ambivalence and strong feelings were rife as unfinished business was dealt with and alternative futures were explored. On one day there would be excitement and enthusiasm about possible futures and the next day there would be gloom and depression.

Tony recognized the importance of reflection on the feedback from his emotions. They became the criteria for choices in his work of re-organization. He learned techniques to identify patterns of feelings and he recognized the need to disidentify from them in order to interpret their messages. He said: 'Last year I would go through cycles of confirmation and doubt. I have been resting with that and trying to write at a deeper level in the journal. I want to talk with someone and haven't felt able to with the comings and goings of my job.' He resisted the temptation to lose patience and opt for quick clear solutions when sweating out the process was required.

In this phase there was mourning and emotional letting go of some aspects of self as new realizations came to birth. Tony spoke about this:

> There was some grieving I hadn't done which came out during this time. I broke down and started crying. It was all about my mother's death and laying the blame. I had never let myself acknowledge that. Guilt, too, about my younger brother and sister. I felt I had abandoned them. So I had to reconcile that. I broke down crying in the end.

The grief of mourning, facing unfinished business and affecting reconciliations gave him new inner strength and self-esteem and the freedom to live in the world of the new perspectives.

Working through experiences of doubting involved successive experiences of the dynamics of disorientation, searching for meaning and peace and self-acceptance. Eventually, it was recognized that old attitudes were changing and new behaviour patterns were appearing. Tom noted such changes in himself around his shyness: 'I have come a long way since last year. I feel different. In past years I would be a retiring wallflower and meet people and not expect them to know who I was. This time I have been almost extrovert in meeting people. I have been pleasantly surprised.' His low self-esteem was giving way to a stronger and more harmonious sense of self. Tom, Tony, myself and others in this study became increasingly aware of a new inner authority and of more accepting and compassionate attitudes towards ourselves. Similarly, we became aware of a more compassionate appreciation of the life struggles of others and a new realization of interdependence and responsibility towards them.

Terry, a teacher and a participant in this study, eventually noted that he had transcended certain contradictions within himself. Part of his doubting journey dealt with the threat posed by students questioning church teaching with which he was not fully comfortable. He noted new behaviours and attitudes which he had developed:

> I now feel much more comfortable with it. I still might not know the answer fully but I would be able to say to the other kids, 'Well there is a good question', and put it back on to the group and let them work it out. Then I would perhaps say, 'Well, the way I see it is'. I am more comfortable in allowing them, in appreciating kids asking why. Because if they don't say why, I had better change to something else to get their interest and get them to ask questions. It is all the reverse now.

His journey into self helped him to perceive reality more in terms of a dialectic and less in terms of polarized opposites. He achieved a new inner balance and harmony in transcending his contradictions yet realized there will be continued tension in maintaining this transcendence.

Mike reflected on a key effect of a two-year doubting period in his life:

> I think that would be the thing I was most missing. I certainly wasn't at home, not only with those outside things but I wasn't at home with myself. My previous time was a peaceful experience in all ways, but I had to grow through turmoil in this. I had to actively identify different facets of me and come to grips with integrating them more fully into me.

Terry also reflected on changes which occurred within himself and he noted after a doubting journey which took several years to play itself out:

> As I look back on it I see the change that came over me, but I still can't escape from it, the acceptance of myself; understanding of who I was. It has given me more confidence in my relationships with people. I would say that more than anything. And a sense of calmness, maybe, or tranquility within myself.

The doubting journey and the learning process of self-transformation for particular crisis periods in the lives of the participants in this study were over when the spiralling series of doubting cycles gave way to the new inner equilibrium, sense of completion and well-being described above by Terry and Mick. Paradoxically, in embracing frightening aspects of ourselves we, the participants in this study, came to recognize our true selves and consequently learned to love rather than fear ourselves. It was in the recognition and acceptance of those fearful aspects of ourselves that we achieved renewed peace and self-confidence.

Relationship to the facilitation of adult learning

To conclude the story of this research and its findings I offer some reflections on the significance of this knowledge about the dynamics of doubting as a learning process of self-transformation to the field of adult learning. Most basically its importance lies in the reality that doubting is part of life's continual process of adjustment of perspectives, beliefs, values and meaning. Facilitators of adult learning and change, be they teachers, counsellors, therapists, friends or learning partners will be more powerful helpers if they are aware of stages of the process and factors which facilitate successful transitions in self-perspectives and factors which block them.

Knowledge of doubting as a transitional learning process is useful to facilitators who are called on to help people change attitudes and perspectives. Perspectives on self and others are not easily changed. Changing attitudes often requires more than giving people new information and much more than merely directing them to change. If facilitators are going to attempt to help learners transform their perspectives it will be helpful to know what the process of change is like, what promotes and what hinders it.

How do I use this knowledge of the stages, dynamics, fears, helps and hindrances of the transitioning process to inform my own teaching? Currently I teach graduate level courses in a university setting and I frequently use the self-directed, emergent design learning group approach in my teaching.

I described my own initial experience of this approach in an earlier section of this chapter. Such an approach frequently results in other learners similarly calling into question many of the assumptions they hold about themselves and others, about learning, about teaching and about knowledge.

Frequently these learners experience a doubting cycle which follows the phases of the doubting process as I described it in my research. These are not life crises of the type described in my research, yet the same pattern is evident. Knowledge gained in this research about the phases, about the necessity to learn with the whole self, about the value of reflection and reflexivity in challenging personal assumptions, about the interconnection of feeling and knowing, about the payoff of autonomous and interdependent learning, and about the usefulness of questioning assumptions all play a part in the way I design my learning experiences and approach the facilitation of learning for adults.

I constantly have learners who return to study after a long time away from formal education. Many of these learners experience low self-esteem. They struggle with their sense of worthiness and competence, they feel inadequate and abnormal, and they use a great deal of energy in trying to hide the seriousness of this inner struggle from me and other learners. My focus is on helping them to achieve the breakthroughs needed to achieve new perspectives on themselves as learners and a consequent bolstering of self-esteem. Overcoming low self-esteem involves transitions in self-perspective. I find that the transitions necessary to overcome low self-esteem and to claim or reclaim inner authority as a learner follow the phases of the doubting journey. This doubting journey can become a learning process of self-transformation.

References

Berger, P and Luckman, T (1966). *The Social Construction of Reality.* New York: Anchor Books.

Griffin, V (1978). Self-directed learners and learning: Part 1. *Learning.* 2, 6-8. 2, 6-8.

Habermas, J (1971). *Knowledge and Human Interest.* Boston: Beacon Press.

Jung, C (1975). *The Structure and Dynamics of the Psyche.* London: Routledge and Kegan Paul.

Mezirow, J (1981). A critical theory of adult learning and education. *Adult Education.* 32, 1, 3-24.

Miller, A (1981). *Prisoners of Childhood.* New York: Basic Books.

Moustakas, C (1974). *Finding Yourself, Finding Others.* New Jersey: Prentice-Hall.

Moustakas, C (1967). Heuristic research. In: J Bugental. *Challenges of Humanistic Psychology.* New York: McGraw-Hill. Reprinted in P Reason and J Rowan. (1981). *Human Inquiry.* Chichester: John Wiley, 207-18.

Moustakas, C (1961). *Loneliness.* Englewood Cliffs, New Jersey: Prentice-Hall.

Chapter 8

Learning from the Perspective of Growth of Consciousness

John Weiser
Ontario Institute for Studies in Education

I want to share some of my ideas about a special type of adult learning that I call *growth of consciousness.* I am using the term consciousness here to refer to the primary frames of meaning with which we interpret our own life and the world. We know that all that we experience is filtered through the lenses of our personal versions of reality, our frames of meaning if you will. Growth of consciousness then is when we alter our version of reality in some permanent and significant manner so that our new understanding calls for changes in attitude, behaviour and even our feelings.

I believe that if I were to ask you if you wished to alter your view of reality most of you would say, No. Our stable sense of reality gives us the feeling of living in a predictable and understandable world. We have trained ourselves to be in this world that we understand and to function efficiently in it. We believe we have the 'correct' version of reality. With little difficulty most of us can become aware of our tendency to maintain the status quo, to hang on to what we believe is true. Yet we have changed our views many times as we have developed into adults. We usually assume that these changes were forced on us from outside. I believe that there is a force within us that wants to move in the direction of an expanded consciousness, that welcomes the environmental challenges for change. Thus there is a dynamic interplay between two countervailing forces. On the one hand our conscious egos are striving for stability; on the other, our own growing or evolving principle is pushing us to expand our consciousness. It appears that some of us can choose to become intensively connected with this direction within ourselves and consequently structure our life, our energies and our will for a considerable period of time towards the development of an expanded consciousness. In particular there is a unique opportunity for graduate students to find support and structure for growth of consciousness within the activities of conducting research for a thesis.

In the social sciences there has been a movement to encourage new approaches to knowledge; consequently a number of research and learning methodologies have been developed which recognize that the intention of the research is to expand the consciousness of the researcher. All of these new approaches to knowledge can be included under the label of qualitative research. This term serves to separate and contrast these approaches from the more familiar methodologies which we label as quantitative research. The qualitative approach seeks to understand the more holistic, relational process, and subjective aspects of human experience. In this approach personal and social history, social context and the individual agency or intentionality of the person are considered to be central to the understanding and meaning of human experience. Even here some of the qualitative approaches will emphasize one of the above perspectives over others. It is not, however, my intention to contrast and describe these many differences. Instead, I will be discussing how these learning projects can be seen as consciousness expanding activities.

It makes sense to me to talk about the expansion or growth of consciousness as occurring in two different directions, the *vertical* and the *horizontal.* Change on the vertical dimension demands a shift of meaning to one that is more inclusive and provides a new integrative perspective. When this happens things that we have been aware of but were seemingly unrelated now may be seen as connected in some meaningful way. In fact, the new perspective places a demand upon us to reorder what we know into a new pattern of relations. In this case we have managed to grasp a whole principle in a single moment. In such times we can know the truth of the principle of the whole being greater than the sum of the parts. The whole provides the meaning of the relationships of the parts to each other. A consequence of this type of shift in meaning is that a new conceptualization of reality is formed, a new framework from which one experiences one's self and world. Because this shift is one of meaning it often occurs with only a minimum of content. One grasps a total concept as true before its implications can be understood. The experience is that of entering a space of meaning without detail, then one is forced to reflect on the concrete events of existence in order to make this new understanding applicable to one's life.

The most dramatic example of this phenomenon for many of us is the experience of becoming conscious of a new view of the experience of women as a result of the consciousness raising activities of the feminist movement. At first many of us had to give up a long held version of reality relating to women and begin to include the basic premises of the feminists as true. If you lived through this process you know personally what it feels like to begin to notice and interpret one's own behaviour and that of others from this new perspective. From these first concrete learnings the demand to re-interpret more and more of life within this feminist framework continues. Now the principles are being applied to the most far reaching aspects of history, economics and religion, for example, and we know we have only begun this work.

I see the horizontal dimension of growth of consciousness as the work of the piece by piece concretizing of a frame of meaning. This is how we come to see and understand where specific events and experiences now fit within it. Here the basic level of understanding is not being challenged but rather filled in. This process occurs in small shifts of insight, of confirming hunches and hypotheses, of adding additional detail so that again our reality becomes an unquestioned given. Eventually and gradually one is again largely unaware of the frame of meaning from which one holds all that is experienced. In terms of types of research, I see most quantitative research as horizontal growth as attempts here are being made to fill in the gaps within an unchallenged larger frame of meaning. I believe that qualitative approaches to research offer a much stronger possibility for a vertical shift of consciousness.

There is an aspect of these experiences of shifts in consciousness that should be noted, and that is, rarely are we shifting or working within a frame of meaning that encompasses all that we believe at any one time. In fact we know we often hold contradictory beliefs. I have found some ideas of Roberto Assagioli (1965) useful in understanding how our personalities keep separate the various levels of meaning that seem to co-exist within us at all times. He suggests that it is not helpful to view ourselves as monolithic identities but rather as being subdivided into parts or smaller identities which he calls subpersonalities. Each subpersonality has its own individual perspective of consciousness from all the others. There is a great deal of overlap and consensus among these entities yet they differ just as you and I agree and differ on many points. Assagioli also points to an organizing centre, separate and distinct from all subpersonalities, which he referred to as the self. In terms of personality development we can all be seen as moving towards the harmonious integration of these smaller identities around this centre. The experience of the perspective of the self includes yet transcends the smaller perspectives. This experience brings the sense of involvement of one's total being to the moment.

Many other writers and theorists, particularly Berne (1964) have referred to this same phenomenon of our having many parts to our personalities. Systems have been developed to understand ourselves that include this tendency to be identified with different aspects of ourselves at different times. What appears to be true is that each identity has somewhat different needs, values, world views, skills, qualities, and in fact are even differing ages in their maturity. Although it appears that we each have a major identity that we are located within for large portions of our time, we do shift into others much more often than we are aware of throughout each day. It is comforting for most of us to sense a constancy or permanency to our personalities, and thus our tendency is not to notice the subtle or even dramatic shifts in identity which we actually make in our daily lives. Each of these identities can experience a shift of consciousness within its limited frame of meaning. Thus each one can experience a sense of growth and maturation in consciousness on either the horizontal or vertical dimension. These shifts can be clearly seen when we find ourselves in differing social roles throughout a day. For instance, I often shift from husband to teacher to therapist to friend during most days. As a teacher in a classroom I may be seen to shift from a teacher to a petulant child in a matter of seconds in response to a perceived challenge from a student. My *petulant child* persona may have matured enough so that it can use the language and skills of an educated man, yet its basic orientation is to defend and protect itself whereas, only a moment before, the basic orientation of the *teacher* might have been seen as that of wishing to share and be open to others. From this example we can see some of the history of maturation in two separate subpersonalities. The 'petulant child' has learned to express its fears and angers in a somewhat socially accepted manner, yet its basic beliefs have remained the same over the years – thus the term 'petulant child' remains appropriate. I will discuss with you later and in more detail how my 'teacher' has changed over time.

My point here is that we can imagine growth in consciousness as taking place totally within the confines of the beliefs of a single subpersonality. This growth could be either on the horizontal or the vertical plane. We can also imagine growth involving more than one subpersonality where each shares the same basic views of reality. Finally, we can imagine growth from the perspective of the centred self. I will discuss this very special type of growth later as I discuss certain experiences of some graduate students at the Ontario Institute for Studies in Education (OISE) while they were involved in conducting qualitative research projects.

In qualitative research one is given the opportunity to become deeply and personally involved in every aspect of the process. By seeing our personalities as multiple we can talk about which subpersonalities are involved in the research and which are relatively uninvolved. We can talk about whether only one or several are involved and we can even imagine that one's most central self may be involved in the discovery of new meaning through the research activities. These notions combined with the understanding of horizontal and vertical dimensions provide an estimate of the degree of commitment and possible difficulties that researchers may expect as they begin their research. At the same time this awareness may provide helpful directions for the researcher and supervisor when or if the researcher begins to experience difficulties.

Up to this point I have been making the case for the term 'consciousness' as a legitimate and useful term to describe a particular set of learning experiences. I have also pointed to the experience of being involved in a qualitative research project as a particularly opportune time for consciousness expansion. I will go even further to state that unless the researchers are open to and actively seeking this change in their own consciousness their research projects will provide only a minimal amount of new knowledge. I would assume that in this case the researcher is involved only at the horizontal dimension of consciousness and in all probability only involving the world view of a single subpersonality. I will provide some examples of this later.

A writer well known to adult educators has attempted to name and describe this type of major change in the world view of individuals. Mezirow (1978) has named this occurrence 'perspective transformation'. Briefly, he says that a perspective transformation involves 'a structural change in the way we see ourselves and our relationships. If the culture permits we move toward perspectives which are more inclusive, discriminating and integrative of experience.' (Mezirow, 1978, p 103.) Here, I believe, he is pointing to the experience of movement on the vertical dimension by using the terms 'inclusive' and 'integrative'. Mezirow is very conscious that personal perspectives are formed through one's interactions with others in the world. He later uses the term 'meaning perspective' in which he highlights the centralness of this assumption. He says, 'A meaning perspective refers to the structure of cultural assumptions within which new experience is assimilated to – and transformed by – one's past experience. It is a personal paradigm for understanding ourselves and our relationships.' (Mezirow, 1978, p 101.) He goes on to state that a change in meaning involves '. . . dimensions of thought, feeling and will. It involves seeing one's self and one's roles and relationships in a consistent, coherent way, a way which will dictate action priorities.' (Mezirow, 1978, p 105.) Here again we can see in his explanation his belief in the necessity of viewing ourselves as being made up of multiple roles. By using the terms 'one's self and one's roles' he points to the possibility of a single coherent identity (self) and then to the phenomenon of smaller differing perspectives. One difficulty that I have had, and has been shared by other readers of Mezirow as well, is to discriminate between those events which could be considered perspective transformations and those which might be a lesser meaning change. I now see the possibility of using the notions of subpersonalities and horizontal and vertical dimensions to assist us in making this discrimination.

Mezirow at another point refers to the experience of a meaning perspective in the following way: 'Feelings and events are interpreted existentially, not intellectually as by an observer.' (Mezirow, 1978, p 105.) John Osborne (1985) in an article entitled *Learning as a Change in World View*, includes this same basic perspective. He says:

> The meaning of learning as a change in world view might best be explicated by disjunctive descriptions. Learning as a change of world view is a change in our relationship with the world (our own world in the case of the phenomenologist). It is a change in our being-in-the-world, in our lived experience, which may include all aspects of our being but especially our perceptual, symbolic and emotional processes. It is more than an intellectual change. It can disrupt the inertia of our prevailing state of consciousness. A change in world view can also be described as a change in attitude or disposition with accompanying feeling states. It is the way we perceive/feel/think about our world(s). (*Osborne, 1985, p 196*)

In the above quote Osborne refers to the 'inertia of our prevailing state of consciousness'. Again the term 'consciousness' is seen as useful to name the phenomenon we are all attempting to describe. There can be no doubt that we are looking at personal change as something beyond, but including, the intellect, yet which also involves feelings, behaviour, relationships and our basic assumptions about reality. He also has a short section relating to qualitative research and in it suggests that researchers are involved in the activity of changing their own world view.

I want to introduce a few statements from Bruce Douglas and Clark Moustakas taken from a recent article entitled *Heuristic Inquiry: the Internal Search to Know* (1985) in which they make clear that what is happening in this form of research is the intense personal involvement of the researcher. What is reported is largely due to the changes that have occurred within the researchers themselves. Although heuristic research is only one of many forms within qualitative approaches, it is certainly a frequently used one, and Clark Moustakas is clearly one of the major pioneers leading us to a new perspective of social science and research.

Douglas and Moustakas state that:

> Heuristic research is a search for the discovery of meaning and essence in significant human experience. It requires a subjective process of reflecting, exploring, shifting, and elucidating the nature of the phenomenon under investigation. Its ultimate purpose is to cast light on a focused problem, question, or theme.

They continue, 'When pursued through intimate and authentic processes of the self, the "data" that emerge are autobiographical, original, and accurately descriptive of the textures and structures of lived experience.' (Douglas and Moustakas, 1985, p 40.) Here they are saying that, although there is a defined intention to find meaning in others' experiences, the researcher is centrally located along with others in the discovery of this meaning. They state this more clearly later when they say, 'The power of heuristic enquiry lies in its potential for disclosing truth. Through exhaustive self search, dialogues with others, and creative depictions of experience, a comprehensive knowledge is generated beginning as a series of subjective musings and developing into a systematic exposition.' (Douglas and Moustakas, 1985, p 40.) An interesting and revealing way of emphasizing the degree of personal involvement of the researcher is in the following quotation: 'When commitment to the search is passionate, it moves beyond the usual energy that we bring to our lives; it carries the urgency needed to reveal and explore shadings and subtleties of meaning.' (p 41.) It is in their use of 'passionate' that a reader can begin to grasp the real depth of personal commitment that is involved. Again we must go beyond the intellectual to include our feelings and tacit understanding in order to gain new meaning. One cannot make this journey with passion and remain unchanged.

Although I have been emphasizing the qualitative researcher's experiences as a model of change of consciousness I have used this as one example of a clearly focused intentional period of changing. I see that these changes occur throughout our lifetime. This can be seen most clearly as we reflect back on our own lives and note the major changes that have occurred in our world views.

My own learning processes

I have been fascinated with the learning process in many contexts for over 30 years. My first experiences as a high school teacher in 1952 brought home to me very quickly the fact that I didn't know much about it. Like many others I soon discovered that I really didn't know how to facilitate learning in others. I had the basic tools gained from my own classroom experiences and what I had been given in teacher training. These tools were satisfactory to a degree but left a great deal to be desired as I encountered students who were learning badly in my classes. I returned to graduate school in the belief that there was a ready body of knowledge to answer my many questions about the learning process. What I found was that there were some answers, but essentially the process remained mysterious. Since that time, I have discovered more answers but I remain in awe of the essential mystery of the process of learning. My experiences with assisting others to learn have been with young adults and adults for the past 25 years. Besides classroom teaching and related group activities I have been very active in one-to-one learning situations as therapist, clinical supervisor and as a supervisor of theses for doctoral students. I am attempting to bring together in this chapter some of the ways that I have come to understand adult learning from these particular types of experience.

Over the many years of this work I have been particularly influenced by a series of approaches to understanding human experience. As I reflect on this process I can see my personal process is an example of the particular type of learning that I am addressing in this paper. My process has been to involve myself within a particular set of premises and to attempt to understand and work with people in their learning efforts within this framework. In each case I found that as I attempted to use a theory or an approach, I learned a great deal and discovered many useful ideas and techniques. Eventually I would become dissatisfied and become aware of phenomena that didn't fit my approach at that time. These experiences led me to explore different approaches that seemed more readily to handle my dissatisfactions.

These theories or approaches to experience have been largely drawn from the field of counselling and psychotherapy. At the beginning of my career I was still interested in classroom learning and was only gradually drawn toward psychotherapy. At that time I was oriented towards an authoritarian model, involving an expert teacher and a relatively passive learner. I was attracted to and used what today would be labelled a cognitive-behaviour approach to learning. The psychology that influenced me was largely a mechanistic approach to learning. Learning was explained by what was done to the learner. Variation in learning success was seen as the combination of the quality of what was done to the learners (teaching strategies) and the quality of the learner – that is, intelligence and previous learning experiences.

By this time I was an adult learner and I was increasingly aware that my own learning did not fit well within this mechanistic approach. Also by this time I was more and more involved in practising and teaching psychotherapy. I turned to Carl Rogers and Abraham Maslow for a different approach to understanding the phenomenon of learning, growth and change. At this time I made a radical shift in my understanding of the learning process. It was a radical shift in that I reversed my understanding of the learning process to one where the learner is the expert and the active participant and the teacher was the relatively passive member of the dyad. In order to accommodate this new understanding I was forced to face up to a number of previously held assumptions about the learner and learning process. In addition, I had to develop an almost entirely different set of 'tools' in order to participate in the learning process in a manner which was satisfactory to my new perspective. Although I have incorporated several different approaches, since then I have never felt the need to change my beliefs about the centrality of the learner in the learning process.

In my attempt to be 'Rogerian' I adapted both my classroom teaching and my counselling styles to fit my beliefs about the process of learning. My attempt was to convey the core conditions for learning that Rogers advocated and in which I passionately believed at the time. After a period of time I became more and more frustrated with the fairly passive role I had assigned to myself, as well as by the frustrations expressed towards me by my students.

It was then that I became enthralled with gestalt psychology and psychotherapy. I found I could still hold my belief in the centrality of the learner and the essentially humanistic and phenomenological models that I was holding about people and their experiences and incorporate the more active elements of gestalt psychotherapy. In particular I found that by allowing myself to develop 'gestalt experiments' I was able to be more active, certainly more creative, and still the learning was centred in the experiences of the learner. I found that by bringing into balance the active and passive aspects of the participants in a learning situation the results were more satisfying and effective. Again I had much to learn and I was once more constantly having to question a number of assumptions I held about the learning process. One of the most important outcomes of seeing this new balance between participants was to recognize that there were really two learners and two teachers in any learner-teacher dyad. I learned to accept responsibility for my own learning and how to integrate this into the flow of the ongoing activity for the mutual advantage of both of us in the situation.

Once again I began to experience frustrations in working within the understandings I had of a gestalt and existential phenomenological framework. I had gained a great deal of respect for experiential learning and I had closely followed the famous suggestion of Fritz Perls that we must lose our minds and come to our senses in order to really learn anything. I now recognized the importance of meaning and values as a part of the learning process. I felt the need to include the 'mind' and yet not in the mechanical understanding of mind that I had previously held.

As I became more aware of my own questions about the meaning of life I recognized this same concern in others. My beliefs at this time were essentially oriented around what could be labelled as an individualistic belief. I structured everything around my concerns for individual responsibility and autonomy. I viewed efforts to learn as essentially motivated to achieve individuality. In fact, I believed that this was all there was available to us. As I began to attend to questions of meaning I became dissatisfied with this orientation. I needed a larger context for myself than personal autonomy. It was here that I discovered psychosynthesis (Assagioli, 1965). Within the psychosynthesis framework of beliefs is the concept of the human spirit. It gave me a framework to search for meaning within a belief in the existence of a human spirit which is both personal and transpersonal. For within psychosynthesis is the belief in a transpersonal self which retains its sense of individuality and also lives at the level of universality. The term 'transpersonal' essentially means to go beyond the personal, or to transcend the personal. At this level we experience from the perspective of the whole where the individual is a full participant and yet only an infinitestimal part. By including the concept of the transpersonal I was able to extend my framework of meaning beyond the individual. For instance, now I see individual development as a part of a larger evolving whole. Although I have been studying and using psychosynthesis for over 10 years, I am still expanding and discovering more all the time. It has provided a framework for me to hold cognitive-behavioural, humanistic, existential-phenomenological, Rogerian, and gestalt beliefs in satisfactory integration.

Perhaps you are able to discern here examples of my own horizontal and vertical changes in consciousness. One can even assume that a number of these shifts had to include several of my subpersonalities joining into a more unified and integrated identification. I have not recounted my story as an example of a unique experience, but rather as an example that we all can tell of our growth in consciousness.

Research students learning at OISE

I studied some students at OISE who had completed qualitative research doctoral theses in the past two years with reference to their growth of consciousness.

The topic each one investigated represented a crisis or difficult situation for the participants. I will discuss some differences I see between students who identified themselves personally as sharing this same difficulty as their participants as opposed to students who did not identify with the difficulties of their participants.

The decision to engage with others in a discussion about their experiences around a crisis or difficulty is a conscious and, I think, important choice. Making this choice offers the opportunity to study the experience of growth of consciousness itself. A crisis can be defined as a situation in which the present attitudes, behaviours and skills of the person are inadequate to resolve the situation or problem. Therefore, there is an opportunity for the person in crisis to find a new perspective which guides the person to a resolution of his or her own difficulty. It is interesting to note that many of the researchers' expectations at the beginning of their work were the finding of change or resolution on what I would call the horizontal plane. Statements of what they were expecting to find in their research often included the discovery of the various coping mechanisms that assisted people in dealing with their difficulty. In my view, a coping mechanism is a way of dealing psychologically or behaviourally with a situation from within a presently held perspective – that is, the *horizontal* plane.

All of these investigators actually uncovered more than this level of meaning in their research. The participants were able to share with the researchers ways in which their beliefs had been altered in minor ways as well. In cases where the researcher was not identified personally with the problem this shift in their participants' consciousness was the ultimate new level of meaning that was reported in the thesis. In reading these theses it is difficult to see a great deal of growth of consciousness on the part of the researcher. The achievement of discovering this new level of meaning on the part of the researcher seems to be limited to a new intellectual understanding of the phenomena. This is of course a legitimate and valuable contribution to knowledge. This process of discovering and sharing knowledge is the normal form in which we assist each other to grow horizontally. Beyond this, most of us can cite occasions when we have read something which seemed to trigger a reaction within us which strikes to the core of ourselves. In these instances we are involved intellectually and emotionally, and a process of deep reflection occurs in which we experience a shift within our present perspective which can be described as a *vertical* growth in consciousness.

In social science research we sometimes seek to find and describe an aspect of humanity which is common to all. Rarely do we attribute our findings to this most fundamental level. More often we cite the limitations of our work due to such things as sample size, age, social class, cultural background, level of education, intelligence, gender and so on. When we describe our research we state which of these powerful influences have been included or excluded or both. Thus we state our findings as applying only to people with certain combinations of these influential factors and we are careful about making generalizations beyond this grouping of people.

In my opinion, many methodological approaches in qualitative research can assist the researcher to penetrate through, below or beyond these known influential layers to something more basic and common to us all. The number of people who are included in this type of study is usually small according to any criteria of size. The researchers are therefore faced with difficulty when asked to what degree they can generalize from their work. In every study that I have been a part of, the researcher's first impulse is to state the usual limitations based on the demographic descriptions of the participants. Yet in every case they have a belief that what they have uncovered can be generalized to a much larger yet indeterminate group of people.

There seem to be several reasons why both the researcher and the reader believe that a study has a larger yet indeterminate generality. In the first place the researchers find that as they have continued to interview participants they find less and less new material. They find the same themes presented within the idiosyncratic form of each of the participants' lives. Thus the expectation is that had the number of participants been increased, little new material would be added. Thus within the limited set of demographic variables of the participants, generalization can be made about the larger number from the smaller.

Secondly, the researchers may believe that they have come in contact with a deeper level of meaning within themselves and their participants which goes beyond influences of personal history. What has been revealed is a piece of our commonality, connectedness, our shared history as a species – that is, the transpersonal level. The experience of contacting this level of meaning is to reach a more inclusive and synthetic understanding. Using my terminology, this is a vertical shift in consciousness which transcends the usual ways we experience ourselves as different owing to ethnicity, gender and culture. I must add that, although these students may sense this to be true, few, if any, have dared to risk a public statement to this effect.

Douglas and Moustakas have pointed to several reasons why this deep level of meaning may be a part of the experience of the researcher. At one point they state that, 'Beyond the pale of ordinary conscious awareness, every person is in touch with numberless sources of knowledge. Subliminal, archetypal and preconscious perceptions undergird all that is in our immediate awareness, giving energy, distinctiveness, form and direction to that which we know.' (Douglas and Moustakas, 1984, p 49.) It appears to me that a number of theses I have read have penetrated through everyday explanations of experience to reveal the basic and common to all level of the archetype. When our experiences are understood at this level our previous beliefs about the experience are seen as partial at best and often irrelevant. I can imagine that any qualitative research project can contact this level of meaning. However, I find that when the researcher has chosen to investigate a more fundamental human experience the odds swing in favour of reaching this level. For instance, I am reminded of two recent studies, one of which looked at the experience of doubt (*see* Chapter 7) and the other the experience of alienation. I perceive these as more basic than those studies which looked at the experiences of women alcoholics or of living with a schizophrenic family member.

In the latter two studies the researchers were able to uncover a core pattern of growth which led to the participants achieving a satisfactory solution to their difficulties. The growth which they describe included a series of shifts of meaning that the participants made about themselves and their world views. Neither of these researchers had imagined that these exact shifts were necessary before their study. Their understanding of the phenomena had therefore been expanded and made richer. Yet there is little evidence that they themselves had undergone similar vertical shifts in consciousness during the course of their enquiry. They continue to hold the view that their studies describe a growth pattern limited to the framework of the participant's situation. They did not find within themselves the same issues and dilemmas as those of their participants. They were therefore unable to penetrate to a deeper, more common level of meaning which would have provided a vision of greater generalization.

In their studies of doubt and alienation the researchers were also able to describe a core pattern of growth which included a series of shifts of meaning. However, these two researchers were themselves co-participants in the study. By opening to their own experiences as well, the descriptions of these shifts were noticeably richer in detail and meaning. As they contacted these new levels through reflection, they were able to see the extensiveness of how these various sets of understandings had profoundly affected their lives. By sharing these deeper, more extensive understandings with the reader, the human communality of the experiences is more readily seen. What is revealed is that the experience of doubt is fundamental to mankind and has affected our historical and cultural development. One is able to grasp the power behind the need for resolution of doubt or the attaining of true relationships that lies behind our individual and collective endeavours to do so. We are able to see that our more fundamental understandings are contained within the collective unconscious that we all share.

However, the focus of the study is only a part of the explanation for the achievement of a deeper penetration into meaning. Again we must look at the efforts of the researcher to understand what has happened. Douglas and Moustakas give us some guidance when they say:

> At the heart of heuristics lies an emphasis on disclosing the self as a way of facilitating disclosure from others – a response to the tacit dimension within oneself sparks a similar call from others. The heuristic scientist, in contact with others, places high value on the depth and sensitivity of interchange, on the promise of 'I-Thou moments', and on the steady movement toward a true intersubjectivity. The concept of intersubjectivity is drawn from existentialism and refers to a communal flow from the depths of one self to another self and to qualities of purity and loving integrity in interactions with others. (*Douglas and Moustakas, 1985, p 50-1*)

What seems to be the essential point here is that an interchange at the level of self to self is fundamental for the uncovering of this layer of humanness. At the level of self to self each is attempting to transcend the level of subpersonalities and to speak from a more basic knowledge which is above all of these smaller identities or perspectives. It is essential in a research process that involves interviews with participants that the researcher must be seeking this level of communication. It can only rarely be experienced as such in the face-to-face encounter. It is therefore necessary for the researcher in the lonely times of reflection upon the transcipts of these dialogues that this level of transcendence can be experienced. It is here that the deeper hermeneutic dialogue can occur between the self of the researcher and the self of the participant. When researchers can find this perspective within themselves the more fundamental questions can be asked of the participants. This process is not one way; the researchers are led to this level from within themselves as the underlying themes in the participants' lives become apparent through relation to and analysis of their stories.

An interesting aspect of this type of work for me has been when the researcher becomes aware that he or she wants to ask additional questions of a participant after reading and reflecting upon the transcripts of a previous conversation. When researchers believe that they are dealing with a question that is only answerable from the perspective of a single person, they either choose to go back to that person or believe that they can never find out the answer to their question. When they understand that they are asking a question which relates to a more basic level of meaning, perhaps common to all, they will ask the question of the next participant with whom they interview. More often than not they will receive relevant responses that answer their question. Over time it becomes clearer that the researcher is dialoguing with a single knowledge which can be found within all the participants. It seems even more profound when the researchers discover that they can uncover this same knowledge within themselves.

Douglas and Moustakas, in their conclusions on heuristic research, state that it '. . . encourages the researcher to go wide open and to pursue an original path that has its origins within the self and that discovers its direction and meaning within the self'. (Douglas and Moustakas, 1984, p 53.) I believe that in this statement they have captured the essence of the process of vertical growth of consciousness. It is at the level of self that polarities can be resolved into a new synthesis. It is here that the borders between subpersonalities are transcended and we can reach out to others to find a commonality of humanness which pushes beyond personal history. This process of 'going wide open' must involve the researchers at many levels of their being. It is described by all our students as uncomfortable, and in two recent cases was described as almost devastating. In both cases the researchers reported the need for support and understanding. One, particularly, cited the special role of the thesis supervisor to supply this support. Both were grateful to family and friends for their caring understanding at these times. In these two cases the researchers were centrally identified with the phenomenon under investigation. In both cases they came to the point of recognizing a truth which shattered a major set of their own attitudes and beliefs. At this moment of realization one could say they had experienced a growth of consciousness on the vertical dimension. At this first realization they were clearly aware of a new level of meaning and could only sense the impact on their lives that this would make. One of the researchers describes this as a vision or direct experience of the ideal which he must now work to fully realize. He emphasized the extensiveness of this vision by sharing his belief that to fully realize it will take years. I believe he is describing here the experience of a large vertical shift in consciousness which I referred to earlier as entering a new realm of meaning with little content. He now must begin the gradual process of recognizing his old perspectives as he experiences himself and his world, consciously shifting the meaning of the moment to this new level of consciousness. I have referred to this as the piece-by-piece growth of consciousness on the horizontal level.

In terms of the subpersonalities 'map', this new level of meaning is held by the self. Each subpersonality identification will still retain the perspectives they previously held and the growth of consciousness that must now take place is the process of the self assisting its smaller parts into accepting and relating to this new level of meaning. This process of working through the horizontal dimension of growth from old to new is often difficult for people. It raises doubts as to whether any shift really happened because one is identified again with a subpersonality. At this point one can 'fall back' to the old and give up the new as unreal. For the researcher here is the opportunity to return to dialogues with the participants, to find the new meaning underlying descriptions of their experiences. This serves to help ground the meaning and confirms its reality for both the researcher and the reader.

I do not wish to suggest that these dimensions of growth of consciousness that I have outlined in this chapter represent an evaluative schema to determine good or bad research. Rather it is my hope that someone beginning this type of research for the first time will be better able to understand some of the implications that may be involved for them and their participants, and be better prepared and sensitive to this process of growth of consciousness. Again it is my hope that those of you who are attempting to understand and participate in the more profound learnings of adults will find these ideas useful.

References

Assagioli, R (1965). *Psychosynthesis.* New York: Viking.

Berne, E (1964). *Games People Play.* New York: Grove.

Douglas, B G and Moustakas, C (1985). Heuristic inquiry: the internal search to know. *Journal of Humanistic Psychology.* 25, 39-55.

Osborne, J (1985). Learning as a change in world view. *Canadian Psychology.* 26, 195-206.

Mezirow, J (1978). Perspective transformation. *Adult Education.* 28, 100-10.

Chapter 9

Research as Personal Process

Peter Reason and Judi Marshall
University of Bath

Why do we get into research?

Why do people get involved in projects and dissertations? Why do students pursue masters' degrees and doctorates? Why is research such an important part of a university's education process?

If we examine these questions carefully we can see a number of different kinds of answers. An orthodox answer is that the purpose of research is to make a contribution to the fund of knowledge in a particular field: in this sense, research is *for them*, for the community of scholars of which the researcher is a member or potential member. But this essentially positivist view has been increasingly criticized in recent years, and a second answer has been suggested by those concerned to develop the 'new paradigm' of cooperative experiential enquiry (Reason and Rowan, 1981). From this perspective, research is *for us*: it is a cooperative endeavour which enables a community of people to make sense of and act effectively in their world.

We wish here to explore a third and somewhat neglected answer to the question: research can also be *for me*. The motivation to do research is personal and often expresses needs for personal development, change and learning. So we must look at academic research as an educative process, and at the enormous potential it holds for personal growth. In this chapter we will consider some of the dimensions of personal development, and illustrate these with examples from the experience of our research students as they have pursued their enquiries. We will also outline how supervision can facilitate this process. But first, we must look a little more carefully at the enquiry process and at the nature of knowledge.

Enquiry and knowing

All good research is *for me*, *for us* and *for them*: it speaks to three audiences, and contributes to each of these three areas of knowing. It is *for them* to the extent that it produces some kind of generalizable ideas and outcomes which elicit the response 'That's interesting!' from those who are concerned to understand a similar field (Davis, 1971). It is *for us* to the extent that it responds to concerns of our praxis, is relevant and timely, and so produces the response 'That works!' from those who are struggling with problems in their field of action. It is *for me* to the extent that the process and outcomes respond directly to the individual researcher's being-in-the-world, and so elicits the response, 'That's exciting!' – taking exciting back to its root meaning, to set in action. Research thus contributes to personal motivation and development.

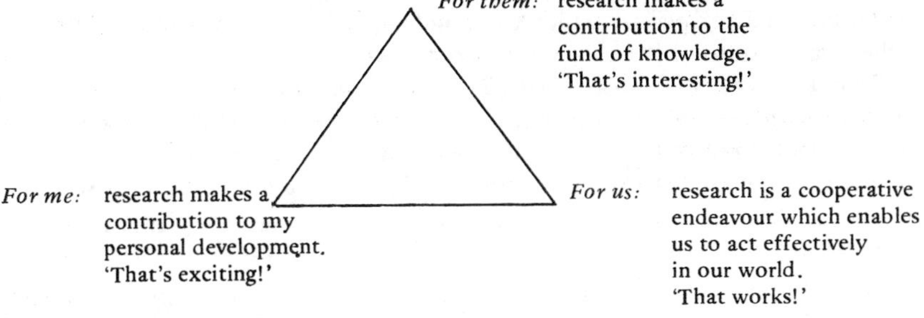
For them: research makes a contribution to the fund of knowledge. 'That's interesting!'
For me: research makes a contribution to my personal development. 'That's exciting!'
For us: research is a cooperative endeavour which enables us to act effectively in our world. 'That works!'

Who is research for?

We regard it as unfortunate and degenerate if any one of these three purposes of enquiry becomes dominant and overwhelms either one or both of the others: all three are authentic and complementary aspects of the research process. Thus this current chapter is written *for me* (there are actually two 'me's') in that it excites us and helps us move and develop as researchers and research supervisors; it is *for us* in that it evolved and will evolve in cooperative discussions with colleagues and research students, and will hopefully contribute to our joint practice or research; it is *for them* in that we clearly intend to influence the academic community at large to view research and research supervision in a different light.

We are working within what has been called a 'post-positivist' perspective (Lincoln and Guba, 1985). This emergent paradigm suggests we can see ourselves as living in an interactive and participatory universe (Skolimowski, 1985). Reality is both one and many, in the sense that we can have only knowledge of 'objective' reality (assuming for pragmatic purposes that there is one, or are some) from many different subjective perspectives; and also, more radically, in the sense that in some fashion we create or choose our reality. Thus valid enquiry rests on critical subjectivity, on the perspective of a personal view from some distance; and truth is multiple and transient, always emerging and changing, and holistic. Also our knowing is not limited to that which we can express in propositions, but can be practical, intuitive, experiential and presentational (Reason and Heron, 1986).

Enquiry in this universe must therefore be participative, qualitative, sensitive. It is enquiry *with* people, rather than research *on* people, a personal process pursued in relation to others. It must be *for me* as well as for us and for them. So in order to understand fully the research process we must have some view of the personal development process, and it is to this we turn next.

Personal development

We will explore the notion of personal development from three interrelated perspectives: firstly, from an existential perspective as the here-and-now struggle with one's being-in-the-world; secondly, from a psychodynamic perspective which views current patterns of experience and behaviour as rooted in unresolved distress from earlier (often childhood) experiences; and thirdly, from a transpersonal perspective which views individual experience as a reflection of archetypal patterns of the collective unconscious.

From the existential perspective we take as our prime concern the individual's current being-in-the-world. Sartre asserted that 'Existence precedes essence': an individual's being is affirmed by and arises out of his or her choices, so that in the extreme, we are our choices. A more moderate existential position asserts:

> There is no such thing as truth or reality for a living human being except as he participates in it, is conscious of it, has some relationship to it. *(May, 1961)*

Existentially, we view individuals as 'thrown' into the world, confronted with a set of issues – problems or life opportunities – with which they have to deal and creating their life through the choices they make in the face of these issues. A central existentialist concern is the relation of being to non-being: the individual's sense of being is enhanced by the courage of his or her choice-making in the face of a world which is in the end unknowable and unpredictable, while non-being is a consequence of avoiding such choices.

So people come to research with their life issues, with the opportunities offered to them by their gender, class, age, race, employment status, and so on; with the need to deal with relationships in various states of development and decay; and confronted by birth, death, and illness. Often they come to the university as a kind of retreat, with a need to take stock and make sense of their life and experience so far.

Life can be seen as a series of commitments to certain ways of being. We make a choice, and live out that choice more or less completely. Yet there comes a time when we turn *against* the old ways of being, when our existing life pattern seems inadequate, when we need to affirm and develop other, neglected sides of our being, and make new choices. Levinson (1978) sees life as moving through seasons, consisting of 'a series of alternating stable (structure-building) and transitional (structure-changing) periods'. It is often these tasks and choices of transition that people bring to a research project.

A psychodynamic perspective complements the existential by pointing out that many of the limitations on being here-and-now have their roots in childhood experience:

> The theory here is that people in our sort of society carry around a good deal of unresolved distress – grief, fear, anger – from past experience, especially from the very beginnings of life and from childhood; and that there is a tendency for this to be projected out unawarely into all sorts of present situations, distorting perception of a situation and/or behaviour within it . . .
>
> Let's look a bit more closely at how this distortion process might work. If as a child I want to express my real nature, my true self, and this urge is repeatedly interrupted and interfered with, I feel the distress of grief, fear and anger. If I am also constrained to suppress these valid distress feelings, then I am conditioned to become false to my real self – and to erect a false and alienated self with which I identify. I then become addicted to projecting on to the world the anxiety of my denied distress, seeing the world as a negative, threatening place which therefore reinforces

my addiction to my false and alienated self. I am stuck in the vicious circle . . .
(*Heron, 1982*)

From this kind of view of individual psychological development, we argue that researchers often choose (consciously or unconsciously) research topics which will restimulate old patterns of distress. Just as we pick at old wounds and worry at hurts in a physical sense, so we are also unable to leave alone our psychological hurts; we are not content with our distorted experience and behaviour. Many theorists of human development have suggested that human beings have a natural tendency or drive toward full realization of the self; we suggest that the researcher often moves into the anxiety of old distress in the choice of research topic and of process, and that this is (intentionally or unintentionally) a bid for personal development.

When this happens, the enquiry process obviously offers an important opportunity to move through and beyond old limiting patterns. Unfortunately, as Devereaux (1967) has pointed out, the usual response to the restimulated anxiety is defensive, so that we project our anxiety out on to the research situation, thus distorting our perspective in a way similar to the effect of countertransference in psychotherapy. Maslow (1966) and Griffin (1978) have shown how this defensive attitude pervades science. Yet this does not have to be so: if researchers are committed to the pursuit of rigorous critical subjectivity, if they are prepared and able to use their subjectivity as part of the enquiry process, if they have the skills and support to manage and transcend this restimulated distress, the response can be creative and developmental. It can be, 'That's exciting!'.

All enquirers need to explore how distress and psychological defences that they are unaware of distort their enquiry. Some systematic method is needed which is powerful enough to reach into the unconscious, draw the distress into awareness and either resolve it or allow it creative expression. Devereaux (1967) suggested that the researcher should undergo psychoanalysis; our own preferred approach is co-counselling (Jackins, 1965; Heron, 1973) which is a method of reciprocal support through which each person, working as client in a pair relationship, can explore the ways in which his or her defences are being caught up with the research thinking and action:

> Keeping some attention in the place of the aware adult in present time, the client in co-counselling reaches down into the hidden places of the hurt child, honours and experiences the pain, and releases it . . . This is the healing of hidden memories, a reintegration of the occluded past. (*Heron, 1977*)

Hawkins (1986) has explored in detail how psychodrama can be similarly used. We have also borrowed on occasion from gestalt therapy (Perls *et al.*, 1951), subpersonalities work (Ferrucci, 1982), and art and dance therapy.

These processes not only contribute to the ab-reaction of distress patterns, they offer also a fundamental stretching of human capabilities: our enormous human capacities for love, for understanding, and for creative action and choice confront a world in which much appears unloving, meaningless and incomprehensible, and many relations are over-controlled. We then experience the existential demand for choice, for commitment, for 'response-ability': we can respond fully – authentically and passionately – to the demands our life places upon us, or choose a more constrained and limited existence. Enquiry in this sense is not a retreat into an ivory tower, but a way of being. To borrow Torbert's phrase, a person must 'undergo a to-him unimaginable scale of self-development' (1981) to fully engage in human enquiry.

A third perspective through which we can view human development is the transpersonal. Here we see the life process as a movement up through levels of consciousness – through consciousness of body, emotions, and mind, the emergence of ego and personality, to the development of intuition and the discovery of the self. As Maslow (1968), among others, pointed out, the discovery of the self in the peak experience is also a realization of the unity of all things; and so the experience of the self is also an experience of the collective.

The self may be approached through the imaginal world (Hillman, 1975; Avens, 1980); it may be seen as a reflection of different archetypal patterns – 'primordial psychic processes transformed into images, where consciousness can grasp them' (Hampden-Turner, 1981). Imaginal work 'eschews causal connections', which it sees as 'literalisms which may trap the psyche' (Hillman, 1985). Rather, it works through multiple imaginal perspectives, different matrices, metaphors and myths to view, deepen and interconnect. As Hillman (1975) says, the task of imaginal psychology is soul-making.

It is important to honour this way of working and to be open to a variety of patterns through which imaginal knowing can emerge and take shape. We might use the I Ching, the Tarot, astrology, myths, stories of gods and goddesses, fairy tales, and so on. Much of the enquiry with which we have been associated has raised issues of masculinity and femininity: stories such as *The Descent to the Goddess* (Perera, 1981), Eros and Psyche, The Grail Myth (Johnson, 1974), and Whitmont's (1983) four images of the feminine principle have been helpful and enriching.

Among the images of the self archetype, which may also be seen as expressing different visions of enquiry, are:

The hero-king – expression of the will to power.
The priest-healer – expression of the will to expand consciousness, to love, to heal.
The philosopher-metaphysician – expression of the will to know.
The scientist – expression of the will to truth.
The magician – expression of the will to manifest.
The idealist – expression of the will to perfection (both saint and inquisitor).
The artist – expression of the will to harmony and the creation of beauty.

Thus from this perspective we can see the enquiry process as part of the discovery and realization of the self in one of its archetypal forms, and as such is an expression of the collective unconscious. The task then becomes that of exploring the images of the archetype arising in the researcher's unconscious – for example, in dreams and fantasy – and active imagination (Hannah, 1981), and manifesting them through the enquiry process. The importance of the transpersonal process lies not in the 'correctness' of its imagery, but in the challenge it throws out to the materialistic and rational world in which we live.

It draws our attention to the unconscious as the essential source of our creativity and to the reality of our imagination.

Thus a transpersonal view offers the possibility of integrating a knowing from psyche or soul with our knowing from intellect and experience (Reason and Hawkins, 1983). As Blake says:

> But to the man of Imagination
> Nature is Imagination itself.
> AS MAN IS, SO HE SEES.

Illustrations of personal development through enquiry

We now offer four examples of the place of personal development in enquiry, each of which illustrates one or several of the three perspectives mentioned above. These examples have been gathered in collaboration with our research students, who are at different stages of the research process, and again illustrate the three audiences of enquiry. They are *for me* to the extent that they help all the students to understand and deepen their own life process. They are *for us* in that they forward our practice of research and research supervision. They are *for them* in the sense that they intend to speak out to, and seek to influence, practice in a wider academic community. (Gill Robertson's chapter in this volume provides another example of this kind of learning.)

Anne

I had been encouraged to take a secondment previously, but I hadn't had a burning issue to work on. One came from Union casework, seeing other people's perceptions of what was happening to them in their work. There were repeated problems for women, who all identified their problems as being with their superior (who was a man) and saw themselves as failing. After helping 30 people through similar problems I realized that their problem was mine, a personal problem, and that the problem was the system. I spent a lot of time trying to persuade these women that they weren't personal failures, they weren't ruining their careers because they weren't doing the right thing, but that the system was constructed in a way that didn't allow for their development. So I wanted to look at why that was.

It was at a right moment because it also fitted with the personal question of myself and developing feminist ideas. I realize now that I had been quite a convert to the system. I believed that if I worked hard and did my best obviously my wonderful qualities would be recognized, and I would advance automatically along. And that was the way I wanted to go. But I had started to question the system: it seemed to do things that I didn't like to people who were taking senior positions in schools. I questioned personally whether I wanted to pursue a career in education, whether education was worth having a career in, or whether I wanted to try to make waves. And it was all getting quite tangled with personal pressures, so the idea of taking a bit of time to think seemed useful.

Doing research has thrown up a lot that has added to the original issues. These ideas are getting confused again at the moment. They seem to be moving onwards so fast, making me question things to such an extent that I do occasionally panic and pull back. The questioning of relationships in work and in my personal life seems so intertwined that it's quite threatening, quite hard to face.

For example, although I'm researching from a developing feminist perspective, I'm very anxious to do that alongside men. I don't want to take a women-only view. That also keys in with reluctance to let go of dependence on the man in my life. Lots of the answers, lots of the things that theoretically I'm considering are ones that I'm reluctant to apply to my personal life – such as the idea of doing your own thing. Being independent has been one of the key issues of difficulty between John and myself, and we really didn't handle it well back home.

This year has involved so much personal growth that I feel I should have done by the age of 21 (and I'm 34). I've got a whole lot of catching up to do, and that's painful because it makes me realize that a lot of difficulties are personal, personal to me in that I've got to go through them. But I'm also very anxious to keep a hold of my idea of a group or system approach, so that I don't run off and do my individual thing. I still have this commitment to doing something which is for others as well, that will have an effect.

As all this happens to me I feel that I am teetering on the edge of various social and ideological groups, not really belonging anywhere very clearly, feeling alone. And because all this questioning leaves one very exposed it's very difficult to proceed with a calm, rational research orientation when there is so much awareness of personal feelings and bias. The one thing I've managed to keep hold of is that I don't see this as wrong. It is a necessary process to go through, but at the same time it's pretty disabling, at least for spells.

All these questions were there before, but they have always been very suppressed. Now it comes too close. For years it's come close on all sorts of issues and I've allowed myself to be diverted to the more immediately obvious next thing to do – there has always been a demand that has not allowed me to explore.

I suppose at some deep level I've learned not to pay attention to my own needs. I learned it where everybody does, in the family. I'm fairly new to raising these sorts of issues. I've been a person who has been very much in control. I've been quite resistant to exploring, because I equated exploring to people being off their heads and out of control. I've come to realize that there's a whole area of me that I've not explored and need to explore before I progress any further as a person. That progression as a person affects my progression as a researcher and my ability to recognize and facilitate similar explorations in other people. That's where I am now.

Marsha

It was important for me to leave the company I was in because of some personal feedback that I got. I learned that I had behaved in ways that I didn't think I ever would. This feedback didn't match my self-concept; it really jarred me. What was I doing in an organization where I was having to be another person from who I felt I was?

I thought of myself as a very participatory manager. But the feedback was that my subordinates didn't feel cared about and felt I was dismissive. I realize I had become pretty much like my boss, and I was scared to death of challenging her. In my next job I went out of my way to be nice to subordinates. I didn't want it to happen again. So again I wasn't who I thought I was.

When I came here to start research I was positive I wanted to work on feedback, on whether people dismissed it or did use it to change. Then I got into circle dance. This got me to look at circles and wholes. I felt OK being part of the circle: I could be a part of something that was all working to learn the same dance; it was empowering. But when I was in an organization and trying to work to the same goal there was a different feeling about how I chose to fit in. I started seeing that it wasn't about feedback but about integration, fitting in and giving up part of myself. And when I started thinking in those terms I started thinking about my relationships with men.

In America my sense of losing myself was happening in the organization and also on a personal level in my relationship with Jim. I stopped going out and doing things, I was sitting around waiting for him. And I don't see me as a person who waits. And when I come to England I get myself into another relationship where for a while I find myself waiting. I seem to let go of some sort of positive image of me in the course of a relationship. So this is a life issue for me, about how I can lose myself in a relationship if I don't stay aware of my boundaries.

It also occurs to me that all I've done is substitute the way I lose myself in an organization for the way I lose myself in the research. It's about doing something I don't want to do, a sense that when I don't have the energy to do it that I really ought to have the energy. Isn't that what was happening in the organization? I think I am less interested in my research than you want me to be, and I think if I had admitted it I was less interested in my work than my boss wanted me to be. There was a feeling that I could never put in enough time to satisfy her; and to some extent, in the research, whatever I do it won't be good enough for you two either. That's the connection, 'O my God, all I've done is transplant my issues from one continent to another!'

It may be connected with being the only child, the only baby, in a family of adults. My parents had me late in life, and my sister was already grown and gone. I was the only child around trying to fit into an adult world, always wanting to grow up faster and faster because I could never catch up with all these adults that were around. So maybe in some sense I lost my childhood? For the last two years I've felt like I've had a great deal of space for me, to re-establish who I am for me, to relearn that in lots of different ways.

I seem to keep sticking myself in situations where I need to integrate. It's a skill that I have, being able to fit in with all kinds of people in different places. In one sense I like that, it's a really good skill to have, and in another sense I think it feeds right into how I lose myself. Being able to fit in is fine, but when it gets taken to its extreme it becomes a fault.

Elisabeth

What I value most about my research is that I've created little dreams: it's about much more than the here-and-now, it's about social imagination or the imaginal in general. So through my exploration of traditional literature, I've tested myself against a more acknowledged way of doing research, but I've also delved into philosophy, religion and different aspects that are not acknowledged to be research.

It's been about something that makes me cringe a bit, and yet I've dealt with it. It was quite a big issue for me, the spiritual side of human beings. Coming from my education, my rejection of a certain way of being presented with religion, I needed to find a model that could express spirituality of human beings. There is a side of spirituality which, for me, is completely different from all accepted religions. There is much more to human beings than consciousness, and the ego and all these different notions that help you deal with the world.

Beyond that there is the soul, the spiritual, the imaginal, the archetypal which expresses another side of our humanity. It's very difficult to research into because there are no criteria for what is valid in this type of research, except for going through the process oneself.

I got into these issues through studying the female, the feminine. Rather than just review the literature I had to assess what it meant to me, challenging myself to find out what my own experience of being female was all about. I discovered enormous resistance to certain aspects of the female which I had denied myself, being brought up in a very strong male culture. I used to think that it was great that I had been educated like a man, but now I'm not sure that it's such a good thing. There are lots of areas and potentials which I discovered through researching into the female which I had sort of resisted as being . . . soft, and these started to make sense and enrich what I was reading and writing about.

This process of discovery requires surrendering to the spiritual aspect of the female principle. It was an experience of freedom, a realization that everything I'd done had been determined by myself, that I could liberate myself from all the limitations I put on myself. And the feminine principle, which is all-encompassing and chaotic and rich and fertile, has liberated me from all these restrictions of experience.

I can't describe a process which has essentially been emotional, irrational; it's very difficult to put into words that are immediately going to make sense. It's just, I suppose, a peak experience, suddenly realizing. A surrender, and yet at the same time, giving up a certain passivity, because thinking that the limitations you find in your life are created by yourself allows you to take charge of all these aspects, as opposed to thinking that you are influenced by your past, which I also believe, but yet you can go beyond that.

The experience was very simple. One night I was thinking on my own, and all of a sudden it just dawned on me. I wasn't in an especially beautiful place, just sitting at home, not even working, just allowing my mind to wander freely, and all of a sudden I had this great big 'Wow!' experience: I am free, I can be in charge. It was as simple and as difficult as that.

The peak experience emerged from struggles, from long quite depressing struggles. And yet there was this process of surrendering: I couldn't resist any longer, I had to let go and see what happened. And that was very rewarding, to discover that there was something very freeing behind it instead of something very chaotic and dark and frightening.

For a long time I got bogged down with the idea that there wasn't much difference between men and women. Then I moved on to believe that there are differences, and explored how I could ground them. There is a difference in experience, but that is not exactly what I'm talking about. Now I see a difference between the masculine and the feminine as archetypes.

One of my struggles has been communicating. Now, even if I don't know how to express what I'm saying, I know I've got things to say and I'm going to say them, even if it's not presented in the best way. Also, I used to think that I was too young to explore and express these aspects of Being. I've been reading about Zen Buddhism and now I'm suspicious of Western culture's linear notion of time, and of maturity that comes in later life. I reckon I can say the things I have to say now, at 25, rather than thinking they will be so much more refined when I've lived and experienced another 40 years.

Peter

I think most PhDs are going to start with the existential choice, like my dilemma of not being caught in an action mode and wanting to move into a reflective mode. That goes all the way through my research, my internal dialogue has always ended up between the acting me and the reflecting me. If you pursue an existential struggle it is bound to take you back into its own pathology, into the psychodynamic issues. Why I am a compulsive do-er has to be addressed as part of the research.

But my experience is that you get to a point where the psychodynamic stops and the transpersonal begins. In terms of phenomenology I have to develop a transcendental ego which will get a perspective on my ego-coming-to-know. One has to posit a notion that there is a transcendental ego, or in Jungian terms a Self that can become aware of persona and ego. Paul Ricoeur doubts whether you can actually do phenomenology without some sort of spiritual perspective and discipline. Otherwise you get caught up in some circularity of ego looking at ego looking at ego.

There was a time where I started thinking I was going crazy. This was a point when my whole dissertation was at risk because I didn't have a known vantage point from which to view things. What I had to hold on to was images, like Heidegger's notion of getting to a clearing. But to get to the clearing you have to actually go through the wood, you have to enter a realm of not knowing, of it not being possible to know. So the questions arose, 'What's the point of doing a PhD?' and, 'Is doing a PhD so caught up with the ego and rational knowing that it is something that has got to be left behind?'

So I've got to look at the whole nature of my being. If I go for my existential dilemma, if I really really push it, I've got to look at all the pathology that's driving it. I look at myself, how I learned in the past, I get insight about myself. But that's looking at me as an object: there is a point at which insight is not enough, so that the me that's looking and the me that it's looking at are trapped within myself, and that dichotomy of self studying self is broken. That was the experience of the Sufi Khankah. I got so disturbed and shaken up by the experiences there that there was no way I could carry on in a mode of being a researcher in my own life. To a certain extent I had been able to use being a researcher as a defence against experience – I do that in life anyway, I dis-associate through insight about my own life. The Sufi community made impossible that mode of being. There was no safe ground from which to watch, and at that point there was a breaking down of my internal self doing research on self.

I'm trying to catch how that makes a difference to the way I do research . . . Having gone through that experience and written about it, I found something cleared in me. After that the PhD was no longer such a struggle at a deep level: it was still difficult, but the whole anxiety of having been caught somewhere and of having to prove something, somehow eased. I think it was that I was choosing to do the PhD from a different place. Quite fundamentally. This is paradoxical, because while that experience broke down my pattern of disassociation, I found I could be more disassociated from the thesis. I could say, 'This is a task that has to be done; it is no longer something with which my identity is tied up.' I could say, 'Yes, this part of me needs to get it done, and I can be OK about that.' Where I am locating myself is slightly different.

I feel some anxiety about the viva, but I also find it quite humorous. I don't feel my whole being is on the line. Yes, it would be bloody annoying if I had to rewrite a couple of chapters – like getting a parking ticket. But I don't really feel an enormous anxiety about it.

The supervision process

How can we as research supervisors help and respond to these developmental processes? Typically, research supervisors adopt one or more of several different stances towards the student. They can be the experienced guide or mentor who has seen the process many times and can give advice; they may be expert in the topic area, someone whose ideas need to be referred to; or they may be the students' friend, or their advocate in the wider system of the university and research community. Our interest here is in the supervisor as process facilitator, and it is this we will elaborate on in this section.

Of course, we are very aware of the many negative and degenerate images of supervision: there is neglect and abdication, where the supervisor is simply unavailable physically, intellectually and emotionally; there are the expert-turned-tyrants, who use students as research fodder to do their own projects, or who bully the student to do research in a particular way. And there are the fools, who are simply incompetent but are supervising research because the system demands it of them. These situations sadden us: the supervisors fail to grasp the possibilities of research as an educative process in the fullest sense of that term.

If we turn to explore the stance of supervisors as process facilitators, we can see that they need to take a particular attitude. Rather than focus on the content of the research, they must pay most attention to the student's intellectual and emotional process: honouring of process is important and significant in its own right, whatever the supervisor actually does. This means following the 'how' of enquiry, rather than the 'what' or the 'why'. It means not being too worried about conclusions, staying with 'here-and-now' events, feelings and meanings. It means trusting that good outcomes will emerge from healthy process. Thus supervision has similarities with the process of psychotherapy, in which the therapist deals with the ways in which clients approach the issues in their lives, rather than concentrating on the issues themselves. Both student and supervisor may attend to process, particularly as the relationship develops. In this chapter we are concentrating more on the role of the supervisor.

In order to be able to work effectively in this fashion, the supervisor needs to be alert to subtle nuances of behaviour, shifts in attitude, feelings of not being really sure what is going on and so on. This of course calls for a skill in attending to process beyond that normal in academic circles. It also helps to have available a number of intervention tactics, and to have the ability to move between them. We find Heron's (1977) six-category intervention analysis helpful in mapping a range of possible approaches. The categories are: prescriptive, informative, confronting, cathartic, catalytic and supportive. All of these can be used creatively or degeneratively; here we will explore some possible uses in the research supervision context:

Prescriptive interventions aim to give advice and direction. We have found that at times we have chosen to instruct a student as to what to read or write or how to deal with a certain problem. Such interventions may also be critical and evaluative, such as when we have read and commented on drafts of dissertations. Prescriptive interventions may degenerate into a 'takeover' of the enquiry project, so that the supervisor attempts to conduct the research through the student, leaving no space to exercise his or her own initiative.

Informative interventions are about giving information, advice and leads on possible ideas, from the supervisor's own experience. This will be very necessary at certain stages in the enquiry, but can degenerate into compulsive advice giving which leaves the student with no room to develop his or her own ideas. Informative interventions can also involve making an interpretative comment on the student's process as seen by the supervisor, for example by pointing to an issue of personal process. This may helpfully alert both parties to explore what is going on, but clearly can degenerate into attempting to turn the supervision into amateur psychotherapy.

Confronting interventions directly challenge the student with the nature of their processes: they may draw attention to restricted intellectual frameworks, emotional attitudes or work patterns; to issues within the relationship; or to positive qualities and attributes which the student is not seeing. Often we have felt the need to challenge limited and limiting definitions of the research topic or approach, which seems more concerned to protect students than expose them to the chaos of creative enquiry. And we have confronted students who persist in ignoring their own competencies. But confronting interventions can degenerate so that the supervisor is experienced as the enemy, blocking the student's own search for expression.

Cathartic interventions are those which speak to the emotional undercurrent in the enquiry and release tension: they prompt the expression of sadness, anger or fear, and help release the student's emotional intelligence. Often they involve intense feelings and so challenge the supervisor's own emotional competence. Cathartic interventions can degenerate by the supervisor attempting to go too deep too quickly; raising issues which neither is competent to deal with in that forum; or raising issues and quickly shutting down, leaving the student with the unresolved and unexpressed emotional debris.

Catalytic, or structuring, interventions provide a framework within which an issue can be addressed. The supervisor might ask the student to write a piece in a particular form, that form being chosen to address an underlying dilemma. Students who appear over-concerned with what they don't know and about how to write perfectly have been asked to write what they do know about a topic area, or to produce a piece which is labelled 'draft'. 'Two chair' techniques have been borrowed from gestalt therapy, where the student is invited to dialogue in the supervision session between apparently conflicting needs in relation to the research. Structuring interventions degenerate when they are used to protect both supervisor and student from those chaotic aspects of enquiry from which creativity often springs.

Supportive interventions are those which contain and provide a boundary for the research process; overall, they assure the student of the supervisor's care and attention, but more specifically may involve active support. Examples of this are encouraging a student to accept and live with the depression of being stuck; giving time and permission for a direction a student is taking which seems tangential to the main research thrust; being alongside and empathizing at times of anxiety, so that the student can work constructively on the issues rather than being swamped by them; and so on. In our work an important supportive strategy has been to form and help develop an effective and caring enquiry group of students and staff. On the other hand, supportive interventions can degenerate into a 'cotton-wool' culture in which there is no challenge, and difficult issues are avoided.

A key skill in all this is knowing when and how to move from one kind of intervention to another. Confronting interventions, if effective, often need to be followed by support; structures may be useful a while, and must then be left behind; tears may need to be followed by constructive problem solving. If the need for supportive interventions continues too long, this may indicate that student and supervisor are colluding to avoid issues which require confrontation. And it is important to know the limits of the supervisor's role, what can appropriately be worked through within the research context, and what may need addressing in a more overtly psychotherapeutic relationship.

We would note in passing that while these process issues are central to supervision, they do at times clash with the demands of the academic system in two major ways. Firstly, timescales may be out of joint so that students require more time to explore an issue for themselves than the academic system allows. Secondly, there are the issues of standards: not only the gross one of whether the work is good enough for a research degree, but also by what standards a personal product should be judged, and how science, art and personal growth should be differentiated.

Conclusion

In this chapter we have explored an aspect of research which is neglected in traditional accounts and yet, for us, is at the heart of creative enquiry. Neglecting issues of personal development may block our ability to move through the 'not knowing' which typically initiates enquiry into a knowing which is both grounded in personal experience and relevant to wider communities of action and knowing. We invite readers, whether researchers or research supervisors, to open up this dimension of enquiry in their own work.

References

Avens, R (1980). *Imagination is Reality.* Spring Publications.

Davis, M (1964). That's interesting! Towards a phenomenology of sociology and a sociology of phenomenology. *Journal of Philosophy and Social Sciences.* 1, 4, 304-44.

Devereaux, G (1967). *From Anxiety to Method in the Behavioural Sciences.* The Hague: Mouton.

Ferrucci, P (1982). *What We May Be: the Visions and Techniques of Psychosynthesis.* Wellingborough: Turnstone Books.

Griffin, S (1978). *Woman and Nature: the Roaring Inside Her.* New York: Harper and Row.

Hampden-Turner, C (1981). *Maps of the Mind.* London: Mitchell Beazley.

Hannah, B (1981). *Encounters with the Soul: Active Imagination.* Santa Monica: Sigo Press.

Hawkins, P (1986). Living the learning. (PhD dissertation.) University of Bath.

Heron, J (1973). *Re-evaluation Counselling: a Theoretical Review* (Human Potential Research Project.) University of Surrey.

Heron, J (1975). *Six Category Intervention Analysis.* (Human Potential Research Project.) University of Surrey.

Heron, J (1977). *Catharsis in Human Development.* (Human Potential Research Project.) University of Surrey.

Heron, J (1982). *Empirical Validity in Experiential Research.* (Human Potential Research Project.) University of Surrey.

Hillman, J (1975). *Revisioning Psychology.* New York: Harper Collophon.

Hillman, J (1985). Comments at Oxford seminar organized by the Champernowne Trust.

Jackins, H (1965). *The Human Side of Human Beings: the Theory of Re-evaluation Counselling.* Seattle: Rational Island Publishers.

Johnson, R (1974). *He: Understanding Masculine Psychology.* Religious Publishing Co.

Levinson, E (1978). *The Seasons of a Man's Life.* New York: Ballantine.

Lincoln, S Y and Guba, E G (1985). *Naturalistic Inquiry.* Beverley Hills: Sage Publications.

Maslow, A (1966). *The Psychology of Science.* New York: Harper and Row.

Maslow, A (1968). *Toward a Psychology of Being.* New York: Van Nostrand.

May, R (1961). *Existential Psychology.* New York: Random House.

Perera, S B (1981). *Descent to the Goddess.* Toronto: Inner City Books.

Perls, F, Hefferline, R and Goodman, P (1951) *Gestalt Therapy.* New York: Dell Publishing Company.

Reason, P and Hawkins, P (1983) *Inquiry Through Storytelling.* Centre for the Study of Organisational Change and Development, University of Bath.

Reason, P and Heron, J (1986). Research with people: the paradigm of co-operative experiential inquiry. (Working paper.) Centre for the Study of Organisational Change and Development, University of Bath.

Skolimowski, H (1985). The co-creator mind as partner of the creative evolution. (Paper read at the First International Conference on Mind-Matter Interaction.) Universidada Estadual de Campinas, Brazil.

Torbert, W (1981). Why educational research has been so uneducational: the case for a new model of social science based on collaborative inquiry. In: P Reason and J Rowan (eds). *Human Inquiry, a Sourcebook of New Paradigm Research.* Chichester: Wiley, 141-52.

Whitmont, E (1983). *Return of the Goddess.* London: Routledge and Kegan Paul.

Chapter 10

Linking Person-Centred Teaching to Qualitative Research Training

Heather Maclean
University of Toronto

Many of the chapters in this book have examined the dynamics of the adult learning process. A number of chapters address approaches to and ideas about research processes that enhance our understanding of both adult learning and of ourselves. In this chapter I will examine how the subject matter of facilitating adult learning and qualitative approaches to the study of experience are closely inter-related. On the basis of my experience in supervising graduate students learning to do qualitative research I have concluded that concurrent experience in a course or courses using person-centred teaching helps them better understand the philosophical and methodological implications of qualitative research.

The students I work with have undergraduate preparation in the health sciences and are interested in using qualitative research approaches to discover more about people's experiences and perspectives on health related issues. These students have a history of education and a view of knowledge that is rooted in a logical-positivist tradition. Sullivan (1984) would locate their experience in the category of empirical-analytic sciences whose primary metaphors are based on mechanical and biological systems. Most qualitative approaches arise from a very different set of assumptions, with the appropriate metaphor being the person, whose essence is communicated through a process of dialogue. Understanding emerges through interpretation which aims to elucidate meanings embedded in human experience. A shift in interest from the empirical-analytic sciences to the interpretive or hermeneutical social sciences represents a significant paradigm shift for students. The shift necessitates a reconsideration of values and assumptions underlying beliefs about scientific truth and the nature of knowledge. Some people would argue, in fact, that the shift entails a major change in one's world view.

My own background is similar to that of my students. Like them, my undergraduate training was in the sciences, and I viewed science, with its emphasis on truth and objectivity, as the means by which we would motivate people to lead healthy lives. The meaning of 'healthy' and the ways in which this end point could be reached were, of course, defined by the scientists and physicians who knew what was best for people. That mass of people known as 'the public' would be sure to fall in line once we had mastered the right techniques of persuasion (or coercion). Our ability to persuade was inextricably linked to our credibility as masters of science and we fought hard to have our professional expertise recognized and certified.

It was from this context that I entered the field of adult eduation in my pursuit of the keys to motivation. I spent six years studying and working in a milieu that had little to do with 'professionalized' health care. During that time I underwent a transformation in attitudes and values that enabled me to see that a system whose *raison d'être* is the care of people was isolated from the everyday concerns of people. I then returned to my old setting with the hope that I could encourage others to take a long, hard, critical look at how we, as health professionals, had cut ourselves off from the perspectives and concerns of the very people we sought to influence. I am trying through the use of qualitative research to bridge this gap and to encourage the development of a new partnership between the public and health professionals.

Challenging the thinking of graduate students is an important facet of this re-orientation process. Are there ways that they can see the professional health care system with a new set of lenses without embarking on a six-year journey into another culture? If they stay inside the system can they comprehend the significance of a person-centred orientation or will they simply learn a set of techniques to be applied in a superficial way? I am still experimenting with approaches to helping students shift their perspectives, and in this chapter will explore my thinking further.

When students initially enter the domain of qualitative research they are rarely concerned with world views. They are simply intrigued by an approach that appears to offer additional insight into their search for understanding of people's health behaviour. They are less aware of the profound changes that are likely to occur that will transform their own value systems. As their supervisor I have wondered how to structure a programme that would help them glimpse the significance of the shift they are about to (unwittingly) undertake. My intuitive response, based on my own experience, was to send them off to take one or two courses in adult education, in addition to research methods courses. They were puzzled by this recommendation because they wished to be researchers, not adult educators. My response was to stress the need for these students to move outside the medical faculty with the hope that the contrast in the two environments would help them recognize their own unquestioned values and assumptions. I hoped they would begin to see the implications of their interest in qualitative methods. In observing what happened to students who took my advice, I discovered that my intuition had been correct, especially when students had the opportunity to take courses that were taught using a person-centred model.

My reflections on the value of combining person-centred teaching with qualitative research training form the basis of this chapter. By examining the similarities between the two activities I hope to encourage my students and others to seek experiences that will help them acquire an experientially based understanding of the fundamental significance of interpretive qualitative research approaches.

A person-centred approach to teaching has long been advocated by adult educators. It is an approach that arises from a consideration, first and foremost, of the conditions that enhance adult learning. It emphasizes helping students to learn and thus begins with a concern for what the learner experiences rather than the factors that contribute to good instruction. Of primary importance is the encouragement of learner autonomy and personal responsibility. Emphasis is placed on personal meaning and the value of knowledge generated through experience. Qualitative research approaches that depend on interpretation have much in common with the values that underlie person-centred teaching. Both activities affirm the personal capacity to generate knowledge in relationships with others in our social world. Both place emphasis on the lived experience of persons and both acknowledge that meanings are often ambiguous and invite interpretation. The ultimate goal of both activities is to enhance human agency. I will now discuss in more detail some of the characteristics of person-centred teaching and interpretive qualitative research. I will then present an assessment of the similarities and conclude with an argument to augment qualitative research methods courses with courses taught using a person-centred teaching model.

Person-centred teaching

A number of adult educators have written about the principles that, when incorporated into a teaching approach for adults, are likely to enhance learning. The following is a synthesis of assumptions about conditions that have been drawn from writings of pioneers in the field (Combs, 1974; Griffin, 1977; Knowles, 1970; Pine and Horne, 1969; and Rogers, 1969).

1. Adult learning is enhanced when learners perceive that the learning process and outcomes are relevant to their own purposes.
2. Adult learning is enhanced in a group setting which allows for the interplay of ideas and hence the potential for 'building' on the combined resources of the group.
3. Adult learning is enhanced when learning is viewed as an evolutionary process which requires time and patience, and where one accepts that goals and directions that emerge may change as people become clearer about what it is they want to learn.
4. Adult learning is enhanced when learners are treated as self-directing, responsible people who are encouraged to take an active role in decision making, planning and implementation of learning activities. Such an approach assumes that adults have a rich accumulation of experiences which can be tapped in the learning process.
5. Adult learning is enhanced when learners are encouraged to trust themselves (including their emotional reactions), to draw from their experience as a source of knowledge and to integrate their personal meanings with external knowledge.
6. Adult learning is enhanced when the learning climate fosters self-esteem, interdependence, freedom of expression, acceptance of differences and freedom to make mistakes.
7. Adult learning is enhanced when evaluation of learning includes self-evaluation – that is, the learner's assessment of what he or she has learned – and feedback from others.
8. Adult learning is enhanced when people are encouraged to be active and

to learn through doing, particularly when emphasis is placed on reflecting on the meaning of what people have experienced.

9. Adult learning is enhanced when it is recognized that some learning cannot be predicted or planned. Some goals, therefore, may initially be ambiguous.
10. Adult learning is enhanced when learners discover their preferred learning styles. As people become more aware of how they learn and become exposed to other ways of learning they can redefine and modify their own styles as they seek ways of becoming more competent and responsible learners.

To apply these assumptions about conditions that enhance learning to a teaching model, facilitators might find it useful to structure their activities around five key concepts. These concepts include the use of an emergent design, the development of a supportive climate, the definition of the meaning of 'content', and the encouragement of reflection and critical self-assessment.

Emergent design

In order to enhance relevance and to use the combined life experience of learners it is important to develop processes to help learners identify and label some of what they currently 'know' (their existing knowledge and skills), and to identify their own learning needs as they relate to the overall course content. It is necessary to allow sufficient time for this self-assessment. In addition, learners should be encouraged to participate in the design of activities to help meet their identified needs. Thus, the course content is not predefined but emerges after a needs assessment. As perceptions of needs may change with time, it is important to make provisions for periodic reassessment and, if necessary, a realignment of the programme plan. Most learners are totally inexperienced in setting their own goals in formal courses and so need encouragement and practical assistance. As well, they will need support to help them cope with the ambiguity of this 'new' approach and their uncertainty about their own needs and goals.

Interdependence

The opportunity to learn from peers is central to a person-centred approach. Other members of the group are valued because they can provide alternative perspectives that contribute to learning. The generative capacities of the group are likely to exceed the creative capacities of individuals. This viewpoint is in notable contrast to the suspicious, competitive attitudes many students have towards fellow learners in more traditional settings. In a person-centred approach much effort is directed towards building group cohesiveness. Then, in a climate of trust and mutuality, learners can take advantage of the opportunity to take risks in testing out new ideas and behaviours. They also have access to feedback and the opportunity to learn from the differing viewpoints of others. Such learnings, however, are likely to occur only if deliberate efforts have been made to promote trust, openness and interaction.

Developing a supportive climate

Because of the emphasis on class participation, on personal agency, on the richness of learning from group activities, and because of the stresses that frequently arise when learners first experience a learner-centred approach, climate setting is a crucial activity. Ways must be found to promote the development of trust, respect and caring among group members, and sufficient class time allocated for activities that build supportive relationships. The facilitator seeks to model respect, caring, self-disclosure, and openness to feedback in his or her own interactions with learners. As well, a tone of informality must be set through attending to the physical arrangements of the room and the facilitator's manner and approach to learners.

Defining content

Learners who are used to a more traditional approach to teaching tend to think of course content as something that exists primarily in written texts and in the lectures and perspectives of teachers. Knowledge is thought of as something 'objective' and is viewed as static as opposed to dynamic. Expanding learners' views of what constitutes knowledge and hence course content is a key task of any teacher who uses a person-centred approach. Knowledge needs to be redefined so that learners think of an open-ended knowledge system that is both relative and creative. The process of relating outside knowledge to what one believes intuitively or knows from experience helps learners discover the personal meaning of ideas. To help learners respect their own experience as a source of knowledge, facilitators frequently suggest learning strategies – for example, laboratory learning, experiential learning, field experience – that encourage learners to engage in activities that generate experiences about which they can then reflect and conceptualize. Learners use these ideas in combination with other sources of existing knowledge about particular concepts to 'learn' the course content.

Reflection and critical self-assessment

The crucial element in the discovery of personal meaning and in the use of an experiential approach is reflection. Reflection implies a conscious consideration of experience and ideas and can serve as a naming or labelling activity. It can occur quite passively by simply allowing things to surface in the course of daily life or it can be structured using discussions with others, journals, self-assessment exercises or reading, or a combination of these things, to trigger one's thoughts. The process involves more than recollection. Learners are encouraged to sort through their experiences and ideas and to develop frameworks for organizing and labelling them. They are encouraged to assess the extent to which their own frameworks could be generalized by discussing them with others, by further reading, by writing and by testing out their practical implications.

In addition to reflection for the purposes of understanding and extending knowledge of the course content, students are encouraged to consider their own learning styles. It is assumed that development of one's full potential as a learner is an on-going challenge and that a reflective orientation will enhance the learners' understanding of their own styles and suggest additional approaches that could enhance their own growth and development.

Summary

Teachers who use a person-centred approach have many additional responsibilities beyond that of effectively communicating a specific body of knowledge. Teachers also have a facilitative role – to act as a catalyst or stimulus to students' learning. They set a climate, suggest readings, and design activities that lead to interaction and self-awareness. They encourage, listen, and support. As well, teachers must model what they expect of students. They need to interact with students, share their own learning agendas, discuss their own insights, and exhibit respect and openness to new ideas. In their capacity as teachers they also face the challenge of providing feedback to students in ways that respect their ideas and kindle their enthusiasm without compromising institutional standards.

Qualitative research

Qualitative research is an umbrella term that refers to certain research approaches that have a number of common characteristics. The term generally refers to interpretive studies designed to investigate human experience and to do so in ways that both reveal its complexity and reflect its historical and situational contexts. The goal of qualitative research is to take the insight and wisdom of people and give it precise expression and logical grounding so that the complexity and dynamics of human behaviour can be better understood.

All branches of the social sciences have traditions of qualitative research. Phenomenology has been associated with psychology; symbolic interaction, and ethnomethodology with sociology; and ethnography with anthropology. Some researchers from each discipline have applied these approaches to educational research. The historical roots of qualitative research in education have been reviewed in some depth by Bogdan and Biklen (1982).

I will not differentiate between the various forms of qualitative research here. Instead, I will provide a brief overview of some of the common characteristics. Qualitative researchers are primarily concerned with meanings. The foundation of such research is understanding and interpretation. Through evidence obtained through interviewing or the written word or both, researchers attempt to understand the intentions and actions of people. Qualitative researchers believe that knowledge is socially constructed. Humans exist in a world of shared action and history and their uniqueness emerges from the common world. They also recognize that meanings reflect multiple realities and that objective 'truths' do not exist. The unit of study is the whole person and his or her reaction to the phenomenon under study. However, individual perspectives cannot be adequately interpreted without an understanding of the context in which they are developed. Thus, it is desirable to observe and document settings in which the research takes place, including the characteristics and values of the broader socio-cultural milieu. Historical perspectives should also be examined so that the current significance of the phenomenon under study is viewed within the framework of its lengthier tradition.

The problems addressed by qualitative researchers are generally directed towards understanding processes as opposed to outcomes or events. Studies can be retrospective or prospective but in either case investigators are concerned with how people make sense of their experience within the on-going framework of their lives.

The design of qualitative studies is frequently ambiguous as often little is known about the nature of the phenomenon before the study. Design modifications are common throughout in response to the needs of participants in the study or because of the nature of the preliminary findings. Questions emerge from the interaction and discussion between the researcher and the interviewee. Detailed knowledge of the phenomenon is not assumed *a priori.* In fact, presuppositions are deliberately set aside so the researcher can remain open to what emerges from the research. As a consequence, the analysis process is inductive. The analysis involves a sifting and sorting of data into categories and then a rebuilding of the material in a way that shows the connections and significance of the various parts when they form the whole. Qualitative researchers take the position that they, themselves, are an integral part of the research process. It is therefore necessary that they identify and monitor their personal assumptions, bias and theoretical predispositions throughout the research process and assess their own effects on the data.

The design and analysis processes are not amenable to a 'cookbook' set of instructions. Processes vary depending upon the interest and orientation of the researchers, the nature of the research problem, the characteristics and responses of the study participants and the nature of the actual data. What is common to all, however, is the interpretive role of the researcher. The data are generally rich and complex and there are many layers of meaning embedded within them. The revelation of these layers emerges only after a long and arduous courtship between the researcher and the data, characterized by periods of intense immersion and contemplative withdrawal.

Summary

Because a detailed discussion of the philosophical and methodological considerations of the many branches of interpretive qualitative research is beyond the scope of this chapter, I would like to draw attention to the following sources: Bogdan and Biklen, 1982; Giorgi, 1970; Keen, 1975; Sullivan, 1984; Taylor and Bogdan, 1984. They are useful for building a more thorough understanding of a range of qualitative approaches.

The common features of the approach that are important to this discussion include an emphasis on the significance of personal experiences and perspectives, the view of person as agent, the attention to the whole person, and to the interactive and interpretive role of the researchers. In the following section I will explore the parallels between teaching and research methods that place the person (be it learner or the research participant) at the centre.

Person-centred teaching and qualitative research

It is at the level of philosophical underpinnings where the first and perhaps the most fundamental similarities exist between a person-centred approach and qualitative research. In both the research and teaching approaches there is an emphasis on the importance of understanding the perspectives of individuals. Further, it is recognized that although each person's viewpoint will be unique and idiosyncratic, it has been shaped within a common world. There is a concern in both settings to find ways to help participants surface and articulate facets of their experience that they believe are significant to them. Personal experience is valued as a means of understanding and learning about phenomena. An examination of the meanings embedded in individual perceptions of experience and a comparative analysis with meanings articulated by other individuals enhances and extends our understanding of the topic of study. In both traditional research and traditional teaching the value of personal meanings as a source of knowledge has been largely ignored or discounted.

This valuing of human experience assumes the ability of humans to be active interpreters of their experience and is based on the concept that humans together constitute the world. This concept of person as agent is fundamental to teaching and research approaches that view people as responsible, self-directed individuals.

Both approaches are concerned with contextual backgrounds. In the classroom, concepts cannot be isolated from issues of practical significance in everyday life. In research, people's viewpoints and experiences on issues have to be considered within historical and situational perspectives. Likewise, phenomena cannot be reduced and studied as isolated variables in an attempt to determine cause-effect relations. Rather, phenomena are studied in their natural setting, and the boundaries of study are defined by what the study participants consider relevant. This is also the case in the classroom where learners have the opportunity to define the relevance of the course content by addressing issues and concerns that reflect what is important to them.

The conventional notion of the researcher as an objective and unbiased observer in the research process is one which is discounted in qualitative research. In this approach the researcher is seen as an integral part of the research process, and it is acknowledged that his or her attitudes and behaviour do in fact influence the course of the research. The presence of the researcher must be accounted for by a thorough examination and reporting of the researcher's assumptions, biases, intentions and behaviour throughout the study. Furthermore, during the interviewing and analysis process the researcher should not be attempting to detach himself or herself from the experience in order to judge the appropriateness of the interviewee's experience. Rather, the researcher actively engages with the individuals or their data or both in order to understand better their experience.

The parallel with a person-centred approach to teaching is that the facilitator, too, must have a detailed awareness of his or her own assumptions, motives and behaviours, and these awarenesses are seen as data for discussion and learning by all members of the group. Like the researcher, the facilitator does not relate to learners in a detached way but as an active member of the group who is viewed as learner as well as teacher.

During the interviewing phase of qualitative research the role of the researcher is primarily facilitative. The researcher is attempting to elicit from those being interviewed all that they see as relevant to their experience of a particular phenomenon. To do the above the researcher must be able to create an atmosphere of trust and mutual respect so that those being interviewed are encouraged to search for and reveal the meaning of their experience. The researcher must be able to suspend prior beliefs and moral judgements and handle the ambiguity inherent in the approach. To work with the data and present a systematic analysis of people's experience requires a person who is sensitive, self-critical and truth-seeking.

The facilitator, too, must be able to set aside preconceived notions and relate to each new group in a way that encourages group members to reflect and learn from their experience. The facilitator must be willing to engage in mutual problem solving and to respect the uniqueness and autonomy of individuals as they identify needs, articulate approaches and engage in learning activities. Facilitators need a sensitivity to others' needs and reactions, an ability to assess their own effectiveness, and a willingness to engage with and learn from other learners.

In qualitative research each phenomenon of study is respected for its uniqueness. The method of enquiry is not the same for each phenomenon but rather emerges from an analysis of how best to acquire an understanding given its characteristics and context. Such an approach is not amenable to a prescribed set of instructions. Using a 'cookbook' type method violates the fundamental attitude – 'the attitude that seeks to meet phenomena on their own terms and not to press them into the mould of preconceptions' (Keen, 1975, p 41). Specific techniques provide useful guidelines for implementing the research approach. However, they should be selected only after a thorough examination of the most appropriate approach to studying the phenomenon and therefore used in response to a need rather than in a prescriptive fashion.

When using a person-centred approach to teaching the same assumption holds true. The actual techniques used to facilitate learning will differ depending on the individual needs of each group of learners. What is consistent from group to group is the facilitator's intention of encouraging learners to discover, articulate and share personal meanings related to the content as they interact with others in the learner's setting.

In conclusion

The similarities outlined above are infrequently explicit in the minds of students taking a course taught using a person-centred approach. Instead, what emerges is a reinforcement of the general principles of qualitative research and an enhanced understanding of their significance because students are forced to confront their implications in an experiential way. The students realize first-hand the value of knowledge that is grounded in experience and generated in dialogue with others. They discover the truth of multiple realities and the potential for growth and development that can emerge from perspectives that incorporate an understanding of meanings. At the same time they experience the degree of difficulty and commitment that must accompany the search to understand the perspectives of others. But they also discover the intellectual excitement of developing frameworks that are grounded in experience and reflect shared meanings. Students learn the importance of honesty, trust and an open mind. They have the opportunity to reflect and learn how to examine their own values and beliefs. They come to understand the meaning of self-awareness and why it is an important facet of the research process. They also acquire a taste of the ambiguity that is part of a science that precludes absolute truths and learn that at best they will only ever completely understand a portion of what they seek to know.

Much of what these students learned would be covered in a theoretical way in qualitative research courses. However, the opportunity to participate in a learning experience that is based on principles of person-centred teaching brings the concepts to life and underscores what they will mean in concrete terms in the conduct of interpretive studies. The learning experience is sufficiently different from what students are used to that it jolts them into thinking about assumptions that had been previously unexamined. This reassessment is an important first step on the road to a new vision of the practice of health promotion.

References

Bogdan, R C and Biklen, S K (1982). *Qualitative Research for Education: an Introduction to Theory and Methods.* Boston: Allyn & Bacon.

Combs, A (1974). A humanistic approach to learning of adults. In: R Bortner, S Dubin, D Hultsch and J Withall (eds). *Adults as Learners. Proceedings of a Conference.* Pennsylvania: The Pennsylvania State University, 51-62.

Giorgi, A (1970). *Psychology as a Human Science: a Phenomenologically Based Approach.* New York: Harper & Row.

Griffin, V (1977). *Principles of Adult Learning.* (Unpublished manuscript.) Ontario Institute for Studies in Education.

Keen, E (1975). *A Primer in Phenomenological Psychology.* New York: Holt, Rinehart and Winston.

Knowles, M (1970). *The Modern Practice of Adult Education: Andragogy versus Pedagogy.* New York: Association Press.

Pine, G and Horne, P (1969). Principles and conditions for learning in adult education. *Adult Leadership.* 108-10; 126; 133-4.

Rogers, C (1969). *Freedom to Learn.* Columbus, Ohio: Charles E Merrill.

Sullivan, E V (1984). *A Critical Psychology: Interpretation of the Personal.* New York: Plenum Press.

Taylor, S J and Bogdan, R (1984). *Introduction to Qualitative Research Methods.* (Second edition.) New York: John Wiley.

Chapter 11

Returning to College Study: Barriers for Adult Learning

Jerold Apps
University of Wisconsin-Madison

Background

In many parts of the world, particularly in North America, thousands of adults are returning to college campuses to complete degrees started years previously or to begin degree work for the first time. These adults experience a variety of problems and challenges. They also face barriers that interfere with their learning.

I have been interested in adults returning to school since 1966 when I enrolled for full-time graduate study after 10 years away from school. As a 32-year-old student I was seen as something of an oddity in some of the classes I took. I was also viewed as a considerable oddity by certain administrators. When I returned I was married and had three pre-school age children. One of the first things I did was to apply for a student loan. I will never forget that experience. After filling out a sheaf of forms, I presented myself to an interviewer. She alternately shuffled through the papers, and looked at me over the top of her glasses. 'Why are you coming back to school?' she asked. She began to sound like my uncle who believed that the only reason anyone ever went back to college was to get out of work – to him work could only be physical labour.

I told the interviewer why I was coming back, at least I tried to. A 'hmmm' was the only reply I received as she continued to shuffle the several forms I'd filled out. 'How come your parents aren't supporting you?' she asked. Trying to contain my anger, I quietly replied, 'They're retired.' 'Retired!' she said. Apparently she'd not run into a student so old as to have retired parents.

And so the interview went on, and I finally got my student loan. But I have never forgotten that day. Those experiences I had as a returning student in a direct way influenced me to do research in this area.

To put into context the research I will be reporting on, my first research project, focusing on study problems faced by adults returning to college, was carried out in 1975. This study and its implications were reported in *Study Skills for Adults Returning to School* (1978). I followed this in 1978 with research which investigated the characteristics of exemplary instructors of returning students. In a series of open-ended interviews with college and university instructors in the United States and Canada, I discovered the teaching approaches these exemplary instructors used, their attitudes towards older students, any conflicts they experienced between teaching and research expectations, and their ideas about changes colleges and universities should make to better accommodate large numbers of returning students. This work was reported in *The Adult Learner on Campus* (1981).

While the work with exemplary instructors provided valuable knowledge about returning students from the instructor's perspective, I believe it important to go directly to returning students to discover what barriers they perceived were preventing them from having richer learning experiences.

Research by Cross and Zusman (1979), Astin (1979) and Carp *et al.*, (1974) suggested the following as barriers listed by potential and actual participants in educational programmes: lack of time, cost, home responsibilities, job responsibilities, lack of access to educational facilities, and seeing oneself as too old to learn. A further trend which cut across these studies was that women identified home responsibilities as major obstacles while men identified job responsibilities.

In 1978 I conducted an exploratory study of returning adult students to learn about their characteristics as learners. From that study I discovered several factors that returning students said affected their learning:

(1) insecurity about ability to learn;
(2) student's marital or family situation;
(3) unpleasant memories of previous formal learning;
(4) expectations that formal learning would relate to life experience;
(5) problems in adjusting to the routines of formal study;
(6) time constraints.

This pilot study gave me some important clues about what I might expect when I conducted a formal study of barriers to learning returning students faced.

The barriers study

Beginning in 1980, our research team (two research assistants and myself) began the study of returning students. A returning student was defined as a person 25 years of age or older, who had been out of school at least three years and returned either for full- or part-time credit study. A barrier to learning was defined as a major problem faced by older students after they returned to school. We defined three categories of barrier:

(a) *Institutional* – practices and procedures used by colleges and universities which excluded or discouraged adult learners (inconvenient schedules, inappropriate locations of classes, full-time fees for part-time study, inappropriate courses of study, or difficulty in obtaining necessary campus registration or graduate information).
(b) *Situational* – barriers arising from one's situation in life at a given time (lack of time owing to job and home responsibility, lack of money, lack of child care and transportation problems).
(c) *Psychosocial* – barriers coming from such internal factors as feelings about being a student, beliefs and values and one's sense of self-esteem; and barriers coming from such external factors as one's level of socio-economic status and such social forces as the opinions of others and past experience in the school setting.

The questions guiding the current research were:

(1) What were the major barriers to learning perceived by adults who had returned to school?
(2) Did those barriers change over time; particularly did those barriers lessen in intensity from the first semester back in school to a year later?

From the review of the literature and reflections on the previous research we conducted, we anticipated the following results:

- Situational barriers would show up more often than psychosocial or institutional barriers as problems for returning adult learners.
- Women would mention family-related barriers more often than men, and men would mention job- and institution-related barriers more often than women.
- Institutional barriers would lessen in severity with time.

Study design

The emphasis of the research was twofold: did returning students perceive a change in barriers over time, and was there a relation between perceived barriers and persistence and withdrawal?

A random sample of 91 men and women was selected from newly enrolled University of Wisconsin-Madison graduate students in the School of Education and the College of Agricultural and Life Sciences (CALS). The sample was drawn over a five-semester period beginning with the spring term 1981 and ending with the spring term 1983. To be included in the sample, the student had to be 25 years of age or older, an American citizen, and have had three years or more between current and any previous enrolments.

These 91 returning adult students were contacted between the sixth and twelfth week of the first semester they were on campus. Data were collected in a one-to-one structured setting, using three questionnaires and 15 open-ended interview questions. The questionnaires included:

(a) a biographical assessment.
(b) a 25-item perceived 'barriers to learning' instrument which included questions related to institutional, situational and psychosocial barriers;
(c) Rosenberg's 'self-esteem scale'.

The instruments were presented in the sequence above, followed by a tape-recorded, open-ended interview session.

One year later the same data were collected a second time from 43 of the original 91 people who were available for interviews. These 43 people are the focus of this report.

Description of students in study

Of the 43 students interviewed twice, 29 were men and 24 were women. Their median age was 30 years with a range of 25 to 61 years. Seventeen students were enrolled in the College of Agricultural and Life Sciences and 26 in the School of Education. Thirty three of the students were married, nine were never married and one was separated. Nineteen were parents. Twenty eight per cent of the respondents were employed full-time, 49 per cent part-time, and 23 per cent were unemployed.

For these 43 returning students, the median length of time out of school was 6.8 years. Twenty four had been out of school three to five years, seven were out six to eight years, and twelve were returning after nine or more years away.

Eighty four per cent (36) said they returned to school for career related reasons. Fifty one per cent wanted new job skills, 28 per cent sought improved current job skills and 5 per cent said they wanted to 'broaden their professional capabilities'. The remaining 16 per cent said they were returning to school for intellectual growth or simply because it was convenient (spouse had obtained a job in the area, for instance).

Fifty eight per cent of the respondents attended school full-time, taking nine or more semester credits as graduate students. Forty two per cent were part-time students enrolling in eight or less credit hours each semester. The smaller number of years a returning student had been out of school, the more likely he or she was to be a full-time student.

Major barriers faced by adults returning to school

Barrier data were recorded twice for each returning adult student. At time one, during the first semester the sample adults had returned to school, these barriers were noted as most important:

	Degree of perceived problems *No of people perceiving problem expressed as a %*		
Situation	*No problem*	*Some*	*Serious/ very serious*
Increase in stress	10	57	33
Parking in and around campus	44	25	31
Balancing family and school time	32	38	30
Balancing job and school time	24	47	29
Spending time with immediate family	31	50	19

Top five barriers to learning – time one

Note that during the first semester they were back to school, 90 per cent of the returning adult students noted 'increase in stress' as a barrier to their learning. Thirty three per cent said it was serious or very serious.

Of the various categories of returning students, stress was perceived as a most serious barrier to learning by those in the School of Education (40 per cent), those 30-34 years of age (42 per cent), for women (44 per cent), for those who were married (41 per cent), those who were parents (37 per cent), those who were unemployed (60 per cent), full-time students (40 per cent) and those who had been out of school six to eight years before returning (71 per cent).

During the interviews we obtained interesting insights into the nature of the stress these returning students were experiencing. Juggling time commitments was one of the reasons for stress. As one student explained:

> I won't have time till the end of the semester. I'm not sure I can get everything all done; I'm not sure I will meet my responsibilities to the people at work and to myself for school and to my husband . . . I am trying to do too much; I really don't know where or if I could eliminate anything. There's nothing I could eliminate. I couldn't drop a course because the department wouldn't let me. I couldn't cut my hours back at work. They are already cut back so far and I have to work to make some money. What really slid was home. I didn't do any cooking and I didn't do any cleaning . . . you just keep going . . . it's like that train in the movie that just slides through to no end. You just slide right up to the end of the semester and you better hope that when you hit the last day or the last exam you can walk away.

'The stresses of school are different from the stresses I felt in my job', another said. 'Tests and examinations are stress. I wasn't evaluated like that in my job. I felt like I could go to work and leave it there, come home and not worry about it and do something else. In school I bring it home with me. I have all these stresses on my mind much more constantly.'

An outcome of stress, change in health, is evident in many student responses. The content analysis of the interview data showed that 45 per cent of the returning students in our research said they were less healthy since returning to school. One student reported the problem this way: 'When I started back to school I experienced a lot of health problems. Apparently it was a shock to my system. I went through a traumatic time. I was on medication and I got infections I could not get rid of. My doctor suggested it was due to stress and suggested I take two weeks off and go away. He told me, "that's the only way you'll get better." I said, "I can't, I've got a job, a family, and I'm in school." '

Another returning student explained: 'My health changed after I returned to school. I was always tired, but I couldn't sleep. I couldn't go to sleep, especially every Sunday night. I would lie in bed and think about work and school and how I was going to fit it all in and I would make a long list of everything I had to do for the week and schedule my monthly calendar. I would still feel rushed on Sunday night and I'd worry, even if I didn't have anything to do on Monday.'

The second most noted barrier, parking, may be an artefact of the Madison campus where parking has been a particular problem for faculty, staff and students for many years. It is an especially difficult problem for part-time students who rush from a job to a class, and then can't find short-term parking. In our interviews, parking problems were most frequently mentioned by women, primarily in the context of safety issues. One woman said, 'I'm conscious of the fact there are problems, but I go where it's well lit, and I walk quickly.' During the research interviews one student noted, 'I shouldn't be interviewing with you today, I just got two parking tickets in an hour.'

Balancing family and school time, the third most serious barrier to learning for returning students, was noted by a significantly larger number of women than men. As one might expect, those with families (77 per cent) noted problems balancing family and school time.

The fourth most serious barrier, balancing job and school time, was perceived as a serious barrier more often by men (44 per cent) than by women (17 per cent).

The fifth noted serious barrier to learning was spending time with the immediate family. This barrier is different from the third one in that it refers to one specific task of balancing school and family time, that of actually spending time with the family. As would be expected, those students with children perceived this as a more serious barrier to learning than those who were childless.

During the interviews, returning students shared many examples of problems. One said, 'Our relationship [between husband and wife] is getting a bit worse. There's really a lot of stress and there are arguments. We went to a marriage counsellor for ten weeks, but going to a counsellor . . . you have to devote time to that too. And you not only have to go, but then you have to work on the problems afterwards. We weren't having the time to follow through with the suggestions so we stopped [going to the counsellor].'

Another said, 'My son does come first. If I start seeing evidence that he's suffering, then I'll drop a course. Because I can't afford child care, I'm trading babysitting with other people. When I'm not studying I'm babysitting, so what's really suffering is my marriage.'

Reflecting on our previous discussion of the categories of barriers to learning – institutional, situational, and psychosocial – we note the following. Among the five most often perceived barriers to learning by returning students, parking is the only one falling within the institutional category. Three of the five barriers can be classed as situational: balancing family and school time, balancing job and school time, and spending time with the immediate family. The major psychosocial barrier noted was increased stress.

We were extremely curious to see if the barriers to learning identified by returning students would change after they had been on campus for some time and had supposedly become adjusted once again to student life. But the same five barriers noted as most serious during the first semester students were back to school remained the most serious one year later.

There were, however, some changes in perceptions of barriers from the first semester back in school and a year later. More students at time two perceived a problem in balancing family time than at time one; fewer students at time two perceived serious problems with registration and with obtaining information from the graduate school and obtaining general campus information; and more students had serious problems with teaching styles of instructors by time two. From time one to time two, returning students saw as less of a barrier problems with concentration, problems with reading skills and problems with study skills generally.

By the time of the follow-up contacts (March, 1985) with the 43 returning students who were interviewed twice, 51 per cent (22) had obtained a degree and 42 per cent (18) were continuing students. Five per cent (two students) had stopped out and 2 per cent (one student) had dropped out.

Comparing results with expectations

- We predicted that situational barriers would be more of a problem for returning students than psychosocial or institutional barriers. Our prediction was accurate. Situational barriers such as balancing time with job and family were perceived more often as barriers to learning than those barriers classed as psychosocial or institutional.

- We discovered no significant differences between men and women concerning family-related barriers and job-related barriers.
- We predicted that institutional barriers would lessen in severity with time. The results were mixed. Such institutional barriers as registration, and obtaining campus and graduate school information did decrease from time one to time two. But one institutional factor, problems with teaching styles of instructors, increased in intensity as a barrier from time one to time two.
- We predicted situational barriers would stay the same or increase in severity over time. We predicted accurately. With one exception, there was no significant difference between time one and time two concerning situational barriers. The exception was balancing school and family time. This was perceived as a more severe barrier to learning by returning students at time two than it was at the time the students were first interviewed.

In terms of demographic characteristics, at the time of the second interviews the following was noted: one married person had been divorced, three non-parents had become parents, and 11 people had changed job status. New percentages of job status at interview time two were: full-time employed, 26 per cent; part-time employed, 56 per cent; and unemployed, 19 per cent. Note that the percentage of unemployed (23 per cent at interview time one) had decreased and the percentage of part-time employees (49 per cent at time one) had increased.

Also at time two, ten students (23 per cent) had changed their student status. At time two, 53 per cent were full-time and 47 per cent were part-time. At time two, of the 43 students in the sample 93 per cent had persisted and 7 per cent had withdrawn.

Discussion

The surprising result in this research was the large number of returning adult students who indicated returning to the college classroom increased their stress. We were even further surprised to see the level of stress increase from time one to time two. In our interviews we discovered some of the implications of this high level of stress: health problems and marital discord.

Although we attempted to examine barriers from the perspective of three categories – psychosocial, institutional and situational – it became clear that there was considerable interaction among the barriers. Balancing time and relationships and commitments to family, school and work clearly contributed to increasing levels of stress. These relationships among the categories of barriers became clear during the interview sessions with adult students.

To understand better the pressures adult students face upon returning to school we examined the phenomenon of multiple roles. Adults engage in a number of primary commitments simultaneously and each is important.

The college classroom becomes but one of these commitments. At times one of these commitments may be emphasized, and another minimally attended to. At another time another commitment is given primary emphasis, and so on. Thus college and university administrators and instructors must be aware that adult students are not only students. Neither are they primarily students – they are workers, spouses, parents and community participants.

Of the study problems noted by returning students (a situational barrier), ability to concentrate was a problem for 64 per cent of the respondents. This problem remained constant from time one to time two interviews. As noted above, returning adult students participate in multiple roles, and multiple roles may make it difficult to keep one's mind on one thing.

Suggestions for practice

(1) The above characteristics of returning adult students challenge college and universities to respond in ways that sometimes must be different from how they respond to the more traditional students. For instance, the timeliness of reading and writing assignments, the dates for test taking, and even a regular attendance at classes may not be met by returning older students in the manner instructors of traditional students may expect.

(2) In-service activities for instructors of returning students should include such topics as information about stress, and how to recognize it, what to do about it and when to refer the student to appropriate counselling services.

(3) Specific problem issues need to be considered by appropriate college and university departments. Firstly, flexible registration times and class times, and availability of professors for returning students who have time schedules influenced by work responsibilities, are needed. Secondly, adequate parking for commuting students, particularly those who are part-time and may need parking for only an hour or two during the week should be provided. Also, the safety issue for women in relation to parking – adequate lighting, and parking within easy walking distance of night classrooms – is important. Thirdly, support groups should be available. Support groups could provide invaluable service for the returning student who believes he or she is the only one experiencing a particular problem. These support groups could also provide social opportunities for returning students who may not have time or the inclination to participate in social activities designed for younger students. Fourthly, counsellors for returning students are needed who understand the multiple roles of returning students and who are prepared to assist with issues that range from discussing how to talk with a child who doesn't understand the parent's return to school to marital counselling. Fifthly, the provision of opportunities for skill-building, including such things as workshops on study skills, reading, mathematics, writing and concentration is needed. Finally, career counselling opportunities are essential, especially for women who have returned to school

and are seeking a career after many years out of the job market.

(4) At the institutional level, colleges and universities often need to examine several fundamental questions concerning mature students. To what extent has the college or university actively recruited adult students but made few adjustments in regular operating procedures to accommodate them? Have they flexible registration procedures; a variety of times for classes including evenings and weekends; and opportunities for learning at a distance using correspondence study, radio, microcomputers or other media? To what extent has the college or university made a concerted effort to solve the unique problems faced by returning students – parking, safety questions, counselling services, etc.

Postscript

It is now more than 20 years since I returned to school. As I reflect on the experiences I had as a returning student, and as I think about the results of my recent research on returning students, two sets of thoughts emerge. On the one hand the old ideas that colleges and universities are primarily designed for young people fresh out of secondary school often still prevail. But on the other hand, some important changes have occurred as well. On most campuses these days, courses are offered so that returning students can find them more readily available. In most instances registration procedures have been streamlined, but more work is necessary here. The society in general is more accepting of mature students and this has helped to improve family acceptance of a parent returning to school.

My research shows that adults returning to school perceive stress as a major barrier to their learning, and something which increases during their course. This is a critical problem that requires further research to uncover its sources as well as discover ways of lessening its effects on the returning adult student. Again, if I may use a personal example, I do not remember stress being a problem for me or for many of my fellow returning students 20 years ago (admittedly our numbers were small, and stress wasn't something one admitted to having in those days). On the contrary, I recall my time of full-time study as challenging to be sure, but also one of the most exciting and pleasant experiences I have had. I remember how excited I was to have time to read and think, and talk with others about matters that were thought-provoking but often highly impractical. It was the opportunity to have this kind of experience that I found most joyful. I hear today's returning students mentioning some of these same positive benefits from returning to school. But I also hear the dreaded threat of stress clouding the joy of academic work for the returning student. Why is this the case? Obviously more work is necessary on this subject.

References

Apps, J W (1981). *The Adult Learner on Campus.* Chicago: Follett.

Apps, J W (1978). *Study Skills for Adults Returning to School.* New York: McGraw-Hill.

Astin, H (ed) (1976). *Some Action of Her Own: the Adult Woman and Higher Education.* Lexington, Massachusetts: Lexington Books.

Carp, A, Peterson, R and Roelfs, P (1974). Adult learning interests and experience. In K P Cross and J R Valley (eds). *Planning Non-traditional Programs.* San Francisco: Jossey-Bass, 11-52.

Cross, K P and Zusman, A (1979). The needs of nontraditional learners and the response of nontraditional programs. In: C B Stalford (ed). *An Evaluative Look at Nontraditional Postsecondary Education.* Washington, DC: National Institute of Education, 1-89.

Chapter 12

The Dynamics of the Learning Community: Staff Intention and Student Experience

Vivien Hodgson and Michael Reynolds
University of Lancaster

In this chapter we describe a postgraduate course which is designed on participative principles and intended to be developmental. It is concerned with enabling students to enhance not only their knowledge and skill but also personal self-awareness through a challenging and supportive learning environment.

Our purpose is to describe both tutors' intentions and students' experience of the course, in particular their experience of the elements of design intended to support the opportunity for increased self-awareness and development. We discuss some of the contradictions and conflicts which occurred between intention and experience as they appeared during the course and as they relate to ideas concerned with libertarian approaches to education.

Our discussions with students throughout confirmed that the course was thought to have been worthwhile. They also show how complex the social dynamics are in a participative design and how important it is to recognize the part they play in the learning process.

The course design

The course is a two-year part-time masters' programme in management learning for experienced management teachers, trainers and consultants. There were 15 students on the course which was divided into five sections. Each section began with a five-day residential event (workshop), broadly focused around some aspect of management learning – for example, determining purposes, design for learning, approaches to research and evaluation, and dynamics of learning relationships. In the periods between workshops, students carried out work-related projects and met at monthly intervals in tutorial groups consisting of five students and a tutor. Assessment was based on seminar papers, a project and a dissertation and was consultative in that as the course developed account was taken of the views of students as well as of the tutors.

The workshops

Only the first day and a half of each workshop was designed in detail by the course tutors. The sessions designed by the tutors tended to be experience-based activities intended to elicit issues, questions or ideas that people could take further. These introductory sessions were followed by the 'open structure' which was designed to present both staff and students with the opportunity to choose what they wanted to work on during the rest of the workshop, with whom, when and by what approach.

The open structure

The following set of procedures was introduced to enable staff and students to plan and choose activities together:

- Each individual prepared a public statement (on a flip chart) of interests, requests – for information or help, and offers – of sessions they would be happy to run based on their research, work experience, etc.
- Everyone then indicated by signing against these statements which of other people's interests etc they would also like to work on.
- Groups of variable size formed around common interests (with or without tutors) and, on a public timetable, recorded their planned activities up until the next review session.

Planned activities included some of the following topics:

designing 'personal awareness' programmes;
what do managers do?;
critique of organizational theory;
assessment within the masters' degree;
career planning;
creating a learning environment;
developing a theoretical framework in management learning;
management development policy;
self-management of learning;
understanding values and 'personal style'.

During the open structure, sessions were run by both tutors and students. Review sessions took place about every 24 hours. At these sessions everyone met to share ideas or issues emerging from the foregoing sessions and to review their experience of the open structure. The next 24 hours were then planned with the same procedures as before. (The review sessions were named 'Taking stock and moving on'.) The intention was that the responsibility for agenda, time-keeping and making the review sessions work should be jointly exercised by tutors and students.

Project work and tutorial meetings

Between workshops, self-chosen tutorial groups met at a time and place arranged by them to exchange ideas and discuss the implications of these ideas for their work. The topic of each student's course work was self-chosen and relevant to his or her role as a management teacher or trainer. So, for example, topics could range from 'learning theory' to 'women in management', or from applying experiential methods in training to the problems of introducing peer assessment in a college of further education.

The role of the tutors

The tutors were responsible for the overall design of the programme, based on a shared set of principles that individuals should take responsibility for their own learning and for helping others in theirs. Within workshop sessions and tutorial groups tutors could contribute from their own research and experience and be co-learners. In the review sessions their role as facilitators could be particularly appropriate and reflected a belief in the value of learning from the experience of being involved in the organization of the course, as well as acknowledging a responsibility in helping everyone avoid some of the potential pitfalls of democratic decision making.

Principles underlying the design

Two guiding principles which were introduced to students at the first workshop were, firstly, that there should be as much opportunity as possible for each person to choose the direction and content of his or her own learning, allowing for the likelihood that each person's ideas might change as the course proceeded; and secondly, that each member of the learning community should accept responsibility for helping others manage their own learning by acting as a resource to them.

There were a number of other values or beliefs which were indirectly involved in these principles:

(1) If individuals were to choose the direction and content of their learning they had to be in a position to influence decisions about policy, structure and procedures within the course.
(2) For this approach to be effective, there needed to be an awareness and understanding of the personal, social and organizational processes which evolve within the learning community and a shared concern for the quality of working relationships which developed.
(3) Learning could be derived from contradiction and difference as well as from similarity of interest or perspective.
(4) Every member of the community, regardless of role, had ideas and experience which could contribute to other people's learning.
(5) Values and feelings were as important as ideas and beliefs in the search for understanding.

The MA in management learning is, as mentioned above, a version of the 'learning community' (Megginson and Pedler, 1976), and belongs within the tradition of libertarian education. However, staff and students may not totally share or adhere to the values and assumptions upon which the design of the course is based. There was, therefore, the familiar dilemma of a participative design being apparently imposed on some who found it cumbersome or may have preferred a more directive approach. Yet although the course contained some internal contradictions – such as procedures centred on the learner but, all the same, assessed by the tutor – it did offer students a share in the responsibility for decision making and afforded them as much choice as we believe is possible in determining both the content and method of their learning.

It is on this aspect of the course which we want to focus by describing the students' experience of taking part in the workshops, and in particular of working within the procedures of the 'open structure'.

Students' experience

In order to find out more about the students' experience of the course and in particular of the workshops, every student from the programme was interviewed during either the third or fourth workshop by one of the authors whose role was solely to coordinate research and evaluation throughout the two years. The second author was one of the tutors.

During the interviews, students were simply asked to describe their current thoughts and feelings about being on the course. The particular emphasis and focus of each interview was very largely determined by the students themselves, the intention being for them to describe those aspects of their experience which were important or significant to them.

We have selected from these descriptions those which specifically refer to students' experience of elements of the workshops' design which were intended to create opportunities for participative learning – namely, the 'open structure'; the roles of staff and students; and aspects of the 'climate' of the course which affected learning. In addition, we have included their descriptions of their experience of learning, either during the workshops or subsequently.

Experiencing the 'open structure'

Perhaps the overwhelming impression of the 'open structure' courses is that the nature and quality of relationships with others was at the core of the students' experience. So, for example, students had different criteria for whom they chose to work with at any time.

> I wanted to attend sessions with those people I don't feel an immediate affinity for and see how they work and how I can relate.

However, another student took the view that it was best to work with people who were of a similar temperament, although not necessarily of the same point of view. As he explained,

> . . . temperament seems to be a more important criteria for working with people than their experience or even their ideas . . . the sort of people I best operate with are business-like, they are there for a clear purpose which is visible. They are intelligent and they don't get involved in manipulation which screws up my learning – they enhance it.

Both of the above statements demonstrate recognition of the importance of social relationships in the learning community approach and, further, that social processes were a significant component of the learning in which they were involved. As one student commented,

> I appreciate learning as being a social process – previously I had thought of it as something that goes on in isolation and as acquired from the written wisdom of other people. I now understand real learning goes on or is more valid when one has worked it out from one's own experience than just reading about it in a book or article.

Overall our impression from interviews was that the procedure for dividing into interest groups during the open structure seemed to work well and allowed people to adopt their own criteria for choosing what to work on and who to work with.

More difficult were the review or 'taking stock' sessions where the entire community met for an hour or so to review individual experiences of the open structure. The rationale for these sessions was that in order to work effectively as a community, problems should be worked out in a public form. If the approach was creating difficulties for an individual or a sub-group, then the membership of the community could only exercise their responsibility to help others in their learning process by being party to the discussion and acknowledging their part in the events from which the difficulties had emerged. Equally important, larger meetings of this kind provided the opportunity to experience the dynamics and dilemmas of being members of organizations and indeed, of society as a whole.

These sessions were, as might be expected, rich in social dynamics. They were experienced by some as providing a forum for power struggles between factions of the community and as such seen as indulgent, wasteful or, at worst, potentially destructive.

> I'm concerned – people see it as a forum for declaring feelings and concerns. They get a kick from doing it – they get value from it. Perhaps they are looking for support or security. They enjoy that and are trying to create conditions where that happens – great for them but not for me.

This does not simply imply that there were different views of the kind of behaviour which was desirable within the community. It indicates that initially at least, some people perceived the review sessions as interfering with their learning rather than enhancing it. Students' experiences reflected both preference and antipathy for working in a collectivistic mode, as the following statements show:

> What I was concerned with was the preoccupation with the learning community itself. I came out of a fairly practical environment. I'm prepared to discuss the learning community, but not at the expense of everything else. I'm prepared to get to a point where we say, look there are certain differences, but get on with the focus of the week, which is not how the learning community was working.

> For me there are two things I'm doing here. One is learning about management training – to some extent I could get that out of books – the other thing I want to learn about is about being a learning community and learning from each other.

Clearly there was a conflict of perceived interest and needs which had a significant impact on the social dynamics of the learning event. In the open structure itself most people seemed to feel they retained sufficient choice and control for this to be a useful procedure. In the 'taking stock' sessions, however, different perspectives and value positions met head on and these sessions were experienced by some as contributing to learning and by some as getting in the way of it.

Either way, the open structure, and in particular the 'taking stock' sessions, were central aspects of the course milieu. Consequently, they received a good deal of attention and attempts were made to resolve the differences which had emerged, differences which were seen as indicating underlying value positions held by staff as well as by students.

> We have surfaced a number of issues to do with paradigms, world views, perspectives – whatever you call them. I contend that there was a dominant paradigm which was being reinforced by a number of tutors and that this was . . . getting in the way of a number of people's learning. I now believe there is a greater understanding on both sides . . . of the need for a different way of working.

Tutor and student roles: questions and responsibility

The difficulties experienced in community sessions were linked with the way in which tutors interpreted their role and carried out assessment.

> There was anxiety and disappointment at the first assignments not having been marked. The vacuum it created, an environment for power play. We felt let down by the tutors. Because of the nature of the workshop tutors were more equal. There was a feeling that they should take more responsibility for content. The content was missing. 'What do we do?' It was fuel for political rivalries.

The ambiguities of the tutor role also preoccupied the staff. On the one hand tutors were responsible for the overall design and course structure, and ultimately were in control of the process of assessment. On the other hand, within the workshops and in particular the open structure, they tried not to take more than their share of responsibility or control for making it work. The difficulties experienced by both students and staff in doing this are reflected in the following comments:

> *(Student)* The tutors are in a way part of the fabric. They are the institution like the books and all that sort of stuff, though much more than that.

> *(Tutor)* There are umpteen strategies, one of which is to say, well that's it – take it or leave it. I'm now no different from anyone else. Or another, if you're committed to something happening is to say, 'Well I'll maintain responsibility for making it happen until there seems to be a general accepted level of responsibility for making it happen.

> *(Tutor)* I think some of the difficulty is people testing out the contract or just how much of it is open and how much of it is not open.

> *(Student)* Anyway it's difficult when there are authority figures, however much they try to withdraw from being such. If you are a member of staff you cannot withdraw . . . it's quite idle to pretend you're on the same level as the other participants except in certain areas of specialized knowledge . . . and they do dish out the brownie points.

Nonetheless, there was recognition by the students that they should share responsibility both for making the method work and for their own learning. If certain students felt they had not got as much from the workshop as they had expected, they did not necessarily blame the tutors.

> I don't think I've got as much out of the workshops, as much as I could . . . I'm wondering why. I think it's something to do with establishing your identity on the programme. I don't think I've done that as strongly as I could have done . . . 'he talks a lot' therefore we expect him to talk and we listen longer. 'He doesn't talk a lot' so we don't give him as much time to talk and we don't give him as much attention when he talks. The dynamics of a group are difficult to break down once it's set – I haven't put my stamp on it as I could have done.

> I have not been successful in tapping into other people's minds or experience, it's an indication that I have not opened myself to somebody else.

The above comments are also a further indication that the importance and significance of social interaction in this learning approach was recognized.

Climate

As we have already seen, in an approach of this kind, the quality and nature of the social milieu or 'climate' is crucial. There is less tutor-direction than students are used to and learning is heavily dependent upon developing productive working relationships with others. The climate of a course is not easy to describe as an objective or easily identifiable entity. It is something that emerges, evolves, and exists in people's experience of very subjective matters such as personal accessibility, risk taking, supportiveness or defensiveness. As such, students' experience of the climate was perceived as having a significant influence on their learning opportunities.

> The fact that the climate was cold was affecting the way we were learning. For example, I was taking many many fewer risks than I would normally take or what I would say to people or interventions I would make or whatever. I was just making decisions not to say anything.

Later the same student commented:

> . . . it's an indication of how careful I'm being . . . that's restricting my learning and what I'm giving to the community. I'm trying to blend in 'cos it's less hassle.

At times the climate of the course was experienced as disconcerting, if not alienating. The following remarks were made by two students:

> Sometimes I close my eyes and think, 'If they want to make an issue of it that's up to them'.

> I don't look for belonging any more because I know I don't feel I belong to the group as a whole. I have a sense of wariness.

As happened with the other difficulties described by students, there were, however, considerable efforts to improve the social climate because it was recognized as being an important part of the particular learning process in which they were involved – one which was worth trying to understand for its own sake and necessary to avoid alienation. Consequently, people tried both to become more open about themselves and to be more understanding and supportive of others. As one student reported later in the course:

> People are becoming franker. Pursuing being themselves and helping others.

Learning

All that we have described so far makes some reference to learning and people's experience of how the different aspects of the programme influenced their learning. But what do the students mean when they talk about learning? What did they perceive learning to be and to involve and, perhaps more importantly, what did they feel they were learning and from what source?

Arguably, students' differing perspectives on learning were at the heart of much of the conflict which emerged within the open structure, For some, learning was seen as:

> Encountering new ideas and a range of views on those ideas very quickly and having my own views challenged.
>
> . . . theory underlying back-at-work practice.

But there may have been a different conception of what constituted useful work during the course for others who saw learning as:

> Trying something you've never done before.
>
> Who am I and what am I taking on, that's learning for me.

People's description of their learning tended in point of fact to reflect more of the second than the first idea and often what they felt they had learned was in relation to their own approach as teachers or as learners.

> I've modified my viewpoint. Before I used to believe you shaped people. I've changed my thinking on that which has affected my practice – very much so.
>
> The biggest single thing is I'm more prepared to let learning happen. I'm more flexible in the classroom. There are objectives still, but I'm less worried about how we get there.

Summary of students' experience

These descriptions demonstrate that the students' experience of the learning community approach centred around the structures, procedures and roles which comprise the design, the social conditions apparently necessary for it to work, and the problems and difficulties they experienced in working with it. The intrinsic dilemmas and potential conflicts of working collectively were recognized:

> X has a right to say, 'I want to explore this' but Y has an equal right to say, 'I'm sorry but that's getting in my way'.
>
> Does everyone want to work in a learning community? That's probably a very fundamental question. It is much easier to operate as individuals. Not only does it take effort and energy and being sympathetic to other people's needs and desires in terms of learning, but it also takes more time. I guess you have got to want to operate in that sort of way.

However, despite the problems, difficulties and frustrations, the method was seen as having contributed to learning that was experienced as significant:

> I've found the learning community very strange and the open sessions because it's very different from anything I've done before – that's everyone's experience I think. It does seem to work in its own way but there's initial frustration.

Intentions and experience

Intentions

As already explained the course was based on the principle that each student should have an opportunity to develop his or her own capabilities in an environment intended both to support this and to provide an experience of working collaboratively.

In its design philosophy, the MA reflects the libertarian traditions of self-development which Archambault summarizes in his account of John Dewey's work:

> Education was the chief means by which those personal capacities were to be discovered and liberated. Education would enable human beings to achieve their maximum distinctive growth in harmony with their fellows . . . (*Archambault, 1966*)

There is, however, a fundamental problem with grand-sounding notions like self-development or growth. They often neither reflect the precise meaning given to them by particular individuals, nor tell us much about the methods intended to bring about their achievement. So, for example, it is possible in practice to trivialize the principles of libertarian education by emphasizing mutual support and trust but ignoring questions of direction or control.

> Under such circumstances . . . self-indulgence becomes synonymous with liberation, and the privatized morality of the classroom becomes an affective antidote for the moral complexities and political problems that characterize the society at large.
> (*Giroux, 1981*)

Nearer the thinking which influenced the design of the MA course is the view expressed by Joel Spring in his summary of libertarian educationalists: 'People must control the learning processes by which they grow before they can truly own themselves' (Spring, 1975). Indeed, the structures and procedures used during the course were part of its content as were ideas or concepts and cannot be separated from them (Hodgson and Reynolds, 1981).

On the MA course, the nature of the engagement between members of the community, tutors and students, was not limited to the exchange and discussion of ideas. Students shared in planning, organizing and decision-making, and inevitably their values and beliefs about education or working relationships were brought into play, as were those of the tutors. As a consequence values and beliefs became a focus for enquiry and debate and as such potentially as important an aspect of self-development as anything else.

Overall the programme could be described as an example of *partial* participation. In some respects it was democratic, in that students had a great deal of influence over the direction and content of their learning. In other respects, such as selection, overall course structure and assessment, it was less so.

Experience

The *partial* model operating within the course did seem to accentuate the difficulties of working with a less than directive tutor role. So, for example, although the intention was to transform the tutor-student relationships within the programme, the tutors' ultimate control over assessment militated against this. Tutors were seen both as traditional authority figures and, on occasions, as failing to exercise their authority.

More broadly, however, it appears to have been the particularly collectivistic aspects of the design which provided the source of so many of the tensions during the course. Basil Bernstein (1975) emphasizes that for this kind of design to work there would have to be 'some consensus' about its adoption. Yet, people's individual definitions of what self-development meant to them and their preferred ways of achieving it differed. Thus, although for some the more collectivistic elements of course design were valued as a source of learning in their own right, for others they were a frustrating imposition.

We would argue that the distinction which underlies this difference is concerned with the focus of control. There seemed to be no problem with the idea that individuals should be responsible for the content and direction of their learning. But there was less agreement about how that might be accomplished. The idea of freedom of choice over content seemed more acceptable than was the prospect of sharing responsibility for the procedures by which those choices were to be made. Yet a starting assumption for us was that those two aspects should not, could not, be separated.

Significantly, this dilemma is paralleled within the professional context. Participation in many organizations has come to signify sharing of responsibility over detail within prescribed areas of activity, and only rarely encompasses more fundamental aspects of the social or political structures within which work is carried out. A consequence of the nature of the course design was that differences in belief about structure and control could be made explicit even if at times they became a source of division within the course community.

Further, some participants felt that a particular value system predominated within the course – one which did not necessarily reflect the views of most students:

> Two tutors were identified as sharing in some way the values and beliefs of the student minority group.

The dominant paradigm, as it was described, was seen to legitimize public expression of feelings – about self or others – and open examination of conflicts within the community. Some found this disruptive and self-indulgent. What was seen by students who identified with the dominant value system as learning about '*being* in a learning community' was experienced by others as 'power play' or 'playing games'.

> They [the taking stock sessions] provide a forum for people to play games. If you join in then you're colluding with their games.

Consequently, the vacuum experienced by some in the 'taking stock' sessions (the least structured) was seen at times to be filled by conflicting views over method which reflected these differing values.

Students who saw the tutors as aligning themselves with the dominant value system, but who did not themselves favour this way of working, were left feeling in conflict with the staff and unsupported by them. Nell Keddie describes this process of 'reciprocity of perspective'. She found that students were not only less likely to challenge tutors who had a similar outlook and view of the world to their own, but were also more likely to have easier and smoother relationships with tutors than students whose perspectives differed (Keddie, 1971). It is not surprising then that on a course where, initially at least, most students did not see themselves as identifying with what was perceived as the dominant tutor perspective, there would be moments of some tension.

The experience of feeling excluded from a predominant value system suggests that a process of socialization operates within the course. Socialization is an uncomfortable concept for liberal educators, who shrink from the thought that they are indoctrinating students, albeit into a more democratic form of working and learning than they may have been used to or wanted.

> On the one hand, they [open educators] very often advocate and self-consciously acknowledge the fact that they are engaged in the building of a new culture . . . On the other hand, advocates of open education are repulsed by the conformity dimension which seems to be inherent in all the proposed definitions of socialization. (*Morgan, 1975*)

Yet the idea of achieving autonomy through some process of socialization is only contradictory within a flaccid doctrine of liberalism where the educators' own values are totally subjugated to students' needs. A participative learning approach will not necessarily succeed just because the opportunity is available. It needs support from staff who believe in it and are prepared to stand by the values on which it is based.

Conclusion

In beginning this chapter we described the intention of the MA course in management learning as being to enable students to develop and increase their capabilities in a challenging and supportive learning environment. The way in which that intention became reality for the students has been examined. Whatever the difficulties experienced by students and staff on the programme, it seems to us that the social processes which are associated with a design of this type are a rich source of personal understanding and development. Ultimately, much will depend on a collective willingness to make values and beliefs explicit and open to discussion. However, this point of view is itself based on a set of values which may not be shared. As tutors we need to be prepared (in both senses) to play our part in enabling members of the learning community to make sense of the social dynamics of the event, both to give collaboration a chance of success and because of the personal learning about work in groups to which it can contribute. In support of this the assessment procedure has also become more collaborative in an attempt to bridge the constraints and expectations of the academic community with the more democratic philosophy of the course design.

It is perhaps unrealistic to think that the difficulties experienced in participative approaches to education could be avoided. More to the point, from a developmental perspective it is not in anyone's interests to think that they should be. To avoid the more problematical consequences of meeting differing beliefs and preferences about work and learning would be to limit opportunities for self-awareness and social understanding. But to benefit from this there will need to be a significant reserve of skill and commitment within the community to understand and work constructively with some very complex social dynamics.

References

Archambault, R D (1966). *Dewey on Education.* New York: Random House.

Bernstein, B (1975). Class, codes and control. III. *Towards a Theory of Education Transmissions.* London: Routledge and Kegan Paul.

Giroux, H A (1981). *Ideology, Culture and the Process of Schooling.* Brighton: Falmer Press.

Hodgson, V and Reynolds, M (1981). The hidden experience of learning events: illusions of involvement. *Personnel Review.* 10, 1, 26-29.

Keddie, N (1971). Classroom knowledge. In: M Young (ed). *Knowledge and Control.* London: Collier-Macmillan. 133-160.

Megginson, D and Pedler, M (1976). Developing structures and technology for the learning community. *Journal of European Training.* 5, 5, 262-275.

Morgan, K (1975). Socialisation, social models, and the open education movement. In: D Nyberg (ed). *The Philosophy of Open Education.* London: Routledge and Kegan Paul. 110-145.

Spring, J (1975). *A Primer of Libertarian Education.* Quebec: Black Rose Books.

Chapter 13

Evolution, Revolution or Devolution: Increasing Learner-Control in the Instructional Setting

Philip Candy
The University of New England, New South Wales

Prologue

This is something of a novel experience for me. For years I have been schooling myself to write from a somewhat distanced, objective and detached point of view – in what is sometimes referred to as an 'academic' style. However, in this chapter, I am going to attempt to examine at least some of the issues around what has been (inaccurately) called 'self-directed learning' from the point of view of learners involved in formal instructional settings. To do this, I will draw on my experience as a learner, as well as what others have said or written of their experiences.

There are at least three aspects of my background which I think it would be useful to share as a preliminary to the substantive content of this chapter: my experience as an adult educator; as an adult learner (in both formal, structured settings and unstructured, or 'natural societal' settings); and as a graduate student.

In terms of my experience as an adult educator, for more than a decade, I have been involved in teaching various forms of adult education, ranging from tertiary level courses for the training of adult educators, to 'liberal' adult education courses on how to trace one's family history. For much of that time, I have been persuaded by the notion that adult learners should accept most, if not all, of the responsibility for their own learning. I have worked at ways of encouraging 'self-direction' in people coming to me as learners; however, I have often had an uneasy feeling that not every learner is willing, or able, to accept the responsibility I am prepared to share.

My experience as a learner can be divided into formal and informal categories. (I am using these terms here in their everyday sense, rather than in the technical way in which they are used by such authors as Coombs (1973), La Belle (1982) or Mocker and Spear (1982).) In the 'formal' category, I include university studies as well as short courses. I have been a student (both part-time and full-time) in various universities for about 16 years. I have also undertaken many short courses – on management, communications, history, group dynamics, religion, military topics – the varied offerings of employers, government departments, voluntary clubs, churches, university extension departments, and other providers of adult education. In all these situations, I have experienced the familiar range of teaching styles, from highly authoritarian and formal, to open-ended, exploratory discussions.

In terms of my informal learning experiences, as what Knowles (1975) has called a 'self-directed learner', Brookfield (1981, 1982) an 'independent' learner and Strong (1977) an 'autonomous learner', I have spent about 16 years researching my family's history. I have read innumerable books and journal articles on genealogical research; spent countless hours poring over faded and musty registers in record offices and churches in Australia and England; peered into the gloomy depths of many microfilm readers; written hundreds upon hundreds of small index cards to keep track of my researches; produced giant pedigree charts which extend along entire walls; and maintained a correspondence with family members and other researchers around the world. All this has resulted in several publications about my own family's history, as well as guides to conducting research; yet all of it occurred 'without participation in externally planned programmes of instruction (such as adult education classes, correspondence courses or professional training courses) in the subject area concerned' (Brookfield, 1984).

Finally, I am (at the time of writing this) deeply immersed in postgraduate studies in adult education, and this has given me the opportunity to read critically and to analyse some of the voluminous literature on both the philosophy and practicalities of learner autonomy in adult education.

No doubt, there are many other experiences that have influenced what I hold to be important (and possible) in relation to increasing learner self-directedness and learner control, but these three seem especially relevant.

Introduction

In recent years, the phenomenon of self-directed learning has been a major focus for researchers in adult education; in fact, in 1984 Brookfield described it as: 'the chief growth area in the field of adult education research in the last decade' (p 59). All this attention has resulted in a veritable avalanche of material on the subject – books, articles, research reports and dissertations continue to appear in increasing numbers each year. In my reading, I have found at least 30 different terms which deal with the same general area. Some of these terms are: autodidaxy, autonomous learning, independent learning, learner-controlled/directed instruction, non-traditional learning, open learning, participatory learning, self-directed learning, self-education, self-organized learning, self-planned learning, self-responsible learning, self-study, and self-teaching.

This proliferation of terms would be difficult enough if they were all exact synonyms, but the problem is made worse by the fact that different authors use the same term to mean different things, and sometimes they use different terms to mean the same thing, and the only way to tell the difference is to delve beneath the surface to what is actually meant in any particular situation. In doing this, one becomes aware of the conceptual confusion which such a range of alternatives embodies. One area of confusion results from the failure to distinguish teaching from learning (Oakeshott, 1967): one must have profound reservations about any phenomenon which can simultaneously be called self-instruction and self-planned learning – for it implies that teaching and learning are interchangeable concepts, which clearly they are not.

It also becomes apparent that, to some extent at least, this sudden upsurge of interest in, and support for, the concept of autonomy in learning is shared by theorists and others who, in other respects, represent different, and possibly even fundamentally irreconcilable, points of view in education (Crittenden, 1978). However, there is no simple way of telling, just from the title of a book, article or research report, whether its authors endorse the notion of developing learner autonomy from a humanistic, developmental perspective or a more reductionistic, skill-oriented point of view. The difference is important because, although they may be using the same terminology, they may have in mind very different ideas of what it means to be 'self-directed'.

Another source of confusion is that there are actually two notions here, but they are lumped together under the same heading. One form of self-directed learning is the kind of enquiry and project I referred to earlier with regard to my family history research – no lectures, no courses and no formal institutional affiliation. The other kind of self-directed learning really refers to a way of teaching, in which more and more responsibility for valued instructional functions is handed over to the learners.

In recent years, largely because of research evidence about the extent of the first kind of self-directed learning, there has been more and more pressure on adult educators to surrender to learners some measure of control over the teaching situation. This demand comes in many guises including open education, self-directed learning, individualized instruction, discovery learning, student-centred instruction, metalearning, learning-to-learn and independent study. At first sight, perhaps, there seems little to unify such diverse themes which, to use Griffin's (1977) phrase, tend to look more like a mish-mash than a movement. However, closer inspection reveals that, although these terms are by no means synonymous, they do seem to constitute a constellation of ideas and practices: collectively they represent an ideology 'in which many more initiatives have passed over to the [learners], who are now expected to be much more independent, self-directed or, in a word, autonomous' (Dearden, 1972, p 449).

When people make recommendations about increasing learner-control, they enlist many arguments. They point to cultural values, such as those of individuality and self-fulfilment; rapid social and technological change and the consequent need for continuous self-development and self-improvement; the emergence and refinement of the notion of lifelong education; legislative sanctions which demand equality of educational opportunity; a liberal sort of humanitarianism which emphasizes personal empowerment; increased costs of conventional formal education resulting in demands for new forms of instruction; and so on.

Sometimes, these arguments in favour of permitting or encouraging learner autonomy are made quite explicit, but at other times they are so deeply entrenched in the ethos of adult education as to be thought 'obvious' or 'self-evident' and thus to be beyond question. A British philosopher, D Z Phillips, refers to these vague and often tacit pressures and values as 'themes in unexamined talk in democratisation'. (I have modelled the style of argument in this chapter on a paper published in 1973 by Phillips.) In the remainder of this chapter, I intend to look at a number of these arguments which are commonly advanced in favour of increasing learner-control in various forms of adult education, and to try to write about them and respond to them, not from the perspective of the committed adult educator, nor of the detached academic theorist, but from the point of view of adult learners.

Assumption No 1 – adults are independent learners

> Considerable research has now established that anything up to 98 per cent of the adult population is regularly involved in independently undertaking self-initiated learning activities outside formal educational institutions (Brookfield, 1982; Caffarella and O'Donnell, 1986; Mocker and Spear, 1982; Tough, 1978, 1979). To fail to recognize and make use of this vast storehouse of learning potential is an affront to adult learners, besides threatening to make formalized adult education redundant through an unwillingness to adapt to the realities of people's learning needs and preferred learning styles.

This line of argument has pervaded much recent writing on learner-control in adult education. Many authors, including Tough in his book *The Adult's Learning Projects* (second edition, 1979), begin from the premise that adult education must adapt itself to the 'natural' learning preferences and established learning styles of these self-directed adult learners. Such a recommendation certainly seems intuitively appealing, but it has several significant flaws.

The first is the assumption that all adults are self-directing. Knowles (1970), for instance, defines adulthood explicitly in terms of self-directedness:

> . . . something dramatic happens to his self-concept when an individual defines himself as an adult . . . His chief sources of self-fulfilment are now his performance as a worker, a spouse, a parent, a citizen . . . His self-concept becomes that of a self-directing personality . . . In fact, the point at which a person becomes an adult is that point at which he perceives himself to be self-directing. At that point, he also experiences a deep need to be perceived by others as being self-directing.

As Collard (1985) observes:

> The first thing one notes is that his argument is tautological: that is, the terms 'adult' and 'self-directing' are used to define each other. An abbreviated form of the above would read 'adults are self-directing people, therefore self-directing people are adults'. Yet is this the case? Would it be possible for someone to perceive themselves as adult, and yet as other than self-directed? Could there be self-directed children?

Thus it appears that the concept of adulthood and self-direction, both of which are central constructs in adult education, are not merely closely related but, at least in the way Knowles uses them, defined in terms of each other.

A second, related problem is the assumption that all adults are necessarily self-directing with respect to their learning. Yet, in the literature, there is much to suggest that many adult learners feel far from self-directing; we have evidence of 'cue seeking' behaviour (Entwistle *et al.*, 1979) and of 'syllabus bound' students (Parlett, 1970); of external locus of control (Rotter, 1966; Lefcourt, 1976); of low self-efficacy (Bandura, 1981); of field dependence (Theil, 1984; Witkin *et al.*, 1977); of fragile or imperfectly developed self-concept; of learned helplessness (Even, 1984, 1985; Perry and Dickens, 1984; Roth, 1980; Seligman, 1975); and generally of docile, passive and acquiescent learners who prefer, or could be held to prefer, other-direction to self-direction. Indeed, Carl Rogers, the doyen of student centredness, has observed that only a third or a quarter of learners are self-directing individuals, most being people who 'do just what they are supposed to do' (Rogers, 1969, cited by Moore, 1972). Moreover, even if the incidence of 'self-directed learning' outside formal instructional settings is as widespread as claimed, this does not necessarily mean that people want, or feel able, to exert control over the teaching situation (Danis and Tremblay, 1985; Taylor, 1980).

As early as 1951, Wispe reported a study which distinguished those learners wanting more permissiveness from those wanting more direction. In a match/mismatch experiment, some members of the 'want-more-permissiveness' group were placed in the structured teaching situation, and some members of the 'want-more-direction' group were given more freedom. Thus, in both cases, some learners were denied exactly what they wanted, and accordingly may have felt quite frustrated. Wispe (1951) writes:

> Realizing the importance of these student classroom needs, what must have been the effects of their frustrations? The want-more-direction students said on the questionnaires that the instructors 'never lectured', were 'poorly prepared' and 'couldn't even answer a question in a straightforward manner'. To the want-more-permissiveness students, the instructors 'lectured too much', 'discouraged viewpoints other than their own', and 'identified with the head of the course'. Every indication is that the frustration in both groups was very intense; but it was especially so in the want-more-direction group. This group, particularly the sub-group wanting more direction, but being permissively treated, held the lowest opinions of sections and instructors . . .

Linked to this is the point that, even if learners do see themselves as autonomous, and would like, ultimately, to take responsibility for directing their own enquiries, they may lack the necessary subject-matter knowledge to make a beginning. Thus, the truly autonomous person may intentionally make a 'strategic suspension' of his or her independence, in order to be taught. Just as many researchers on self-directed learning point out that adult learners may opt to undertake their learning projects specifically to avoid the constraints and restrictions imposed by formal providers, so those people who deliberately enquire into, seek out, enrol in and pay for planned programmes of instruction may have very specific expectations about the type and degree of direction they are likely to receive. To ignore these legitimate expectations, and instead to force learners into a self-directed or learner-controlled mode for which they may feel unprepared seems, to me, every bit as unethical as denying freedom when it is demanded.

Assumption No 2 – learner-control allows for different learning styles

> It is now established beyond question that individual learners differ from one another in significant ways, and that these differences in fact increase, rather than decrease, with age. Accordingly, it is vital to develop and use methods of instruction which emphasize individual differences. Approaches to teaching which rest on the autonomy of the learners, and

which seek to give them control over the teaching situations, do allow for such individual differences between learners.

Any person who has taught adults for any length of time, or indeed who has participated in courses of adult education, does not need to be reminded that adult learners differ from one another in ways which affect their learning. Indeed this recognition is such a commonplace that it has become part of the folklore of adult education. The question, however, is whether handing over control of certain valued instructional functions really does allow for different learning styles as claimed.

At one level, learner-control clearly allows for individual differences – indeed it is predicated on the existence of such differences – but there is little if any evidence to suggest that it reduces inherent inequalities by compensating for such differences (Snow, 1980). In fact, to the contrary, giving freedom of action to those able to deal with it may well increase their natural advantages, while placing those lacking self-confidence at even greater relative disadvantage. McClintock (1982) writes: 'Perhaps self-set study is an education designed to perpetuate privilege and to create elites. By this means, the rich may get richer, the powerful more powerful, the cultured more cultured, while the common man gets more common yet . . .' (p 51).

A second problem is the widespread assumption in the literature that, on the whole: 'all [learners] should want or, under certain specifiable conditions, would want, more autonomy' (Dearden, 1972). Very frequently, programmes which seek to increase learner control do so from an ideological point of view (Candy, 1985), and learners who actually want or need more direction are not very well looked after. What the teacher, trainer or facilitator is really saying is that it would be 'good' for learners to exert more control, irrespective of what the learners themselves might think. It seems ironic that individual differences in learning style can be enlisted as a justification for increasing learner control, yet it appears, as Dearden points out, that there is no room for individual differences in respect of people's willingness to be self-directing.

Sometimes, the push by instructors for increased learner-control is not ideological, but pragmatic; they cannot easily cope with the enormous diversity within a group of learners, and so effectively abdicate responsibility by handing control to the learners. However, I know from my own experience as a learner in adult education activities, that I do not expect the teacher or trainer to throw up his or her hands in exasperation at the range of different learning styles, personalities, experience bases, interests and so on within the group. Instead, I expect that person to make the most of such differences, to have the more experienced helping those with less knowledge in the group, or undertaking advanced or enrichment activities while the rest of us are struggling with the basics. Simply handing over the reins to us as learners is only likely to lead to frustration and disappointment.

Even if the teacher or trainer were genuinely concerned to adapt his or her instruction to learner demands, there still arises the problem that if I, as a learner, have only ever experienced certain approaches to teaching and learning, then my perception of what is possible is likely to be restricted. Accordingly, to limit educational offerings to what I already know about, is a potentially stultifying action. Cross, in her book *Accent on Learning* (1976), discusses the advantages and disadvantages of matching teaching styles to learner preferences, and she observes:

> . . . the simplicity of the 'matching' concept is . . . likely to trouble research psychologists. In the first place, they may question the assumption that it is desirable to place students in learning environments geared to their predilections. In the second place, they may question the assumption that the student's profile remains constant and that the institutions are infinitely flexible. For example, if we know that a field independent learns best and most pleasantly in independent study, are we necessarily serving him well if we offer him a steady diet of independent work? Maybe he needs to learn to work cooperatively with others. 'Matching' him to his own style or preference may push him toward further field independence, and that may be maladaptive in certain social situations. Maybe we should expose him to a 'challenge match' – that is, place him in an uncongenial or conflict setting, so that he is forced to develop an area of weakness or at least some flexibility in dealing with uncomfortable situations . . . *(p111)*

This situation may be likened to coaching people to play tennis: if they already have a strong forehand, then playing to this strength is unlikely to lead to an improvement in their backhand. And if, indeed, they have never ever been shown the backhand, this is a double disadvantage for they may excel at something of which they are presently unaware.

Finally, to adopt the stance that adult educators should modify their offerings (sequence, pacing, mode of presentation, level of content and so on) to the demands of learners is to relegate adult education permanently to the status of a reactive field – determined entirely by the whim or preference of learners who, by definition, may not be in a position to direct their own education.

Assumption No 3 – increasing learner-control increases motivation to learn

> It is widely recognized that people are more likely to be committed to activities and ideas they have had some hand in developing and shaping; indeed, they may feel opposed, simply on principle, to being subjected to situations over which they feel they have little, if any, control. This is particularly true of adults who, as Knowles points out, have a self-concept of self-directedness which is violated when their autonomy is disregarded. Self-directed modes of instruction have the dual benefit of avoiding imposition on learners of unwelcome direction *and* fostering motivation in learners who have been responsible for selecting or shaping their own direction.

The so-called 'motivation question' is one of the most intractable in education. Essentially, it involves encouraging people either to learn something for which they see no purpose or, alternatively, to undergo certain experiences which lead to a desirable goal, but where the connection between the activities and the ultimate goal is unclear to the potential learner. It is often claimed that allowing learners to decide their own direction solves the motivation dilemma, because they are then pursuing a course of action which they have had a hand in determining. However, as Hamm (1982) observes:

> The solution to the motivation problem is not allowing [learners] to choose what they want to do. Being motivated to do what one wants is either a tautology or not a problem. Instilling in [learners] the desire to pursue what is in their interest to pursue when they lack that interest initially is the motivational problem in education. *(p 96)*

To some extent, Elton (1973) answers this criticism, for he argues that the method of instruction, as distinct from the content of instruction, can be inherently motivating:

> By this, I mean that one devises learning situations in which the student feels himself involved, and in which he is active, perhaps through some form of self-study. The hope is that these situations, which in general appear to be designed in the main to achieve cognitive aims, lead to such student involvement, that he is carried over into the affective domain. *(p 76)*

This is an appealing argument. It maintains that handing over control of the learning situation is an inherently motivating thing to do, and that the excitement and pleasure it engenders will carry over to an enthusiasm for the subject matter itself. If this were true, however, the many research studies which report increased enjoyment from various forms of learner-control (for example *see* Gruber, 1965; Caffarella, 1983) should also report enhanced learning outcomes, yet this is rarely the case. Wispe's pioneer study, to which I have already referred, clearly demonstrates the capacity of learners to distinguish the constructs of enjoyment and achievement in learning tasks.

Moreover, this line of reasoning is something of a double-edged sword, for if positive feelings about the process of learning are expected to spill over to the content, then there would seem to be no reason why negative attitudes might not do the same. Thus, learners with unhappy or unsuccessful experiences in learner-controlled instruction may feel inept and uncomfortable when confronted with the demand that they direct their own learning. Their feelings of frustration, anger and disappointment, derived from being placed in an uncongenial learning situation, could 'spill over' and contaminate their learning outcomes, and perhaps even lead to dropout or attrition. It would indeed be ironic if a teaching strategy designed to increase autonomy and learner satisfaction, actually led to feelings of frustration, impotence, and ultimately of failure.

Assumption No 4 – learner-control contributes to the development of the 'whole person'

Although adult education stands outside the mainstream of the 'formal' education system (and, in some cases, may be directly opposed to it), nonetheless it is devoted to certain ultimate purposes, including the development of autonomous, self-actualizing adults. Such traits and characteristics, to the extent that they are educationally attainable, are usually thought of as synonymous with the definition of effective self-directed learners. Accordingly, the use of self-directed approaches to instruction is seen as one method by which adult education can fulfil some of its more global objectives.

What people usually mean when they argue this way is that the use of self-directed or independent learning methods will lead to desirable social outcomes and the development of broader skills and attitudes both of critical judgement and of autonomous action. Mezirow (1981), for instance, has written:

> It is almost universally recognized, at least in theory, that central to the adult educator's function is a goal and method of self-directed learning. Enhancing the learner's ability for self-direction in learning as a foundation for a distinctive philosophy of adult education has breadth and power. It represents the mode of learning characteristic of adulthood. *(p 21)*

This quote embodies a serious error of thinking, namely that 'of mistaking the means for the end . . . making no distinction between the characteristics of an ideal end product and the characteristics of the process that is supposed to lead to such a product' (Hamm, 1982, p 102). Does the use of methods which encourage learner control lead to more global qualities such as critical judgement, autonomous action and self-initiated enquiry? Lewis (1978) points out:

> To approve 'autonomy' as an ideal for students is one thing: to commend 'autonomous' methods of learning is another – however autonomy is defined. If, for the purposes of argument, we gloss it as independence, it is not quite obvious that independent methods of learning promote independence – auxiliary casual relationships must be established. *(p 152)*

In response to this view however, Boud (1981) has written:

> We should be careful in following this path too far. Although it may be in doubt that independent methods of learning in themselves promote independence, it is certainly unlikely that dependent teacher dominated methods would do so. *(p 23)*

At the heart of this controversy is the useful distinction made by philosophers and logicians between *necessary* and *sufficient* conditions. A simple example would be that the presence of water vapour in the atmosphere is a necessary, but not a sufficient condition for precipitation to occur.

With reference to the issue of autonomy, Dearden (1972) has analysed the relationship between freedom and autonomy and he argues that the absence of external constraints is a necessary but not sufficient condition for the development and exercise of autonomy. He cites the example of a prisoner who, having his freedom restored after a long period of incarceration, 'exhibits only anxiety and withdrawal in the state of freedom, rather than the capacities of self-direction and choice which are characteristics of autonomy' (p 451). He goes on to argue that, 'the granting of various freedoms by a parent or teacher might simply have the result that his direction is replaced by that of some other agency still external to the [learner] . . .' (p 451).

In summary, although the use of autonomous methods of learning may encourage the development of autonomy, the relation is by no means automatic. It is clear that a person may be exposed to so-called autonomous methods of learning, without internalizing the values of autonomy, or necessarily being enabled to think and act autonomously (Campbell, 1964; Torbert, 1978). Conversely, it may be possible to develop autonomy without recourse to autonomous methods. If, for instance, autonomy is defined as the ability and willingness to approach situations with an open mind, to suspend critical judgement and to act in accordance with rules and principles which are the product of the autonomous person's own endeavours and experience, then, paradoxically, as Dearden argues, it might be precisely a student's upbringing and previous educational experience, with relatively little freedom, which does develop autonomy (Dearden, 1972, p 452).

It seems that the distinction between autonomous learning as a goal (or teachable capacity) and autonomous learning as a method (or learning experience) is a crucial one for the practising adult educator.

Assumption No 5 – learner-control recognizes the equality of adult learners and adult educators

> One of the distinctive features of adult education is the equality of teachers and learners. In our political system, for instance, we expect each person's vote in the democratic structure to be exactly equal to each other person's vote. Extending this idea to education, if the process of education is to be truly democratic, each person (teacher or learner) should have the same weight in deciding the direction of an educational event or experience. The principle of learner control gives equal respect to the needs of each individual learner.

At first sight, this argument seems quite plausible. So deeply ingrained are our notions of political equality, that we easily and unwittingly apply the same criteria to other domains of our lives. Moreover, many authors have an almost instinctive reaction against the notion that one adult might have, or be seen to have, power over another and the inequality which such a situation implies is anathema. According to Phillips (1973), such conceptions of equality are usually based on one or other of a number of analogies, and these do not really stand up to critical scrutiny.

The first of these is the political analogy which claims that in a democracy there is the principle of 'one person, one vote', and that this should likewise apply in education. Phillips explains the invalidity of this proposition as follows:

> If I am awaiting an operation, I shall express justifiable concern if I see a group which includes experienced surgeons, new doctors and students take a popular vote to determine who shall perform the operation. Similarly, if my car breaks down I should be worried if those who happen to be on the premises at the time hold a popular vote to determine who shall attempt to repair my car. Given that certain people were elected to perform the operation or to repair the car, I should protest on the grounds that they are not qualified to do so. If asked to expound what I mean by this, I should refer to the fact that the person elected is not a qualified surgeon or a qualified car mechanic respectively. What we mean by 'qualified' in these contexts will be elucidated in terms of the skills, knowledge, expertise and standards involved in the field of surgery and car mechanics respectively. It is extremely important to notice that the notion of being qualified in these fields can be understood quite independently of the popular vote. It does not derive its meaning from such a vote, but from the content and standards of the disciplines concerned . . .
> *(Phillips, 1973, p 136)*

In adult education, the authority of the adult educator (Weber, 1985) does not (for the most part) derive from a show of hands, but from having expertise in the particular subject area. And just as I would be dismayed if a surgeon or mechanic denied his or her special expertise in the name of a spurious democracy, so I would be justified in feeling cheated if, having enrolled in a course of instruction, the instructor suddenly denied that he or she had any special knowledge of the subject, and insisted instead that I had the ability (and indeed the responsibility) to discover things for myself, to plan my own programme of enquiry, and to identify my own learning goals.

This disappointment, however, should not be construed as meaning that I accept the right of the adult educator to dictate to me in other areas, for we may well be equals in other domains of life. But I can recognize and acknowledge a lack of equality with respect to the subject being taught and learned without it detracting from my self-concept of autonomy overall. Thus, there is '. . . no analogy between the notion of democracy as used in the context of parliamentary representation, and talk of so-called democratisation in academic institutions' (Phillips, 1973, p 137).

A second source of confusion, claims Phillips, rests on the notion of intellectual equality, and the moral right of people to be treated equally and to be listened to: 'I have a right to have my say and my say should count, simply because I am a human being.' Phillips states that although this proposition is far from nonsense in many realms of human affairs, it is most emphatically nonsense in the domain of education:

> . . . the advocates of democratisation . . . speak as if the mere fact that someone is an individual makes what he says intellectually worthwhile. This is to deny the very meaning of intellectual enquiry. Where matters of the intellect are concerned, it is fatal to confuse the statement 'I can say something' with 'I have something to say'.
>
> Certainly, a teacher must think it worthwhile listening to what his pupils say, but the relationship between the teacher and what is said must be a critical one and it is in terms of intellectual criticism that a distinction appears between what is said and what is worth saying. Without such a distinction, there can be no academic standards and hence no deep inquiry into any subject. *(pp 139-40)*

There are certainly some domains of adult education where the expertise of the adult educator is in his or her knowledge of group processes, for instance, or where the subject is one (such as philosophy or religion) where each person is truly entitled to personal beliefs and there is no one 'right' or 'correct' answer. Yet even here it is reasonable to expect the adult educator to know (at least at the outset) more about the subject than the learners, and to accept a leadership role, rather than handing over control to the learners and expecting them to identify learning needs in an area of which, by definition, they are ignorant, or at least less competent than the instructor.

According to Phillips, a third mistaken proposition rests on the assertion that, because each adult learner is unique, each has the right to determine what is worth learning, and not to have any curriculum imposed: '. . . the confused view put forward by some advocates of democratisation, namely, that the student should be the person who determines what subject should be taught or what parts of a subject he wants to study' (p 141). As Phillips says, to the extent that learning involves developing a critical stance in relation to the subject being studied, then a learner can assert his or her essential intellectual autonomy with respect to the subject either by accepting it or rejecting it, but such a choice must be 'determined by critical standards inherent in the subject itself' (p 141).

Finally, there is a paradox relating to the notion of learners setting their own goals and making reasoned choices from amongst alternatives:

> The democratic ideal requires knowledge and an ability to decide between a range of possibilities. When this ideal is applied to situations which involve learning, we face the paradox that by definition, what has not yet been learned is not yet known, and the potential learner can only at best dimly perceive what he wants to know more about. He is not therefore fully in a position to judge and decide what he shall do and he is inevitably placed in the position of having to learn from somebody and that 'somebody' is a teacher whether he be so called or not. *(Lawson, 1979, p 26)*

This is a point which has frequently been overlooked by writers in adult education. Except in those rare instances where adult education 'is taken to involve no values whatever about what is learned, to refer to no standards of performance or achievement but to remain at the level of subjective personal insights which have no external intersubjective points of reference, . . . the positive conception of a teacher has to be introduced . . .' (Lawson, 1979, p 26).

Assumption No 6 – learner-control models a changed power relationship

> Adult education has long been associated with the activist tradition (Selman and Kulich, 1980; Welton, 1986) of social emancipation (Johnson, 1979) and personal empowerment (Freire, 1972). The use of self-directed and learner-controlled methods not only models such changed power relationships, but equips learners with the skills and expectations to deal with potentially oppressive situations encountered elsewhere in their daily lives.

There is no doubt that truly handing over power to learners can result in a dramatic shift in the locus of responsibility for educational events. This, in turn, may lead to increased capacity and willingness to take responsibility for other aspects of one's life (for example *see* Hovey *et al.*, 1963, p 351). However, the link is by no means certain, and several points of caution are indicated.

The first is that adult educators should not embark on programmes designed to increase the autonomy or self-directedness of learners, unless they are able and willing to cope with their consequences. The justification for increasing learner-control rests ultimately on the essentially Marxian interpretation of social structures, and has quite inescapable ramifications for the teacher or trainer who embarks on a programme of increasing learner-control. This is because, in the final analysis, it demands nothing less than the dismantling of existing structures of knowledge, and power relationships, in favour of a more democratic and egalitarian approach to the creation, distribution and 'ownership' both of knowledge and of means of production.

This relates to the second point, which I refer to as 'pseudo-autonomy', based on Kremer's (1978) notion of 'pseudo-progressivism'. Because of the very strong groundswell of support for increasing learner-control, many adult educators find themselves caught in a conflict of values: on the one hand they want learners to accept more responsibility; yet on the other hand, they fear that the more successful they are at doing this, the more likely they are to become redundant.

Not everyone would go as far as the professor cited by Wight, who calls learner-control 'the fool for a master school of education' (Wight, 1970, p 273), but many would find themselves nodding in agreement with the tutor quoted by Abercrombie and Terry (1978):

> Is participant tutorage going to reach the goal I want at the end – that I shall not be of use any more, that I've passed on all my experience, my experience has developed the students so they can operate by themselves to be self-learning people? *(p 92)*

The net result of this ambivalence is often a capitulation to the demands for increased learner responsibility, while at the same time maintaining control over certain crucial functions. For instance, 'Holland (1969) has pointed out that providing choice for certain dimensions of learning (for example, mode and pacing) is something of a sham if the objectives are not manipulable by the students' (Geis, 1976, p 262), and Hamm (1982) asks:

> . . . is there not a deception in the suggestion that teachers 'set expectations', 'help students to explore alternative activities', 'provide a general program structure', 'setting realistic goals and deadlines' (Gibbons and Phillips, 1978, p 298) and so on, while letting students think they are making the important decisions? Is this more than merely an aura of freedom? If one is not by those techniques attempting to convey the sense of freedom without actually granting the freedom, there is little difference between it and conventional teaching. *(p 102)*

Others argue that control over the assessment of learning is the real crux. Heron (1981), for instance, points out that:

> If there is no staff-student collaboration on assessment, then staff exert a stranglehold that inhibits the development of collaborations with respect to all other processes. Once varying mixtures of self, peer and collaborative assessment replace unilateral assessment by staff, a completely new educational climate can be created. Self-determination with respect to setting learning objectives and to programme design is not likely to make much headway, in my view, without some measure of self-assessment. *(p 63)*

I am not suggesting that adult educators are guilty of deliberately misleading learners as to their intentions, but rather that they are often unaware themselves of the dissonance between their 'espoused theory' and their 'theory-in-use' (Argyris and Schon, 1974; Torbert, 1976, 1978). Miller (1986) and his associates, for instance, write about an experimental course in which they genuinely wanted learners to accept responsibility for a number of curricular and methodological decisions.

Afterwards, as part of the evaluation, they invited feedback about the approach, and one of the students commented: 'To my mind, one situation was simply exchanged for another – staff were in full and undisputed possession of the decision not to have a typical academic programme. This was never open to negotiation, at least definitely not at the start of the . . . sessions.' Another wrote: 'I believe that we were not free to choose – staff had made the choice of the process for us. The argument that at the beginning of the course the group could have opted for the traditional teacher-learning situation is not, in my opinion, true.' (Miller *et al.*, 1986, p 441).

There is no getting away from the fact that, when an adult educator decides that learners should exert more control over the instructional events than hitherto, he or she is imposing a value just as surely as if he or she had decided not to consult them. From the point of view of the learners, any attempt to ignore or deny the value-laden nature of such a choice may come across as insincere, contradictory or, worse still, hypocritical.

A third point to note concerning the modelling of changed relationships is that such an approach cannot be carried out in a vacuum, because it may place learners and instructors alike into a conflict situation, either with other instructors or even with the dominant organizational ethos. For instance, if I work within a highly structured, formalized and authoritarian organization (such as the armed services) there would be a certain incongruity or dissonance if the training personnel engaged me in collaborative learning, discussion and self-directed enquiry. This is because I would be manifesting one sort of behaviour and value system in the training environment, and quite a different model in my day-to-day life. On the other hand, formal, directive approaches are just as dissonant in more open-ended contexts such as clubs, churches and voluntary associations (Thomas, 1967).

Conclusion

My intention in preparing this chapter has been to examine the evidence both for and against increasing learner-control in adult education and to compare this with my own experience. Many observers have noted the disinclination of adult leaners to accept responsibility for instructional functions and decisions. Some maintain that this is just a temporary state of affairs, and that experience will eventually transform the dislike of responsibility into a tolerance, and perhaps even a preference, for independent intellectual work (for example, Gruber, 1965, p 5).

A second interpretation is that some people are simply more independent than others, and that this is a function of intelligence, personality or some other innate quality or characteristic. In this view (which is widespread amongst learners and teachers alike), the teacher or trainer must do whatever is necessary to extend each individual learner to the limit of his or her potential, but must also accept the inherent limitations of some people, and thus be prepared to take a more active role in 'teaching' them if this seems called for.

A third view holds that the preference for dependent learning is not innate, but is itself learned. The construct of 'learned helplessness' is frequently invoked to explain why adults might prefer to be 'taught' rather than to take responsibility for their own learning. The argument is that the more people have things done for them, the more 'institutionalized' they become, and the more institutionalized they are (in both a figurative and a literal sense), the more dependent, helpless and passive they are. It is argued that years of passivity in educational settings deprive many people of the confidence to take charge of their own learning, but as Even (1984) points out, 'If such human conditions are learned, they can be unlearned' (p 280). Accordingly, what is demanded is a sort of educational approach which breaks the 'passive set' for learning, and encourages people to feel potent and competent with respect to their own learning (for example, *see* Campbell, 1964, p 357).

Although there is probably some truth in each of these positions, it seems to me that most explanations of learner dependency ignore one vital element, and that is the ability of adults to make rational choices for themselves. In their collection of materials on independence in learning, the Nuffield Foundation Group for Research and Innovation in Higher Education advocate the use of the term 'autonomy in learning' to describe situations in which the learner is able 'to choose between dependence and independence as he perceives the need' (Nuffield Foundation, 1975, p ii). There are several circumstances in which a learner might choose to 'be taught'.

To begin with, in 'examination-oriented institutions, most students will probably prefer directive-type teaching' (Wispe, 1951, p 185). This is a finding which is supported by the research of the Goteborg Group in Sweden and of the Institute for Research in Post-compulsory Education at Lancaster University in England (*see* for example Hounsell and Entwistle, 1979; Marton, Entwistle and Hounsell, 1984): learners are highly attuned to the tacit criteria for success in any learning situation and tend to adapt themselves to those variables which maximize their chances of succeeding.

However, it is not necessary to turn to such pragmatic considerations to find examples of voluntary 'learners', for anyone who is unfamiliar with a subject or topic may well choose to submit to being taught, at least at the beginning. This does not necessarily imply any pathological lack of self-confidence, but rather an acknowledgement that the best way to master the rudiments of a new area is to be taught by an expert.

At the beginning of this chapter, I stated that I have long been committed to the idea that 'adult learners should accept most, if not all, of the responsibility for their own learning', although 'I have often had an uneasy feeling that not every learner is willing or able to accept the responsibility.' Now, as a result of this enquiry, I am in a better position to explain my point of view more clearly. I am still firmly convinced that adults are responsible for their own *learning*, but what I have come to reconsider is whether all should be responsible for their own *teaching*. My experience, as both an adult educator and an adult learner, leads me to believe strongly that when adults enter an instructional setting, they have every right to be treated with courtesy and respect. They should expect to be listened to and consulted, for they commonly have a valuable reservoir of experience which they can, and do, draw on in learning new material. Most important of all, however, adult learners are not mere passive observers or objects of teaching, but are active construers (Candy, 1980; Goodman, 1985; Thomas and Harri-Augstein, 1985).

Although it may be true that adult learners have the capacity to direct their own learning, and many also to direct their own instruction, they also have a right to avoid what one author had dubbed 'the tyranny of self-direction' (Frewin, 1976). After all, learners, too, make ideological judgements about the adequacy and acceptability of learning situations, based on 'pedagogical expectations [which] are culturally influenced ideas people have about the kinds of . . . educational activities that are recognizable . . . as valid learning activities . . .' (McKean, 1977, abstract). And in the final analysis, their willingness to accept increased control will depend on whether or not, in any particular case, they judge it to be a valid strategy and a situation from which they can learn.

References

Abercrombie, M L J and Terry, P M (1978). Reactions to change in the authority-dependency relationship. *British Journal of Guidance and Counselling.* 6, 1, 82-94.

Argyris, C and Schon, D A (1974). *Theory in Practice: Increasing Professional Effectiveness.* San Francisco: Jossey-Bass.

Bandura, A (1981). Self-referent thought: a developmental analysis of self-efficacy. In: J H Flavell and L R Ross (eds). *Social Cognitive Development: Frontiers and Possible Futures.* New York: Cambridge University Press, 200-39.

Brookfield, S D (1981). Independent adult learning. *Studies in Adult Education.* 13, 1, 15-27.

Brookfield, S D (1982). Independent adult learning. *Adults: Psychological and Educational Perspectives No 7.* Nottingham, England: Department of Adult Education, University of Nottingham.

Brookfield, S D (1984). Self-directed adult learning: a critical paradigm. *Adult Education Quarterly.* 35, 2, 59-71.

Boud, D J (1981). Toward student responsibility for learning. In: D J Boud (ed). *Developing Student Autonomy in Learning.* London: Kogan Page, 21-37.

Caffarella, R S (1983). Fostering self-directed learning in post-secondary education: the use of learning contracts. *Lifelong Learning: an Omnibus of Practice and Research.* 7, 3, 7-10, 25-6.

Caffarella, R S and O'Donnell, J M (1986). *Self-directed Adult Learning: a Critical Paradigm Revisited.* Proceedings of the Twenty-seventh Annual Adult Education Research Conference, 23-25 May 1986, Syracuse University, Syracuse, New York. 37-42.

Campbell, V N (1964). Self-direction and programmed instruction for five different types of learning objectives. *Psychology in the Schools.* 1, 4, 348-59.

Candy, P C (1980). *A Personal Construct Approach to Adult Learning.* Adelaide, South Australia: Department of Technical and Further Education, Adelaide College of the Arts and Education.

Candy, P C (1985). *The Ideology of Autonomous Learning: an Attempt to Cut the Gordian Knot.* Proceedings of the Fourth Annual Conference of the Canadian Association for the Study of Adult Education, 28-30 May 1985, University of Montreal, 59-76.

Collard, S (1985). The self-directed andragogue is alive and well and inhabiting discourse. (Unpublished paper.) Vancouver: Department of Adult Education, University of British Columbia.

Coombs, P H (1973). How shall we plan nonformal education? In: C S Brembeck and J Thompson (eds). *New Strategies for Educational Development: the Cross-cultural Search for Nonformal Alternatives.* Lexington, Massachusetts: Lexington Books, 145-7.

Crittenden, B (1978). Autonomy as an aim of education. In: K A Strike and K Egan (eds). *Ethics and Educational Policy.* London: Routledge and Kegan Paul, 105-26.

Cross, K P (1976). *Accent on Learning.* San Francisco: Jossey-Bass.

Danis, C and Tremblay, N (1985). *Critical Analysis of Adult Learning Principles from a Self-directed Learner's Perspective.* Proceedings of the Twenty-sixth Annual Adult Education Research Conference, 22-24 March 1985, Arizona State University, Tempe, Arizona. 138-43.

Dearden, F R (1972). Autonomy and education. In: R F Dearden, P H Hirst and R S Peters (eds). *Education and the Development of Reason.* London: Routledge and Kegan Paul, 448-65.

Elton, L R B (1973). Motivation and self study. In: C F Page and J Gibson (eds). *Motivation: Non-cognitive Aspects of Student Performance.* Papers presented at the Eighth Annual Conference of the Society for Research into Higher Eduation, July 1973. London: Society for Research into Higher Education, 75-9.

Entwistle, N J, Hanley, M and Hounsell, D J (1979). Identifying distinctive approaches to studying. *Higher Education.* 8, 4, 365-80.

Even, M J (chair) (1984). *Symposium on Adults Learning Alone.* Proceedings of the Twenty-fifth Annual Adult Education Research Conference, 5-7 April 1984, North Carolina State University, Raleigh, North Carolina, 279-84.

Even, M J (1985). *Adult Classroom Locus of Control.* Proceedings of the Twenty-sixth Annual Adult Education Research Conference, 22-24 March 1985, Arizona State University, Tempe, Arizona, 157-62.

Freire, P (1972). *Pedagogy of the Oppressed.* Harmondsworth, Middlesex: Penguin.

Frewin, C C (1976). The relationship of educational goal-setting behaviour to the conceptual level model. (Unpublished dissertation.) University of Toronto. [Canadian Theses on Microfiche No 35207]

Geis, G L (1976). Student participation in instruction: student choice. *Journal of Higher Education.* 47, 3, 249-73.

Gibbons, M and Phillips, C (1978). Helping students through the self-education crisis. *Phi Delta Kappa.* 60, 4, 296-300.

Goodman, D (1985). *The Influence of Self-concept as Learner on Participation Patterns of Adult Learners.* Proceedings of the Twenty-sixth Annual Adult Education Research Conference, 22-24 March 1985, Arizona State University, Tempe, Arizona. 177-81.

Griffin, V R (1977). Self-directed Adult Learners and Learning. Paper presented at the Adult Educators' Lyceum, 15-16 July 1977, Pewaukee, Wisconsin.

Gruber, H E (1965). The future of self-directed study. In: W R Hatch and A L Richards (eds). *Approach to Independent Study. New Dimensions in Higher Education No 13.* Washington, DC: United States Department of Health, Education and Welfare, 1-10.

Hamm, C (1982). Critique of self-education. *Canadian Journal of Education.* 7, 4, 82-106.

Heron, J (1981). Assessment revisited. In: D J Boud (ed). *Developing Student Autonomy in Learning.* London: Kogan Page, 55-68.

Holland, J (1969). The Misplaced Adaptation to Individual Differences. Paper presented at the Annual Convention of the American Psychological Association, 1969, Washington, DC.

Hounsell, D J and Entwistle, N J (eds). *Higher Education*, 8, 1 [Special issue, July 1979]

Hovey, D E, Gruber, H E and Terrell, G (1963). Effects of self-directed study on course achievement, retention and curiosity. *Journal of Educational Research.* 56, 7, 346-51.

Johnson, R (1979). 'Really useful knowledge': radical education and working-class culture, 1790-1848. In: J Clarke, C Critcher and R Johnson (eds). *Working-class Culture: Studies in History and Theory.* London and Birmingham: Hutchinson in association with the Centre for Contemporary Cultural Studies, University of Birmingham, 75-102.

Knowles, M S (1970). *The Modern Practice of Adult Education: Andragogy versus Pedagogy.* Chicago, Illinois: Association Press/Follett Publishing Co.

Knowles, M S (1975). *Self-directed Learning: a Guide for Learners and Teachers.* New York: Association Press.

Kremer, L (1978). Teachers' attitudes towards educational goals as reflected in classroom behavior. *Journal of Educational Psychology.* 70, 6, 993-7.

La Belle, T J (1982). Formal, nonformal and informal education: a holistic perspective on lifelong learning. *International Review of Education.* 28, 159-75.

Lawson, K H (1979). Avoiding the ethical issues. In: K H Lawson. *Philosophical Concepts and Values in Adult Education.* Milton Keynes: Open University Press, 17-25.

Lefcourt, H M (1976). *Locus of Control: Current Trends in Theory and Research.* Hillsdale, New Jersey: Lawrence Erlbaum Associates.

Lewis, H A (1978). A teacher's reflections on autonomy. *Studies in Higher Education.* 3, 2, 149-59.

Marton, F, Entwistle, N J and Hounsell, D J (eds) (1984). *The Experience of Learning.* Edinburgh: Scottish Academic Press.

McClintock, R (1982). Reaffirming a great tradition. In: R Gross (ed). *Invitation to Lifelong Learning.* Chicago, Illinois: Follett Publishing Co, 47-78.

McKean, R B (1977). Adult learners' pedagogical expectations about level of formality and type of learning experience (Unpublished PhD dissertation.) Michigan State University. [Dissertation Abstracts International. 38(10A), 5850]

Mezirow, J D (1981). A critical theory of adult learning and education. *Adult Education.* 31, 1, 3-24.

Millar, C J, Morphet, A R and Saddington, J A (1986). Case study: curriculum negotiation in professional adult education. *Journal of Curriculum Studies.* 18, 4, 429-43.

Mocker, D W and Spear, G E (1982). *Lifelong Learning: Formal, Nonformal, Informal and Self-directed.* Information Series No 241, ERIC Clearinghouse on Adult, Career and Vocational Education. Columbus, Ohio: The National Center for Research in Vocational Education, The Ohio State University.

Moore, M G (1972). Learner autonomy: the second dimension of independent learning. *Convergence: an International Journal of Adult Education.* 5, 2, 76-87.

Nuffield Foundation Group for Research and Innovation in Higher Education (1975). *Towards Independence in Learning.* London: Nuffield Foundation.

Oakeshott, M (1967). Learning and teaching. In: R S Peters (ed). *The Concept of Education.* London: Routledge and Kegan Paul, 156-76.

Parlett, M R (1970). The syllabus-bound student. In: L Hudson (ed). *The Ecology of Human Intelligence.* Harmondsworth, Middlesex: Penguin Books, 272-83.

Perry, R P and Dickens, W J (1984). Perceived control in the college classroom: response-outcome contingency training and instructor expressiveness effects on student achievement and causal attributions. *Journal of Educational Psychology.* 76, 5, 966-81.

Phillips, D Z (1973). Democratization: some themes in unexamined talk. *British Journal of Educational Studies.* 21, 2, 133-48.

Rogers, C R (1969). *Freedom to Learn: a View of What Education Might Become.* Columbus, Ohio: Charles E Merrill.

Roth, S (1980). A revised model of learned helplessness in humans. *Journal of Personality.* 48, 103-33.

Rotter, J B (1966). Generalized expectancies for internal versus external control of reinforcement. *Psychological Monographs,* 80.

Seligman, M E P (1975). *Helplessness: on Depression, Development and Death.* San Francisco, California: W H Freeman.

Selman, G R and Kulich, J (1980). Between social movement and profession – a historical perspective on Canadian adult education. *Studies in Adult Education.* 12, 2, 109-16.

Snow, R E (1980). Aptitude, learner-control and adaptive instruction. *Educational Psychologist.* 15, 3, 151-8.

Strong, M (1977). The autonomous adult learner: the idea of autonomous learning, the capabilities and perceived needs of the autonomous learner. (Unpublished thesis.) University of Nottingham.

Taylor, M M (1980). *A Conceptual Representation of Learning from the Learner's Point of View.* Proceedings of the Twenty-first Annual Adult Education Research Conference, 7-9 May 1980, University of British Columbia, Vancouver, British Columbia. 193-8.

Theil, J P (1984). *Successful Self-directed Learners' Learning Styles.* Proceedings of the Fourth Annual Conference of the Canadian Association for the Study of Adult Education, 28-30 May 1985, University of Montreal. 317-37.

Thomas, A M (1967). Studentship and membership: a study of roles in learning. *The Journal of Educational Thought.* 1, 1, 65-76.

Thomas, L F and Harri-Augstein, E S (1985). *Self-organized Learning:*

Foundation of a Conversational Science for Psychology. London: Routledge and Kegan Paul.

Torbert, W R (1976). *Creating a Community of Inquiry: Conflict, Collaboration, Transformation.* London: John Wiley.

Torbert, W R (1978). Educating towards shared purpose, self-direction and quality work: the theory and practice of liberating structure. *Journal of Higher Education.* 49, 2, 109-35.

Tough, A M (1978). Major learning efforts: recent research and future directions. *Adult Education.* 28, 4, 250-63.

Tough, A M (1979). *The Adult's Learning Projects: a Fresh Approach to Theory and Practice in Adult Learning.* Toronto: Ontario Institute for Studies in Education.

Weber, B (1985). Authority of the Adult Educator: Clarifying our Role. Paper presented at the North West Adult Education Association Conference, 18-20 April 1985, Ashland, Oregon.

Welton, M R (1986). Vivisecting the Nightingale: Reflections on Adult Education as an Object of Study. Discussion paper prepared for the Fifth Annual Conference of the Canadian Association for the Study of Adult Education, May 1986, Winnipeg, Manitoba.

Wight, A R (1970). Participative education and the inevitable revolution. *The Journal of Creative Behaviour.* 4, 4, 234-82.

Wispe, L G (1951). Evaluating section teaching methods in the introductory course. *Journal of Educational Research.* 45, 3, 161-86.

Witkin, H A, Moore, C A, Goodenough, D R and Cox, P W (1977). Field-dependent and field-independent cognitive styles and their educational implications. *Review of Educational Research.* 47, 1, 1-64.

Chapter 14

Self-Directed Learning: More than Meets the Observer's Eye

Marilyn Taylor
Concordia University, Montreal

Introduction

I was drawn to the study and practice of adult education by its emphasis on fostering the fullest possibilities of each person. Its medium seemed consistent with its message. Respect for the interests and judgements of adult learners was reflected in the attention to learners' views in the organization of adult education programmes. I noticed that this principle had a considerable history in the field. In 1926 Eduard Lindeman was writing:

> In conventional education the student is required to adjust himself to an established curriculum; in adult education, the curriculum is built around the student's needs and interests. *(p 8)*

I was privileged to have studied with people who have a practical understanding of how to assume their responsibilities as educators in light of these convictions. One of these people is Virginia Griffin whose course served as the setting for the research which will be reported later.

When I came to the literature on learner-oriented education, however, I found that, as a learner, the popular discussions about adult learning, independent and self-directed, notably in Knowles (1970, 1975) and Tough (1971), did not seem to represent adequately my experience as an adult learner. I eventually realized that the concerns of *learners* in a learner-oriented educational approach were based largely on observations of the *educator* in such works as Bergevin, Morris and Smith (1968), Knowles (1970, 1975) and, later, Smith (1982).

I had a hunch that if, studied closely and carefully enough, the experience of learning, in this case for self-direction, would have a commonly experienced pattern. The research reported here is a study of self-direction in the classroom based on reports of the learners themselves. I thought that if learners' views on what is to be learned is a sound basis on which to orient educational programmes, their perspectives would be equally important as a basis of understanding how that learning occurs. I thought that identification of an 'inside-out' pattern would enable both learners and educators to intervene more effectively to aid learning.

In fact it was possible to identify a pattern common among learners; a pattern can be seen as a process of learning to take responsibility for one's own learning. It consists of a chronological series of essential features which constitute its four phases and four-phase transition points.

In the first portion of this chapter I will present the pattern of learning for self-direction which was identified and some background about how I conducted the study. In the latter portion, I will discuss how I now understand my disjointed relation to existing literature on self-directed and independent learning – that is, how this research is situated in my own search for understanding.

About the study

The study is based on the experiences of eight learners (six women and two men) from a 13-week graduate course which promoted self-direction in course work. Since the instructor judged the class too large for her purposes, it was then divided into two separate sections at the end of the third week. The activities in each of the sections evolved differently yet the process of learning which was identified in the study occurred in the experience of participants in both sections. It is, therefore, evident that this experience of learning is not simply an 'effect' of particular activities.

The age range was from 24 to 50, and all learners had extensive training, experience and education in such professions as education, social work, library science, nutrition and counselling before enrolling in this course. The learning process described here can be regarded as a transition experience between what Lindeman in 1926 called 'conventional education' and self-directed adult learning. Most of them knew this particular graduate course by reputation and valued the notion of 'self-direction' in adult education. Nevertheless, participation in the course where people were expected to take primary responsibility for their own learning created shock, confusion and ambivalence. Argyris and Schön (1975) have described this incongruity between what is valued intellectually and what is practised as the discrepancy between 'espoused theory' and 'theory-in-use'. In this study, evidence of the difference was the beginning of learning.

Two researchers interviewed the learners at weekly intervals throughout the course and once following the completion of the course. Study participants were asked to describe their experience as thoroughly as possible each week. Beyond this, care was taken to minimize interviewers' influence on the content of the interviews which ranged in length from 45 to 90 minutes, averaging about 60 minutes. The interviews were tape-recorded and later transcribed verbatim.

A comparative inductive analysis was done on the 1600 pages of transcript. Each participant's set of 14 interviews was taken as a unit, and the conceptual framework was generated from intensive study of four participants' transcripts. Data analysis was not approached with a preconceived conceptual framework; rather, the transcripts were studied and reorganized until constructs emerged which seemed most relevant to the research question of 'how learning happened'. The framework described was generated out of an intensive study of four people's data; it was then examined for relevance in interpreting the data of the remaining four people.

The study context

The course, called 'Basic processes in facilitating adult learning', was intended to enable course participants in developing their capabilities to help other adults learn in group situations. This included examining one's own notions about learning and education as well as having opportunities for practical involvement in designing and leading class sessions. Course participants were expected to learn from their experience of the course as well as from discussions, presentations and books in the bibliography.

The physical environment and procedures of the course were organized to promote involvement and interaction. The class met in a comfortable carpeted room with movable furniture, chairs being arranged in a circle for the beginning of the class. Coffee and tea were available in a corner of the room. There was a table displaying relevant reading materials each week from which people could borrow materials. Each class began with a 'transfer in' period in which people chatted with a person next to them either to divest themselves of external dis tractions or identify concerns related to the class that may have needed to be discussed. The agenda and its rationale presented at the beginning of class enabled people to join in more fully. After the first three weeks of the course, volunteers from the class (usually different people each week) joined with the instructor to plan and lead class sessions based on objectives which were developed in the class as a whole. Evaluation sheets were most often filled out at the end of each session and taken into account in the planning of the next session. The results were also reported at the beginning of the subsequent class. Leadership modelled in the class emphasized *facilitating learning* and the development of the learning group rather than teacher-oriented instruction.

The first three weeks of the course were designed to 'give participants an opportunity to uncover some of the needs they want to work on . . . and help them get acquainted with each other well enough and with what other people wanted in the group sufficiently well to make decisions about how we would use our time together in the class most effectively'. (Comments from an interview with Dr Griffin after the course about its design and her views about her role and purposes.) The first class was oriented to informing people about the course information and procedures, including how the instructor understood her role and beliefs about teaching and learning, and to otherwise addressing what Dr Griffin observed to be the usual student concerns and worries at the beginning of this course. People had an opportunity to meet in pairs and foursomes to choose and discuss which of a list of elements in learning they were experiencing as important at the moment. At a later point in the class people assembled in four different areas of the room which reflected how clear or unclear they were about what they wanted from the course. Both activities had the multiple purpose of introducing people to each other, of promoting thought about their own learning, of legitimizing differences in the class, and therefore of maximizing a comfortable climate. During the second class session, participants began to identify and communicate their learning interests, first in small groups and then with charts on the walls for the entire class. During the week people obtained copies of the 'interests inventory' which was generated, and completed questionnaires on learning style and educational philosophy.

During the third class session, the class was asked by the instructor to decide whether to split into two sections because the group was very large. After the decision was taken to do so, the results of the questionnaires were interpreted and discussed in the two respective sections of the course. From this week on, the sections met separately (on different days of the week). Also, this was the point at which learners participated in planning the classes with Dr Griffin. This aspect of the course both promoted learner responsibility-taking in the course and provided an opportunity for people to experience and practise designing and leading activities.

Additionally, each learner was responsible for developing his or her own learning contract with the instructor so that course work would be uniquely suited to his or her goals. 'I don't press them to work on those early in the course . . . but that those individual goals will change and emerge over time . . . A little over half the way through I suggest that people ought to be firming up what they want to do individually and talk with me about it,' said Dr Griffin. The contract is then negotiated in light of the grade that the learner wants for it.

The shift to learner direction-setting took place, then, on two levels – namely, the class session planning and individual work. It should be mentioned here that the study context was special in that, the subject matter of the course being learning *per se*, the experience of learning was the focus of discussion. Whether or how much this pattern would be found in the experience of students in courses in subject matter areas unrelated to the topic of learning has yet to be established. Further, it should be remembered that participants in this study were learning to deal with self-direction in a formal classroom. It is not self-direction *per se* which is described here but, more specifically, the transition to self-direction.

What people were learning from their experience of this course

Course participants were learning a new way to learn and teach, a new way of understanding learning and themselves as learners and teachers, characterized by learner involvement and responsibility-taking.

> I used to be a receptacle learner. I spewed it out but I only spewed it out in the way it came in. But now it's more a cyclical thing. It's coming in and it's getting processed in some way and the way it's coming out is unique to me . . . There was nothing of *me* in learning [before] . . . I didn't behave differently.

Knowledge is not something simply 'outside' the self, but something that learners are involved in shaping. Because knowledge is constituted in part by personal meaning and perspective, it is not static and fixed. The learner has an active role and responsibility in shaping the process and its outcomes with others.

> Learning is not as great as when I do some struggling on my own and then I start struggling with some other people . . . Then it's just like the quantum leap stuff that was happening this morning.

What participants were learning resembles the changes Perry (1970) described as a 'revolution in a person's address to the nature of knowledge and the origin of values' (p 28), the reorientation of a view of knowledge from absolutism to relativism. Corollaries in that learning included a valuing of one's own experience in learning, the importance of collaboration with others, the importance of personal reflection and increased confidence in oneself.

Applied to the 'teaching side of the coin', this new perspective involves understanding oneself as an assistant to people in their learning without having to be the source of knowledge and control in the learning setting.

> . . . I see in the real practice of adult education that the mutuality of it, the mutual learning aspect of it, is a way of helping without condescension.

Corollaries of this kind included the issues of professional standards, expectations by others that one has the answers, and the congruence between principles and practice.

The following describes the common sequence of experiences in how this major re-interpretation of learning and teaching took place over the period of the course.

The learning process toward self-direction

The study reveals four different seasons or phases of the experience in learning. The phases occur in a consistent order around a particular learning theme or problem being worked on. For six of the eight participants the problem was how to behave and understand oneself as a self-directed learner in a professional educational setting where one expects to be directed and evaluated. For two of the learners it was the problem of how to be a helper to others' learning without having to be an infallible and only source of direction (conventional instructor role). In all cases, learners were challenged to make a major reorientation in their assumptions and expectations about learning and teaching.

The four phases and the phase transition points through which this change of perspective occurs are briefly summarized as follows:

- Disconfirmation (phase transition) – a major discrepancy between expectations and experience.
- Disorientation – a period of intensive disorientation and confusion accompanied by a crisis of confidence and withdrawal from other people who are associated with the source of confusion.
- Naming the problem (phase transition) – naming the problem without blaming self and others.
- Exploration – beginning with relaxation with an unresolved issue, an intuitively-guided, collaborative, and open-ended exploration with a gathering of insights, confidence and satisfaction.
- Reflection (phase transition) – a private reflective review.
- Reorientation – a major insight or synthesis experience simultaneous with a new approach to the learning (or teaching) task.
- Sharing the discovery (phase transition) – testing out the new understanding with others.
- Equilibrium – a period of equilibrium in which the new perspective and approach is elaborated, refined and applied.

The sequence is most adequately represented as a cycle or helix because the disorientation phase arises out of an experience of equilibrium similar to the final phase described here. The sequence can be visually represented as a series of eight critical points.

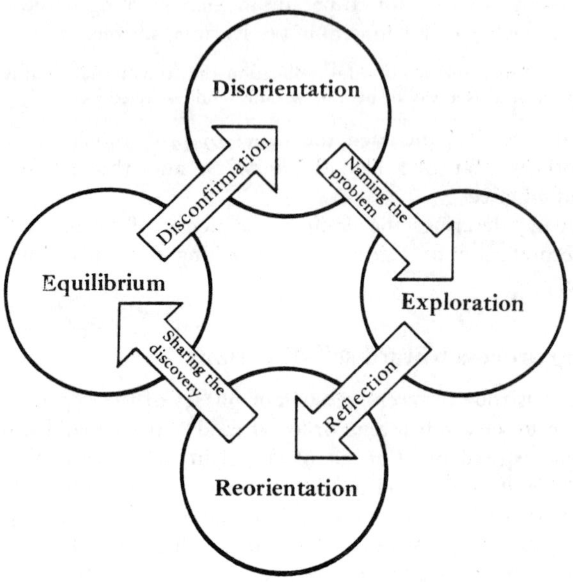

1. Learning process sequence

Critical features in the learning process toward self-direction

Learners enter the course in the equilibrium phase, observing and fitting their experiences into existing conceptual categories.

Critical point 1: phase transition from equilibrium into disorientation

The learning process begins with the collapse of the learner's frame of reference or 'assumptive world' (Parkes, 1971) as an adequate means of understanding his or her experience. This event is associated with different aspects of the classroom environment for different people. One person was disrupted by the first class activity and course description; another by several attempts in the first several weeks to accomplish something and get himself organized in his course work; another by some concepts discussed during the third class. Whatever the event and timing, the occasion marks the beginning of the change sequence.

Critical point 2: disorientation

Disorientation results when the learner's experience diverges from his or her existing assumptions, expectations and preconceptions. This phase is identified by four characteristics: confusion, anxiety and tension, a crisis of confidence, and withdrawal from others with whom the learner associates the source of confusion.

Confusion results from the absence of an adequate conceptual 'map' for what one is experiencing – the loss of a meaningful link between concept and experience. One learner exclaimed:

> Nothing was clicking and it was at that point that I came to realize that the course was not going in the direction that suited [me].

Feelings of tension and anxiety are expressed implicitly and explicitly: 'I could feel myself tensing up and getting anxious at a lot of moments.'

A crisis of confidence also characterizes this phase. Self-accusing comments like the following are common:

> If these underlying philosophies were being accounted for in this theoretical model and I didn't recognize it, how dumb could I be? If this is so important to me, how dumb could I be not to recognize it?

The fourth identifying feature is the reduction in the quality of relationships with others associated with the source of confusion. It is a social pattern of psychological (not necessarily geographical) withdrawal from other people. One person reported:

> I just sat there like a lump with a dissatisfied expression on my face . . . I just couldn't participate in the group and couldn't talk. That's not like me.

The phrase, 'that's not like me', underlines an observation made during this phase: the learners' experiences and expressions at this point were not present in other periods during the course. Problems with self-esteem, confusion, anxiety and relationships with others were phase-related rather than person-related, though individuals may have had unique ways of experiencing these moments.

For most learners, there is a period during which they tend to deny their confusion, a tendency likely to be related to cultural prohibitions against expressing of confusion in professional environments. One individual attempted to 'frame out a reasonable workload' but this proved unsatisfactory. The next week he reported that 'other people in the class seemed to be putting it together a bit better' than he was. Comparative, even competitive, statements tend to occur at this point, but not at other times.

During this period, the problem is defined in terms of who to blame. Aggravation and hostility are expressed toward others, particularly the instructor. One learner threatened to go to the graduate instruction committee about the way in which the course was being taught. Some learners tended to blame themselves. One person was worried about his lack of productivity: 'It strikes me as something that . . . could be very disturbing – that [I] don't finish things.' For another it was her integrity, and for yet another it was her correctness.

Critical point 3: phase transition from disorientation to exploration

Two events are associated with the learner's movement out of the disorientation phase. One is that the learner is able to identify the general nature of the problem and its relationship to himself or herself. Some learners communicated this event in the interview almost in passing; others reported it as a momentous event. In either case, it is the first significant 'naming' of one's experience in the sequence. The following is an example:

> . . . I realized finally that what was happening in her class was that . . . I was working in an actual 'freedom-to-learn' situation . . . She [the instructor] was the living embodiment of Carl Rogers' approach to education which I had just been reading . . . *Freedom to Learn.* All the while I was reading it I was saying, 'Oh yeah, that's good.' And all the while I was experiencing it, I was saying, [sounds like 'ayie-e-e'].

Naming the problem is one of the essential elements in moving out of the disorientation phase; the other is having some affirming contact or exchange, however brief, with others who are significant to the learner in the light of the problem being experienced. One learner whose concern was whether her uniqueness would be appreciated or acceptable, stated:

> I think I felt very anxious right at the beginning but then talking it over with a couple of other people and with the teaching assistant, I realized that I was quite *pleased* that I was confused about it. *[Learner's emphasis]*

Critical point 4: exploration

The exploration phase begins when the learner relaxes with the problem without having resolved it or having thoroughly understood it. One learner observed:

> The first class [during her disorientation phase] left me sort of very confused. I didn't know *what* was going on. Last week things came together. I still don't know what's going to happen. [Learner's emphasis]

She described herself as being willing to 'throw out all assumptions and presuppositions and be sort of free floating . . . I'm more interested than anxious, more excited than tense.'

The exploration phase is identified by five characteristics:

(1) An intuitively-guided exploration.
(2) A predominantly present-oriented time sense.
(3) Collaborative relationships with others.
(4) A series of 'insight episodes'.
(5) A gathering of confidence and satisfaction.

The learners feel confident they are on the right track without knowing where they will 'end up'. The exploration is intuitively guided and decisions are made as situations arise instead of from a previously made plan. One person stated:

> I'm willing to proceed with learning at the moment in the sense of going after things that are interesting to me rather than some great big huge design that I have to complete.

The same person described his approach to choosing reading materials:

> I started just flipping through the bookshelves – some of the things I had. The chapter headings [of the book he chose] looked interesting and were what we were into.

This description seems in stark contrast to another learner's statement (during an earlier phase of the sequence) that he was 'mowing down the bibliography'. As a part of this intuitive approach to decision-making about learning activities, the emphasis is present-oriented. One learner stated:

> When I came into the class my main goal was . . . to get something out of this that I can take back and apply. Well, I still want to do that, but I'm much more generally interested and also much more interested in what's going on in the weeks now. It's not quite as future-oriented. More kind of here-and-now sort of situation.

The social pattern which characterizes this phase is one of collaboration, exploring questions and thoughts with others who have similar or complementary interests. The class structure provided occasions for course participants to share thoughts and questions with other students in discussion either as a whole class or in small groups. A more cordial atmosphere developed in one section of the course than in the other. Course participants from the less supportive section sought their colleagues outside the class sessions in order to fulfil their need for collaboration in their exploration, suggesting that this element of the learning process is necessary.

Insight occasions can develop from collaborative questioning and discussions. The following statements from several learners describe these experiences:

> People were saying fantastic things. Some people said things that just summed up for me a lot of what I had been thinking and not been able to verbalize . . . I mostly connected with what I was thinking . . . Just the whole fact that there were all these connections being made . . . between half-formed ideas that I was having and the fact that I could put them into concrete form . . . It was one of these things. Everything was right on.

Finally, the exploration phase is identifiable by a gathering self-confidence and sense of satisfaction.

> . . . *I* felt good about talking to other people and I was being very verbal . . . which is being my old self again . . . I've got ideas and they were coming out there. I was very *pleased* with myself. [Learner's emphases] . . . I find it interesting that I can click out of that 'hey-I've-got-to-be-as-good-as' mind frame.

Critical point 5: transition from exploration to reorientation

The close of the exploration phase is marked by a withdrawal from collaborative activity with others. One person described:

> . . . There was just the tiredness of working with those people – in spite of the fact that we'd done good work together.

Comments which suggest retrospective reflection begin to appear in the discussion:

> . . . I know there are still some more things but it feels like it's been so much . . . such an immense amount of stuff I learned – that I'm still sorting out in my head – things I don't realize I've learned. It just occurs to me every once in a while, 'Yeh. I have perceptions about this now, perceptions about that. I can conceptualize such and such that I couldn't have before.'

A shift to solitude takes place, not as a conscious decision but apparently as a 'felt pull' or tendency. This often occurs in relation to reading or writing. This is also a point where resistance is expressed. One learner who did not move out of the exploration phase by the end of the interview period stated:

> I don't find learning in classes hard work . . . If I'm with other people a lot of reflection, conceptualization, and experiencing happens quite fluently and flowingly, and with feelings and laughter. My whole theme this year is that doing it by myself is hard. It is one of the things I'm tired and angry about. I don't know how to get out of that bind. It feels like I'm the one who has to initiate that and create that, and I don't know how to go about it.

The week before she had identified what seemed to be a real fear of stepping out on her own and taking that kind of initiative. She said:

> If I do a lot of learning and get very excited with doing that, I think, 'Oh where am I going? Am I going to be left all alone doing that?' . . . The scare is something like standing on my own two feet – being responsible for all that stuff. I have such a glorious wish to lean and hang on to everybody – 'Please tell me what to do. Am I doing it the right way? Tell me I'm okay.' Striving through life in a carefree way, taking on a question, is not my style . . . I have the feeling that if I take that on I'll really be on my own.

Critical point 6: reorientation

Out of the reflective review of experience emerges a major synthesis, a new understanding, a sense of resolving the issue which arose in the disorientation phase. The intensity of this phase parallels that of the disorientation phase though the phases are opposites in the sense that the first is 'falling apart' and the other is 'coming together'. Nevertheless, the ecstasy of creation might be expected to be as difficult to acknowledge in a public discussion as the agony of loss and confusion.

A new approach becomes acted upon simultaneously with the major insight; several people described the experience of simultaneity. One person's major insight occurred in the interview. A few minutes before, she stated:

> . . . I am realizing that what I said to you before – the closing of the time lag is starting to happen. It's not taking three hours, six hours, five days. It's closing. Sometimes it's almost simultaneous but it's getting there. It's starting to come together.

Another learner reported how she was able to describe the synthesis experience to her colleagues in the class as a rapid interplay of experiencing and conceptualizing experience.

The reorientation phase synthesized experiences and ideas into a perspective. This sometimes takes several weeks, punctuated with several reflective occasions of remarkable intensity. A learner whose major insight was provoked by reading a particular book in combination with a class activity, reported:

> It was one big connection all the way through . . . Something about reading that book and listening to that exercise made it very clear in my mind and everything's fine. It's resolved.

She went on the next week to label the nature of the process she had been involved in. She described the period of reflecting by herself, during which the insights about her learning process occurred, as follows:

> I had a telephone conversation till midnight and couldn't go to sleep afterwards. I tried reading and I got all these ideas on experiential learning and started writing down all these things.

Another learner described her experience to the interviewer as it was occurring since it happened partly during an interview. She noted a physical pressure in her chest: 'It makes it hard for me to talk at times.' She stated the next week that after the interview she, too, could not sleep. 'All these things just fell together. I couldn't *believe* it.' She described the end of the insight experience a week later as follows:

> I didn't feel the kind of physical tension that I feel when I'm really learning something in the sense that I didn't in the [last] interview but there was certainly a heightened awareness or heightened tension that sort of said, 'I don't ache physically,' but there was something that said, 'You've got to stay up and keep going – there's more coming.' It's like delivering a baby and I finally thought, 'God, it's out and it's breathing on its own. Now I can go to bed.'

The reorientation phase produces a profound conscious acknowledgement, which is simultaneously expressed in action, that learning is a process in which learners are the actors. It can be facilitated by teachers and classrooms and books, but *they* are 'where learning happens' and *their* views and judgements are centrally involved. An initial intellectual agreement with this perspective becomes a much deeper, more pervasive understanding. Comments which reflect this include:

> My understanding of content has expanded. . . It's no longer just this knowledge that exists in books or in the lecturer – or outside myself. It now exists within me as well as in group process. But to get that process I have to do it. It's not something that anyone else can hand me on a platter . . . The content still comes out 'cause often I like the ideas. The content relates to the process. I'm talking of them as if they're separate but they're not separate any longer. They're all integrating so everything is tying up.

The learners who reached the reorientation phase experienced the major insight by enacting their agency as learners. One had initially taken a logical approach to developing his learning contract. His reorientation experience occurred in relation to planning his contract in an entirely different way. He said:

> I had written one a couple of weeks ago and hadn't liked it . . . I started . . . to write objectives and again they were dry and I didn't feel any sense of connection to them . . . I decided to take a different tack. [A colleague] had been talking in the basic processes course about generating goals and objectives out of a person's feelings rather than out of what makes normal, logical sense on how to approach the problem . . . So what I did was just took a piece of paper and for both courses I just kind of wrote down whatever feelings I just generated toward the course. Just as they hit my mind I just scribbled them down on paper and kept going . . . That's the order [pointing to the sheet] they came out in everything – the only exception being . . . before I gave them to [the instructor], I kind of expanded them a little bit because the way I had written down originally . . . it said something to me but not necessarily to anybody else. The objectives for the rest of the course just kind of jumped off the page at me because it was fairly obvious where *my* interests lay in terms of completing things that I felt were not complete but I wanted to complete. It just happened so easy, it amazed me.

Critical point 7: transition from reorientation to equilibrium

The transition from reorientation to equilibrium is marked by sharing the major insight with others significant to the learner in the light of the discovery. Unlike the close of the disorientation phase, the learner is not in need of self-affirmation, but rather affirmation of the intelligibility of the new perspective or insight, even though the 'product' has an implicit authority for the learner. One learner's major insight came in constructing his learning contract for the course:

> I think one of the satisfying things I found was – *I* did it and it felt good to me and it *made* sense and it *looked* proper and it looked whole and all that kind of thing. And when I went into that meeting with [the instructor] yesterday, we just talked a bit and I told her what I had done and I gave it to her to read. And it *seemed* to communicate to *her* where I was, fairly clearly, in the course, you know. That seemed to be a good kind of validating experience for me. I would have been very frustrated, I think, if she had said, 'What the hell is this?'

A third learner had to go out of her way to find an occasion where she could discuss her discovery. She was unable to do this within the class because of tension and discomfort she felt there. She was aware of a sense of incompleteness:

> . . . So far the classes have given me very little chance for conceptualization and reflection . . . if we can get through [describes the class's agenda] we may get to that next step which is to say, 'Let's take a look at what we've done and what we can draw out of it.' I imagine that *could* pull the class together for me. *[Learner's emphasis]*

This did not happen, however. It wasn't until the next semester in the advanced course on the same topic that she found the appropriate group of people and the moment to share her insight to bring her a sense of resolution and completeness.

Critical point 8: equilibrium

The equilibrium phase is characterized by:

(1) The activity of consolidating the new perspective, applying and refining it.
(2) Much less emotional intensity.
(3) Preconceived involvement with others.

Several learners described this phase by contrasting it to earlier periods in the course:

> I think there's a distinction from last term . . . Last term was far more exploratory, far more open, far less self-directed, far more experiential . . . Last term was far more interior . . . relying much more on my own subjective experience than this term has been . . . This term it would revolve more around reading and writing and talking as opposed to doing and thinking and reflecting. I am reflecting this term. I am doing it privately . . . [The second term is] not as wide open, which in one sense decreases one's sense of wonder. On the other hand, I'm kind of more confident of my ability to explore because I can see paths to do it. *[Learner's emphasis]*

> . . . The kind of emotional turmoil that characterized me in the first month here [was one of] disintegration . . . The ambiguity was incredibly exciting . . . And [now what I am experiencing] is the opposite of the spectrum. The excitement of being integrated – re-integrated. And I'm just feeling incredibly good about myself because I'm realizing that I *do* have sort of – that there is some sort of direction, some sort of central purpose in me, and I've connected up with a lot of resources to further this feeling – this direction . . . I'm feeling incredibly good about it – so good that I really don't want the reading and the enlarging upon this to stop. *[Learner's emphasis]*

Learners in this study proceeded at different paces in this cycle though the sequence of experience was common as described above. All the learners experienced disconfirmation, but it was provoked by different experiences at varying times in the course. Similarly, the affirmation associated with transition out of disorientation came from different persons on different occasions for each participant, and so on. Figure 2 indicates the pace of learners in phases of the learning process.

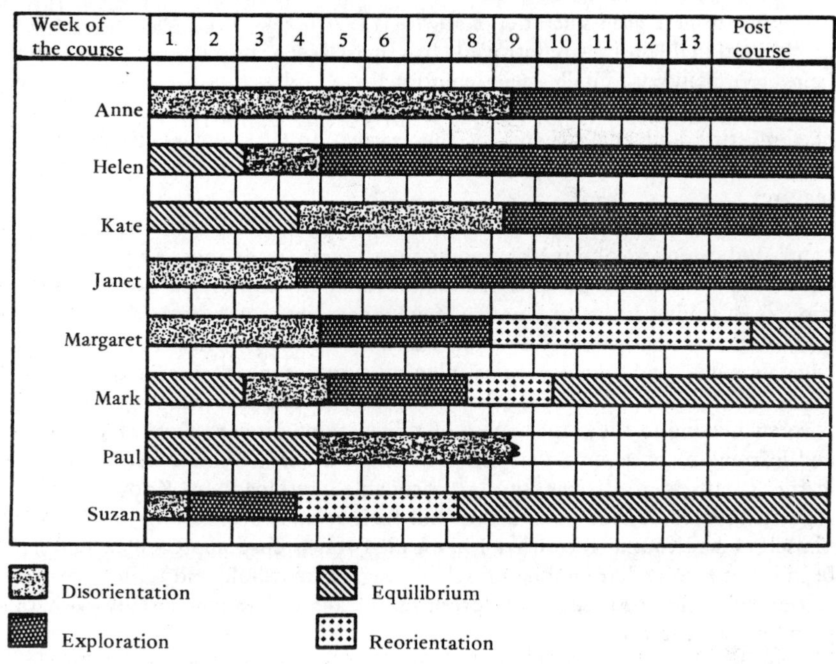

2. Learners' paces through the sequence

Reflections on the results of the study

'Finding some missing pieces'

There are four dimensions of the experience of learning for self-direction evident in this study which were absent or 'under-represented' in the literature I looked to as a learner.

The first of these is *emotionality.* The experience involves the agony of loss – the loss of a frame of reference, a way of doing things and, consequently, confidence in oneself. It includes the fear of uncertainty and mental chaos, as well as of the possibility that one will be discovered by others to be inadequate. Although this is alluded to briefly in the literature (Knowles, 1970; Smith, 1982), this aspect of the process does not get equal time with discussion of the more rational activities. Reading these presentations, in the midst of confusion and anxiety I could easily assume that there must be something wrong with me and become even more defensive and isolated. Likewise, the relief and excitement of being in a discovery process, gradually accumulating insights into the nature of this unknown world, and the outstanding experience of the integrative understanding which signals the close of the process remain unmentioned in existing discussions of what is involved in learning for self-direction. Through studying the experiences of learners in this study, I learned that the ecstatic moment of conceptual clarity that *I* had experienced was neither incidental to the process nor idiosyncratic. Knowles (1970) acknowledges that learning is 'an internal process controlled by the learner and engaging his whole being – including intellectual, emotional and physiological functions' but then collapses this into the notion that 'learning is described as a process of need-meeting and goal-striving by the learner' (p 50), obviating further discussion about the nature of these intellectual, emotional and physiological features.

The second aspect of this learning experience which has been missing, indeed contra-indicated, in observers' accounts is the important role of *intuition*, that apprehension without an apparent logical reason. Smith (1982) identifies intuition in learning as 'an alternative way of learning' but not as a constitutive feature of learning for self-direction. Paradoxically, it is logical that one cannot envisage a goal and derive a logical plan of activities in the absence of a relevant frame of reference. It is precisely this frame of reference which is lost or discovered missing in the initial phase of this learning process. Goal identification and learning plans assume that one is oriented in one's experience. Indeed, one learner's efforts to 'frame out a reasonable workload' as Knowles (1975) suggests seemed to lead him further and further away from being able to orient himself. I had found, too, what I had called this 'stepsy approach' would have been at one point like pulling myself through a knot-hole and quite irrelevant. Rationality and logic seem inappropriate means of dealing initially with this kind of disorientation.

Thirdly and, again paradoxically, the learner's perspective draws into focus the *relational quality* of learning for self-direction. Indeed, it would be incorrect in this perspective to represent this process as something which is generated by the educational context or the individual learner. Rather, both the environment and the individual are constitutive of the result. When the individual is withdrawn during the disorientation phase, he or she is withdrawn from a very specific social context. During the exploration phase and the building of a new perspective, there is an implied sociocultural network which serves as a stabilizing and sustaining system for learners which, not unlike the root system of a tree, is not evident to the observer. Finally, while the integrative understanding of this approach to education is clearly a highly personal construction in the reorientation phase, evidenced by the personal power which is experienced in this event, it is also a social construction in that intelligibility of the discovery to particular others is essential to a sense of completion. This integral role of relationships with others better explained my relationships to people in my learning than the instrumental notions of '*using* another person as a resource to learning' (Smith, 1982, p 100, emphasis added), and 'to see [peers] as resources . . . to give them help and receive help from them' (Knowles, 1975, p 61).

The implicit image of the competent learner in adult education literature is that of an independent individual, governed by his or her own rationally derived decisions. To expect to interpret learning for self-direction as an accomplishment of an individual alone, even using others as resources, would seem to underestimate the complexities and contingencies of the experience.

Yet another paradox is that an essential feature of an educational environment which fosters self-direction is the presence of people credible to the learner authorities, people who are able to provide the affirmation that releases him or her from a struggle with confusion into a creative discovery process. This dimension, an aspect of the *politics* of learning for self-direction, is also missing in existing popular discussions of self-direction. Institutionally-recognized people, the instructor, teaching assistants, senior students, are in a strategic position to promote or inhibit learners' responsibility-taking in their education. The learner is *in relationship* to the instructor, and it is through this and similar relationships that the locus of responsibility and authority is transformed and reinterpreted from being external to the learner to being shared in by the learner. I now had a basis for understanding the feelings of profound appreciation when affirmed by instructors I saw as models. I also understood the terrible anguish I felt when affirmation did not come from a field supervisor who, as I, did not understand her importance to me at that moment. I later experienced these unacknowledged and often unrecognized demands on the instructor when I began to teach, particularly when students were organizing their own activity and not simply following detailed instructions. An understanding of this role of authority in the learners' processes of learning would seem to be pivotal in effectively facilitating that learning.

Another aspect of the political dimension in learning for self-direction will be noted here rather than be fully discussed. Because this approach to teaching contravenes usual institutional educational practice, it is important to understand the nature of support for the teacher of such a course within the institution.

A different frame of reference

In the seven years since this study was completed I have become more distinctly aware of how these 'missing dimensions' are quite related to one another as part of a perspective quite different from that represented in adult education literature on self-direction. I found that I had what might be called an ecological perspective in which even the phrase '*self*-direction' seems somewhat inadequate. I was heartened and energized by reading the work of people like Bateson (1972) who are oriented to the study of relationships and social contexts in contrast to the study of objects and individuals, who questioned the 'purposive consciousness' which does not include itself in the world it describes and acts upon, and who observed that 'the most important task today is, perhaps, to learn to think in a new way' (Bateson, 1972, p 462).

Writers like Miller (1976) and Gilligan (1982) helped me to recognize that, as a woman, I might be disposed to construing 'learning' as process (events in meaningful relation over time), as an 'inside-out' structure (order and pattern evident from within), and as a relation between person and environment (an act of communication). The ideas which have currency in educational literature are those which tend to assimilate everything to a frame of reference of individual, logical and externally observable behaviour. I found it instructive to note that this was the quality of what I called the 'equilibrium phase' in learning for self-direction, the phase being characterized by purposiveness, conceptual clarity, analytical and logical thinking. Equilibrium is the acceptable state in our culture, a culture which reflects primarily a male gender perspective (Gray, 1982; Miller, 1976; Gilligan, 1982). The experience and practical realities of the first three phases of the *transition* to self-directed learning such as confusion, emotionality, intuitively-guided search, integral involvement of others, and reflection on experience are largely obscured in this perspective. Qualitative features and challenges which characterize those first three phases, as reported by learners in this study (both men and women), are highly related to aspects of the human experience which have been culturally attributed to women and thereby made invisible, reduced in apparent value in the culture. These include 'vulnerability', 'emotions', 'participating in the development of others', 'cooperation', 'creativity' (Miller, 1976), orientation toward connection and relationship (Gilligan, 1982), familiarity with transitions (Gray, 1982).

Applications

To my knowledge there have not been studies that have been conducted to identify this or similar learning process patterns in other classrooms, whether learner-directed or not. Therefore, empirically and strictly speaking, it is not possible to assess how widely applicable this process model of learning from the perspective of the learner is and under what circumstances. There are observations from a theoretical viewpoint and from practice that suggest it is rather widely relevant.

From a theoretical point of view, the process model resembles a number of conceptual formulations of change or learning processes. Similarities in the model can be drawn between this model and the pattern of 'psychocultural transformation of perspective' experienced by women returning to school described by Mezirow (1978), the process by which people shed 'illusions of safety' through adulthood (Gould, 1978), adult transitions as described by Adams *et al.* (1976) and many others (Taylor and Gavin, 1984). There is a need for the careful work of documenting this kind of learning process in relation to other specific learner-oriented educational programmes. It would also be instructive to have process patterns documented from the learners' perspectives in more traditionally instructed programmes and courses.

Indications of the relevance of this process pattern come also from practice. One indication of the applicability of the model is its 'recognizability' to learners. The process model described here has been used in a number of adult education courses, at the Ontario Institute for Studies in Education as well as other graduate programmes in adult education in Canada, because learners can identify this pattern in their experience.

As a teacher, this learning pattern has served as 'language' which helps me to interpret students' behaviour and to make course plans in the light of what I think learners are experiencing. The process model helps me to refine my hunches about the best timing of activities and course work. I know that there are periods in a course when people will not be able to work productively on tasks and other times when things more easily fall into place. I know that there are times when opportunities for contact with me are especially important and other times when it will not particularly matter. There are times when opportunities for learners to work with their colleagues will generate great bursts of energy and excitement, and there will be other times when discussion groups in class would be of little interest. I know there are times when reflective writing tasks will be very catalytic in clarifying thoughts, and other times when they would be impossible. There are times when learners can tell me what they are experiencing and other times when I have to go on my best hunches. While there is something of a critical mass of the group at various points in the sequence to whom class plans must be oriented, I look for clues to what is happening for individuals who have a different pace. I find these clues in how they speak of their work, how they relate to me, how their course work is done, their behaviour in class, and their apparent relationship with other people in the class.

I have come to appreciate the authority I have as a teacher as a precious ingredient in people's learning rather than as inhibitive. I have a better sense of how to relate to people who are in a conflicting relationship with me and of when my attention and support are critical to learners. I understand better who I am to people in my classes and, while I think I have become much more effective as a teacher, I am also acquiring an appropriate humility about the limits of my influence.

References

Adams, J, Hayes, J and Hopson, B (1976). *Transition: Understanding and Managing Personal Change.* Oxford: Martin Robertson.

Argyris, C and Schön, D (1975). *Theory in Practice: Increasing Professional Effectiveness.* San Francisco: Jossey-Bass.

Bateson, G (1972). *Steps to an Ecology of Mind.* New York: Ballantine.

Bergevin, P E, Morris, D and Smith, R M (1963). *Adult Education Procedures: a Handbook of Tested Patterns for Effective Participation.* Greenwich, Connecticut: Seabury Press.

Gould, R (1978). *Transformations: Growth and Change in Adult Life.* New York: Simon and Schuster.

Gilligan, C (1982). *In a Different Voice: Psychological Theory and Women's Development.* Cambridge, Massachusetts: Harvard University Press.

Gray, E D (1982). *Patriarchy as a Conceptual Trap.* Wellesley, Massachusetts: Roundtable Press.

Knowles, M (1975). *Self-directed Learning: a Guide for Learners and Teachers.* New York: Association Press.

Knowles, M (1970). *The Modern Practice of Adult Education: Andragogy versus Pedagogy.* New York: Association Press.

Korzybski, A (1933). *Science and Sanity.* Lakefield, Connecticut: International Non-Aristotelian Library.

Lindeman, E C (1961). *The Meaning of Education.* Montreal: Harvest House.

Mezirow, J (1978). *Education for Perspective Transformation: Women's Re-entry Programs in Community College.* New York: Centre for Adult Education, Teachers College, Columbia University.

Miller, J B (1976). *Toward a New Psychology of Women.* Boston: Beacon Press.

Parkes, C M (1971). Psycho-social transitions: a field for study. *Social Science and Medicine.* 5, 105-115.

Perry, W (1970). *Forms of Intellectual and Ethical Development in College Years.* New York: Holt, Rinehart and Winston.

Smith, R M (1982). *Learning How to Learn.* Chicago: Follett.

Taylor, M (1979). Adult learning in an emergent learning group: toward a theory of learning from the learner's perspective. (Unpublished doctoral dissertation.) University of Toronto.

Taylor, M (1986). Learning for self-direction in the classroom: the pattern of a transition process. *Studies in Higher Education.* 1986, 11, 1, 55-72.

Taylor, M and Gavin, J (1984). An examination of individual and community adaptation to Atlantic fishing industry reductions using the 'Taylor model'. A research report submitted to the Department of Fisheries and Oceans, Ottawa, Canada.

Tough, A (1971). *The Adults' Learning Projects: a Fresh Approach to Theory and Practice in Adult Learning.* Toronto: Ontario Institute for Studies in Education.

Chapter 15

Evolving Perspectives of Learning, Research and Programme Evaluation

Lynn Davie
Ontario Institute for Studies in Education

During the past 20 years I have witnessed an evolving understanding of the nature of learning. Our ways of investigating learning have undergone a profound transformation, and through these different perspectives and approaches, our understanding of human learning itself has evolved.

There are a variety of ways to investigate the structure and meaning of learning. We may ask adults about their experiences; structure settings in which learning might occur and then investigate the changes in the adult through either interview or measurement; or collect information about learning during the process of programme evaluation.

This chapter is an autobiographical exploration of my own changing concepts of learning. It is based on my experiences as a faculty member in departments of adult education. In that role, I have supervised graduate theses and conducted research and programme evaluations. I have seen changes in the research approaches to understanding learning and in the kinds of evidence which scholars in our field will accept for both research and evaluation standards.

In a sense, my own experience parallels the changing knowledge and assumptions of the field. It might be helpful to review the changes in the past few years in order to bring some perspective to our current knowledge and beliefs.

No one's understanding is ever complete, of course, and the chapter ends with my current understanding of learning and how best to go about studying and evaluating it. I will share with the reader my puzzles and the difficulty I have in understanding learning and its importance. In the course of the journey, I hope that I will be able to raise questions and help the reader think through some of the important issues as well.

Qualitative research and naturalistic evaluation

Qualitative research is a generic term which has come to be used to describe a family of approaches such as hermeneutic enquiry, phenomenological enquiry, ethnographic research and various kinds of field research. These terms are not synonyms. Proponents of each approach have very different epistemological beliefs about knowledge, different points of view and different approaches. In many ways, they differ as much in their beliefs about the organization and meaning of reality as they differ from the quantitative researchers. Nevertheless, the qualitative approaches have some similarities in the kind of data that they collect, their relationship to their informants, and some of their approaches to analysis.

Our understanding of this family of approaches has come primarily from the disciplines of sociology and anthropology with their attempt to understand different cultures. In the study of other cultures we come immediately face to face with the problem of subjectivity. Can we describe another culture from an objective point of view, or what Putnam (1981) calls a 'God's Eye' point of view? Or must the observations of another culture always be cast only within the perspective of the observer. Smith and Heshusius (1986), reporting the arguments of Dilthey (Ermarth, 1978), say:

> This meant the investigator of the social world could only attain an understanding of that world through a process of interpretation – one that inevitably involved a hermeneutical method. The meaning of human expression was context-bound and could not be divorced from context.

The important difference between qualitative research and various positivistic approaches is not the methodology, nor the kind of research material, but rather with epistemology. By epistemology, I mean an individual's beliefs about the origin and methods of the gaining of knowledge. The qualitative approaches are based on the assumption 'that reality is mind-constructed and that facts cannot be separated from values' (Smith and Heshusius, 1978, p 5).

This essential difference between these two views can be stated simply. Those who approach research or programme evaluation from a positivistic point of view believe that there is an independent reality and the goal of the researcher or programme evaluator is to discover, describe and understand this independent reality while controlling for various external influences. For those who approach research and programme evaluation from the qualitative point of view, there is no independent reality. Reality is constructed by the observer and is inherently limited by the observer's values and point of view.

Does this distinction matter? How would our approach to understanding the nature of learning differ if we approached it from the two different epistemological bases? What differences in approaching the assessment of learning or programme evaluation would be required by the different points of view? For this chapter, I will make a distinction between the assessment of learning and programme evaluation. The assessment of learning refers to attempts to identify and collect or measure student learning. Programme evaluation often contains the assessment of learning, but also includes attempts to study the effect of programme structures on student learning.

I believe that these questions are best explored in a description of my changing understanding over the past decade. Guba and Lincoln presented a paper at the November meeting of the American Evaluation Association's meeting in Toronto (1985). In this paper, they describe four generations of evaluation: (*1*) technical; (*2*) description; (*3*) judgement; and (*4*) responsive. As I read this paper I found that it described in rough terms the growth of my own understanding of programme evaluation and the assessment of learning. I have used their description of evaluation generations to organize a description of the change in my own understanding that forms the heart of this chapter.

Evaluation of learning as measurement

In the 1960s, I was trained first as a secondary school teacher and then later as an adult educator. Learning was seen as complex, but it was conceptualized as essentially linear. The important questions had to do with whether the student learned the information and concepts identified in the teacher's goals. Student assessment and programme evaluation questions centred on finding out how much a student had learned. Knowledge was seen as a commodity, a thing to be possessed. The primary responsibility for programme evaluation was that of the teacher, and the evaluation was always conducted from the instructor's point of view. The attempt was to objectify the knowledge of what students had learned. Efforts were made to create objective tests that removed or limited the teacher's subjective decisions. The view of knowledge was positivistic. There was an objective reality, and the goal was to construct objective measures of this knowledge.

The most important evaluation questions centred on how to construct objective tests that would measure higher order cognitive accomplishments. Bloom's taxonomy was very important, for it identified the need to measure not only recall but application and evaluation as well (Bloom, 1956).

Learning was seen as the result of teaching and the teacher's responsibility was to *cause* learning at the highest cognitive level possible. There was some talk of the other domains (affective and psycho-motor) (Krathwohl *et al.* 1964) but there was far less emphasis on these areas.

The problems for adult educators were twofold: firstly, to develop good objectives, and secondly to find acceptable ways to measure learning in terms of these objectives. In the area of objectives, Tyler (1950) was king, and Mager (1962) and others who argued for specific behavioural objectives were the princes.

There was a good deal of difficulty in measuring adult learning, as the adults resisted typical paper and pencil tests. One needed to find ways of assessing the learning that maintained the importance of the objectives, but was palatable to the adults.

As with education within the school system, there was also the problem of collecting evidence of higher level cognitive learnings. A major difficulty was that the adult learners did not always share the importance of the objectives. They argued that stated objectives did not represent significant learning from their perspective, and there was an immense resistance to the breaking down of objectives into the smaller, more specific behavioural objectives against which learning could be measured.

My main professional challenge during this period was to help practitioners to develop alternative forms of testing which would meet the technical concerns of validity, reliability, discrimination and power in forms that would be acceptable to adults. We experimented with case studies of different forms, carefully structured role plays and problem-solving case studies. In every case we were trying to make the testing instrument or activity simulate real life as closely as possible.

One particularly interesting approach was a device we called the *anasynics* case study. We coined this word to refer to both the analytical and synthetic skills needed to study the cases. In this instrument, we presented a learning group with a short case study that did no more than set the scene. Individuals or small groups then decided what additional information they needed to solve the problem and submitted written questions to the facilitator. The facilitator provided answers according to a predetermined scheme, and when the individual or small group decided they had enough information to solve the problem, they provided a solution based on their prior learning and the information they had collected. Feedback was provided for the students based both on their information search strategies and the adequacy of their solution.

However, adults during this period continued to express dissatisfaction with the testing methodologies. They felt disadvantaged by the predominant multiple choice format of testing instruments, and they also expressed some frustration with the alternative testing methods we were developing. The concerns centred on the control being exerted by the facilitators through the complex structures and they felt that the testing did not take their goals and interests sufficiently into account.

During this early period I was also involved with postgraduate education. Theses that I supervised during this period tended to reflect the predominant research paradigms. Theses were either needs assessment exercises or, in some cases, programme evaluation studies. The evaluation theses concentrated on the measuring of student learning. Numerical data, often from surveys or questionnaire studies, were highly valued. From the point of view of a faculty member, thesis supervision seemed straightforward. Standards from the field of measurement or of descriptive and inferential statistics were known and could be applied to judging the theses.

These theses were safe in that other academics could understand the research strategies. The only issues were the appropriateness of predominant theories and the strategies for solving practical measurement problems.

During this period my understanding of learning reflected the major research paradigm as well. Learning was a complex phenomenon, but its significant components involved cognitive structures. The major differences in understanding learning from an adult educator's point of view was centred on taking into account the relationship of the new learning to the complex underlying cognitive structures. Learning was a phenomenon to be understood by cognitive psychologists.

Evaluation of learning as description

Towards the end of the 1960s and the beginning of the 1970s, the predominant model of adult education was centred in the human potential movement. The learner defined what was most important to learn, although the human potential movement also stressed feedback to the individual. Learning was defined as change, and adult educators often called themselves change agents. The focus was on significant learning and significance was defined in the final instance by the individual.

There was a change in the role of the professional. Instead of *causing* change, the professional was seen as a *facilitator.* The facilitation role was analogous to a coach or helper rather than a director. There was emulation of Carl Rogers' style of providing supportive, but non-directive feedback. Adult educators attempted to help adults make their own decisions about goals, methods and assessment of their learning. Both what was to be learned and how much was to be learned were under the control of the learner.

Research and evaluation studies were also entering a new era. While the predominant model of academic research was still positivistic, we were beginning to see the first grounded theory researches based on the work of Glaser and Strauss (1967). In their seminal work, *The Discovery of Grounded Theory*, they argued against the utility of applying grand theories to the understanding of social behaviour. Instead, Glaser and Strauss believed that we needed to develop 'grounded theories' or theories that were both closer to and derived from actual experience. The proper technique was to collect a great deal of qualitative data in the form of open-ended interviews and field notes, and then to construct theories that were grounded in the data. These theories would be better because they would be more valid – that is, the theory would be closely related to the actual experience of the individuals and social settings being studied.

Those involved with student supervision, more familiar with positivistic paradigms, were hesitant and often required that much of the thesis be devoted to a defence of the legitimacy of the qualitative research paradigm. However, the absolute position of the positivistic paradigm of research was weakening and faculty supervisors began to consider it legitimate to examine learning (or at least the conditions for learning) from the perspective of the learner rather than solely from the perspective of the teacher, facilitator or programme planner.

The limitations of programme evaluation being solely focused on student testing were also acknowledged at this time. The emphasis in programme evaluation was turning to description. Case studies were an important form of evaluation in this area. For the assessment of individual learning, the predominant form of evaluation was self-description. The individual was asked to describe what he or she had learned. There was a major push in schools and universities for self-grading, for who else knew better what had been learned and how important that learning was than the student?

In one sense the epistemological basis for programme evaluation and grading had changed from an external, positivistic stance to a phenomenological one. There was no reality outside of the perception of the learner and hence no valid basis for external evaluation.

This approach to programme evaluation had both its strengths and weaknesses. Its major strength lay in the recognition that although education may be a social and political activity, learning was private. The important aspect of learning was in the social meaning of the cognitive connections between new learning and the already existing cognitive structure.

The strength in the self-evaluation approach lay within its recognition of the importance of the personal context of the learning. Self-evaluation recognized that the significance of learning was deeply related to the individual's values and that learning could not be assessed from a purely external position.

The problems of self-evaluation became most critical when the self-evaluation was linked to self-grading. The weakness of self-evaluation lay in the lack of recognition that grades had social and political purposes as well as self-reporting. Grades were used by individuals other than the students themselves and had symbolic meaning external to the learning itself.

In formal educational settings, there were at least three major problems with the evaluation as description approach. First, there was some resistance by adults to the requirement that they be responsible for their own curriculum and from some for the assigning of their own grades. Second, there was the inequity between the students who honestly described their own failings and assigned themselves lower grades to reflect their recognition of what remained to be learned, and those students who assigned themselves higher grades, through a lack of understanding of their learning, out of a confusion of effort with learning, or out of a need for higher grades for other purposes. Finally, the prospect of being the sole judge of one's own learning raised issues of self-doubt, loneliness and despair among the adult learners.

The professional challenge for programme evaluators in formal settings at this time involved finding better ways to gather descriptions of learnings. The keeping of personal journals or writing personal accounts of learning were seen as important. There were many attempts to describe (and some attempts to measure) the learnings involved in human potential groups and programmes. Change in the individual was seen as most important, and there were many claims of deep, fundamental changes. However, these descriptions of fundamental change were often in conflict with a lack of results when positivistic measures were employed. Thus, the two epistemologies produced quite different results and the different approaches to reality added a significant element to the confusion concerning the effects of the human potential movement.

Research and programme evaluation tended to be unsynchronized with the human potential movement. Although the focus of the learning was personal or interpersonal, research tended to be positivistic. There were countless attempts to measure the outcomes of learning using conventional psychological or sociological instruments. Because it did not seem possible to measure the significance of personal change, attention was turned to attempting either to measure differences in behaviour within groups, or to define a set of behaviours as skills and to measure increases in interpersonal skills.

It should be clear by now that these eras or generations of programme evaluation and learning do not come and go. During the period of the human potential movement, there was still much emphasis on an external reality, at least in terms of the research and, to a lesser extent, in programme evaluation. This is still true, and although I will argue that we are at present in the fourth generation of evaluation, we can still see the earlier evaluation models present. Some individuals also strongly believe that those earlier models are the most important or, in some cases, the only appropriate ways to conduct research or programme evaluation.

Graduate students with whom I worked during this period were quite varied in their epistemological approaches. There were several theses which attempted to measure the outcomes of various human potential movement strategies. In the positivistic tradition, these theses attempted to predict behaviour in small groups using current sociological or psychological theories. Although we learned a good deal from some of these theses, most of the results were negative. The theories available to us did not correspond to the outcomes either in terms of described learning or changed behaviour. While there were some attempts to interview participants, the resulting qualitative data were viewed as less scientific than quantitative measurement, and if the qualitative analysis contrasted with other forms of measurement, the qualitative data were discounted.

A few graduate theses attempted to examine learning from the grounded theory perspective espoused by Glaser and Strauss (1967). These studies remained difficult to supervise in that it still seemed necessary to defend the basic approach. In addition, it was difficult to know what academic standards to bring to bear on the thesis.

Programme evaluation during this period was often descriptive as well. Numerous evaluations comprised a straight description of programme activities and descriptions of student learnings gathered in interviews or through the use of open-ended questionnaires.

My personal understanding of learning had begun to change slowly. I began to appreciate the understanding gained through some of the grounded theory research. I accepted the importance of seeing the learning experience through the eyes of the learners. Yet, at the same time, I believed that the positivistic approaches had the value of slowly building our cumulative understanding of human learning. Surely, the careful testing of theories would allow us to understand the conditions under which significant and important learning occurred.

Evaluation of learning as judgement

During the late 1970s, acceptable research paradigms in education began to broaden. Many of the qualitative approaches in all of the social sciences, and in education in particular, were beginning to be accepted. More emphasis was being placed on an analysis of the context of learning and on interpretations of learning from a variety of ideological stances.

During this period, programme evaluation was also in another phase. Evaluation was seen as a process of judgement or decision making. The basic programme evaluation model was to compare data to a set of criteria or values. This judgemental process differed from the first two programme evaluation processes (measurement and description) in that a programme's objectives were subject to evaluation as well as the outcomes of the programme (Wolf, 1979; Stake, 1967).

The programme evaluator was essentially external to the learning process, and there was little linking between what was going on in the theory of programme evaluation and the evolving understanding of learning from the learner's perspective.

Adult educators were trying to bridge the problems of the earlier models of facilitation by constructing learning contracts that would include both the learner's and the teacher's objectives. Effort was directed towards helping the learner develop personal learning goals that were helpful in providing a structure to the learner and which would accommodate external requirements to the learning. Thus, personal goals and external goals were negotiated and the results of the negotiation were set out in a learning contract.

As with earlier approaches there were both strengths and weaknesses to the judgemental approach. On the positive side, learning contracts required the learner to think about problems that he or she wanted to solve and to plan carefully to link learning with the solution of those problems. In addition, the learning contract allowed for planned negotiation between the learner and the facilitator about goals, resources and observable outcomes before the learning activities were undertaken. This planning helped to clarify misunderstandings and avoid activities and results which were unacceptable to either the facilitator or the adult learner. Programme evaluation models could focus on the quality of the learning contract and the extent to which the contract was fulfilled.

On the other hand, there were problems with the learning contract approach as well. Firstly, there was the problem of how to construct a learning contract in an area where the learner had little previous learning. How could one formulate clear, precise and detailed learning goals and objectives in an area where he or she did not know the underlying structures of the information? Secondly, both the learner and the facilitator had to come to terms with the fact that as the learner progressed, objectives might change. Too often the learner felt locked into a contract which contained an earlier, now outdated perspective of the desired learning. Facilitators tried to deal with this conflict by allowing modifications to the contracts, but dissatisfaction remained as too much time was being spent on the unproductive activity of modifying the learning contracts.

In addition, there was the problem that programme evaluation was lodged outside the learner. Thus, there was too little attention paid either to the significance of the learning to the learner, or the changing perspective of the learner. While some attempt was made to encourage reflection on the part of the learner, too often these activities were separate from the assessment of the activity.

Educational research was split into the two main streams of quantitative and qualitative research. There remained some dissertations which were focused on a positivistic attempt to measure outcomes of learning and some dissertations focused on understanding the process of learning by examining the self-reports of individual learners. None of the theses that I saw were working on the issues of blending the external and the internal as were the programme evaluation studies.

Part of the problem was that the two research approaches had underlying assumptions that were antithetical to each other and, as a result, it was not clear how one could approach the gap between the public and the private in learning.

During this period a team of researchers at the Ontario Institute for Studies in Education were working on the shared process evaluation system (SHAPES) (MacKeracher, Davie and Patterson, 1978; Davie, 1983). This system, which was primarily designed to help evaluate community development programmes, provided a systematic process for describing community development programmes and their results. It is not a measuring device, but rather a series of procedures and approaches which helped to assemble the extensive data available about community programmes in a format that can be used by programme evaluators to make judgements about the efficacy of community intervention strategies.

system was most often used by external evaluators, the displays of the data were clear enough that programme participants could make their own judgements about the progress of both their learning and the effectiveness of applying that learning to community problems.

SHAPES relies on interviewing various key informants in the community and collects information about who was involved in a project, a history of the project and a report of project outcomes. The outcomes could be decisions, or individual learnings, although most people report decisions or actions that are seen as a benefit to the community or individuals within it. Although these decisions or actions were almost always preceded by individual learning, the learning was seen as incidental to taking action.

In some ways the results from the SHAPES process are descriptions and the approach belongs to the era of descriptive evaluation. However, programme evaluators using SHAPES typically work with the community to help the community state clearly its values and objectives. A community might identify that participation by a wide variety of citizens would be desirable and, in that case, the SHAPES data can easily be used for an evaluation judgement that is clearly within the evaluation as judgement era. It is also possible that a community might see its goals in terms of a desired economic outcome, such as the development of a hundred new jobs. Again, the information collected could be easily compared with the goal. Both of these examples include a good deal of learning by community participants. In the first instance, the learning might be about techniques of communication and organization. In the later case the learning might well be about sources of funds to establish new businesses or skills in the organization of the business.

While the SHAPES process was designed primarily to track learning in a community development context, it was used in a number of student projects to track, display and understand learning in academic or training settings. The SHAPES system could be used to help facilitators and learners make judgements about learning.

I supervised several theses which used the SHAPES approach. These theses helped us understand something about the necessary structure of community programmes as well as the relationship of community programmes to societal goals such as democratic decision making.

During this period, my understanding of learning developed into a full appreciation of knowledge which resulted from learning being a constructed reality. Information could be taken in by the learner from his or her environment, but knowledge was constructed by the learner by fitting the information into a cognitive structure. This fitting in was controlled by the learner's values and epistemological beliefs. Thus, belatedly I came to accept the major tenet of the qualitative approaches, that reality is constructed.

Evaluation of learning as a description of different agendas

In the past few years, there has been an emphasis in the evaluation literature on what Stake calls responsive evaluation (Stake, 1975), and what Guba and Lincoln have variously called responsive evaluation, naturalistic evaluation

(Guba and Lincoln, 1983) or naturalistic enquiry (Lincoln and Guba, 1985). This approach recognizes that there are different stake-holders in an educational programme. Each stake-holder brings his or her own agenda, and each has a different level of risk involved in the outcomes. The different stake-holders have different (sometimes conflicting) needs and values in the evaluation as well as different meanings for the learning. Each stake-holder places the learning into a unique set of values and thus judges the significance of the learning from his or her own perspective.

The role of the programme evaluator is still external in the sense that he or she is seen as facilitating the different stake-holders in their attempt to clearly state their own agendas. The evaluator's role is seen as one of mediation between the differing views. There seems to be a similarity between this approach to evaluation and ethnography (Spradley, 1979), which describes the setting from the point of view of the inhabitants but which builds an overall perspective out of the constituent parts. However, there is an important difference between the programme evaluation approach and the research of ethnography. In ethnography differences are noted and preserved where important, but there is no compelling reason for judging one perspective right and another wrong. The ethnographical description preserves the difference and reports them as interesting detail. In evaluation, however, it is often important to decide between the values of different stake-holders in order to decide between implementing further intervention strategies or continuing the educational programme.

A problem with responsive or naturalistic evaluation is that it depends heavily on the reflection of the individuals and their ability to know and to be able to state their own agenda. As such it places stress on cognitive learning and ignores what we have been learning about reflective learning, intuitive learning and the learning cycles or phases that learners report going through (Taylor, 1979; Denis, 1979; Fales and Boyd, 1983; *see also* the accounts by Denis and Taylor in Chapters 2 and 14).

Student theses written during this period have continued to expand in response to a wide variety of qualitative approaches. There have been theses that continue to describe learning from the learner's perspective, a phenomenological approach. There have been theses which have focused on the researcher's changing perspective as he or she interprets the data, a hermeneutical approach. In addition, we have theses attempting to build grounded theories of learning. Supervision is becoming easier, or at least more consistent, as the faculty becomes comfortable with the different approaches. There is little need to justify the qualitative approach, although it is still important to explain in detail both the epistemological assumptions and the techniques of the research.

My understanding of learning in this most recent era has continued to develop. I continue to be aware of the complexity of human learning. In every situation I see a buzz of different players with different agendas, belief structures and meanings attached to their learnings. I see the political effects of learning of new skills and concepts. New knowledge brings with it new power. This resulting power fundamentally changes the relationships between participants. It is important not only to recognize the different mind-constructed realities, but also to find ways to help individuals to teach each other about their realities and to construct an intellectual space of shared reality.

Naturalistic evaluation helps us to be sensitive to each other's agendas and provides us with alternate views of reality to consider. This programme evaluation approach stresses the links between learners and the ways in which we may facilitate each other's learning.

Evaluation of learning as learning and communication

As I review my learnings over the past decade, I have come to view programme evaluation as a kind of meta-learning. It is a way of learning about learning. It involves reflecting on what one has learned (or on what others have learned) and communicating our learning as well as the meaning that learning has for us to other stake-holders. Programme evaluation asks us to reflect on what has occurred, what needs to occur, and the meaning of learning which is occurring. It recognizes that the evaluator is also a stake-holder, whether that evaluator is an original stake-holder such as a student or a teacher, or an external agent who becomes a stake-holder by participating in the life of a programme as an evaluator.

Evaluation, then, has three important functions. Firstly, through reflective activities one comes to know what one knows; secondly, one comes to understand the meaning and value of what one knows; and finally, one communicates this new learning to others. The purposes of the communication vary, but it seems that the purposes may be either political (to convince the other to provide some resource) or simply an attempt to support the human community through sharing information of value. Evaluation is a human response to the problems of being alone. It is a communication of the values in life.

Thus, I view programme evaluation as an essential part of the process of learning that goes on within the structure of the community of learners. It is the layer that floats on the complex learnings that are taking place in educational programmes. Through the process of programme evaluation, we reflect on our individual learning and strive to achieve a shared understanding of the world.

There are still some puzzles that remain for me. I am concerned that an idiosyncratic view of learning leads less directly to findings that can be applied to a variety of settings. I am concerned that the negotiation of individual learning agendas may over-emphasize the political power of the already powerful to the detriment of the less powerful.

Nevertheless, an examination of programme evaluation has much to teach us about the predominant conceptions of the meaning and importance of learning. Our understanding of learning and its meaning to adults is changing. We need to step back and see the pattern of those changes and reflect on where we should direct our attention in the future.

It is my hope that my reflections on the developing understanding of the meaning of learning in these past few pages have been helpful to the reader. I believe that this kind of reflection is important if we are to come to a deeper understanding of this complex, pervasive and important phenomenon.

References

Bloom, B S and others (eds) (1956). *Taxonomy of Educational Objectives. Handbook 1: Cognitive Domain.* New York: Longmans.

Davie, L E (1983). Community development in the cooperative extension service. *Journal of the Community Development Society.* 14, 2, 95-106.

Denis, M (1979). Toward the development of a theory of intuitive learning in adults based on a descriptive analysis. (Unpublished doctoral dissertation.) University of Toronto.

Ermarth, M (1978). *Wilhelm Dilthey: the Critique of Historical Reason.* Chicago: University of Chicago Press.

Fales, A and Boyd, E (1983). Reflective learning: key to learning from experience. *Journal of Humanistic Psychology.* 23, 2, 99-117.

Glaser, B G and Strauss, A (1967). *The Discovery of Grounded Theory.* Chicago: Aldine Publishing.

Guba, E G and Lincoln, Y (1983). *Effective Evaluation.* San Francisco: Jossey-Bass.

Guba, E G and Lincoln, Y S (1985). The countenances of fourth-generation evaluation: description, judgment, and negotiation. (Paper presented at American Evaluation Association meeting, November, Toronto, Canada.)

Krathwohl, D R and others (eds) (1964). *Taxonomy of Educational Objectives. Handbook 2: Affective Domain.* New York: David McKay.

Lincoln, Y S and Guba, E G (1985) *Naturalistic Inquiry.* Beverly Hills, California: Sage Publications.

MacKeracher, D, Davie, L and Patterson, T (1978). Evaluation and community development: the SHAPES approach. *Journal of the Community Development Society.* 7, 4-17.

Mager, R (1962). *Preparing Instructional Objectives.* Palo Alto, California: Fearon Press.

Putnam, H (1981). *Reason, Truth and History.* Cambridge: Cambridge University Press.

Smith, J K and Heshusius, L (1986). Closing down the conversation: the end of the quantitative-qualitative debate among educational inquirers. *Educational Researcher.* 15, 1, 4-12.

Spradley, J P (1979). *The Ethnographic Interview.* New York: Holt, Rinehart and Winston.

Stake, R (1967). The countenance of educational evaluation. *Teachers College Record.* 68, 7, 523-40.

Stake, R (1975). *Evaluating the Arts in Education: a Responsive Approach.* Columbus, Ohio: Charles E Merrill.

Taylor, M (1979). Adult learning in an emergent learning group: toward a theory of learning from the learner's perspective. (Unpublished doctoral dissertation, University of Toronto.)

Tyler, R W (1950). *Basic Principles of Curriculum and Instruction.* Chicago: University of Chicago Press.

Wolf, R L (1979). The use of judicial evaluation methods in the formulation of educational policy. *Educational Evaluation and Policy Analysis.* 1, 3, 19-28.

Chapter 16

Naming the Processes

Virginia Griffin
Ontario Institute for Studies in Education

The contributors to this book have named the processes they, as learners, and adults whom they have studied, have experienced in a significant aspect of their learning. The reader might ask, 'Do I have to be skilled in doing qualitative research to name learning processes that I and other learners experience?' My answer, after ten years of intense effort to understand the learning process, is, 'No! You don't need to have training in doing qualitative research to name your own, or others' learning processes, or to help learners with whom you work learn to name their own learning processes.' Maclean (Chapter 10) has drawn parallels between qualitative research and learner-centred teaching. I would add that you have a head start on naming the processes if you are learner-centred in your teaching or learning. And if you have read any of this book, it is likely that you are learner-centred in your approach, or you are somewhat attracted to learner-centredness.

I have been learner-centred in my teaching for many years, and am recognized as such by my students, but I have only recently come to my current understanding of the importance of learners naming their own processes. In my first phase of learning about learning processes, I thought it was my responsibility to name the processes learners would experience – because only I would know what I meant by learning process. Now, I feel my responsibility is to help learners learn how to name their own learning processes and to explore the importance of their doing so.

I now see my development and learning as being in three phases. It has not been an easy journey, and it is not finished. My current phase is full of unanswered questions. But knowing what the questions are is exciting and giving direction to my learning. I can illustrate my development and learning with the following anecdote.

When we started putting this book together, I wondered how I would resolve a great dilemma. I had supervised the theses that form the basis of seven of the chapters in this book. It had been important to these researchers that they did not start their studies with a conceptual framework, but that they waited to see what emerged from what the people studied told them about their experiences. In most cases, they ended up with an analysis in the form of a model or conceptual framework. I thought these were excellent and very useful studies. But I was left with my unresolved dilemma. If these researchers had been unwilling to start with a conceptual framework, how could they or I promote the use of their resulting conceptual framework by other learners or researchers? This is no longer a dilemma for me because I see their work as useful to other learners who may want to: (*1*) broaden their ideas of what is possible to experience; (*2*) find words to express what they have experienced; or (*3*) find the courage to say, 'No, that is not what I have experienced. For me, it has been different.'

That naming the learning processes is of value to many learners and empowering to them is not only something I have experienced in myself, and observed in students with whom I work, but was described by Boyd and Fales (1983) as a finding of a number of studies they did with reflective learners. They report that highly effective reflective learners had not thought about how they reflected; once they became aware of their natural processes they named those processes – a significant aid in their use of reflective learning. They also found they had more control over their learning, and also experienced a surge of energy in their learning.

In the remainder of this chapter, I will first discuss the concept of 'process', ways it is often used in adult learning, and then what I mean when I use it. I will then present examples and characteristics of learning processes. Following these examples and characteristics, I will discuss phases I have gone through in understanding and enlarging this concept. I will mention how I have used the idea in my teaching in each phase, including my dreams and failures in each. In addition, I will highlight how research has been generated in each phase and, in turn, informed the work.

Because my current phase is to encourage learners to name their own processes, I will discuss ways of helping learners to do this naming.

What is a process?

So what is the concept? *Process* is a word, commonly used in adult learning, often in many different ways and with different meanings. We process a structured exercise – meaning we debrief and review what we have learned. We lead a class through a particular activity or method, and call it a 'process'. We talk about the learning 'process', meaning the stages of learning within any particular approach to learning or teaching. We analyse the group process to understand, among many qualities, the development of group norms, relationships within the group, sources of leadership and power within the group, and stages the group goes through. Cognitive psychologists study mental processes or thought processes. Wittrock (1986, p 297) summarizes research on student thought processes of perceptions, expectations, attentional processes, motivations, attributions, memories, generations, understandings, beliefs, attitudes, learning strategies and meta-cognitive processes.

I have been working on building, understanding and teaching a new use of the word 'process'. I have signalled its difference by calling it 'basic learning processes'. Basic learning processes are inner happenings or experiences the learner has when engaged in learning. These inner happenings will occur, whether the learner is in a group, with a friend, or alone; when reading a book, listening to a lecture, or reflecting on his or her own experience.

In these chapters, many of the preceding authors have given examples of what I mean by processes. Denis reports a list of 18 processes of intuitive learning (Chapter 2) and Keane (Chapter 7) lists three learning processes:

(1) developing autonomy in searching;
(2) trusting the harmony of the whole self;
(3) learning how to learn more effectively.

He then elaborates on several aspects of each of these processes, including how one learner became empowered as he learned to look for patterns in his behaviour, and came to recognize what type of help was useful to him.

Examples of learning processes can be found in each of the other chapters, although they may not be labelled as such. Rather than form a synthesis of all of these processes, I will tell you about my efforts to understand and use the concept of processes. These efforts have been grounded in graduate courses focused on adult learning and facilitating. Students in these courses usually have had experience in facilitating adult learning. This, plus the fact that they have chosen to study at OISE, are the only factors they have in common. They have taught in different settings; the subjects they have taught are extremely diverse; and the learners with whom they have worked are as diverse as the adults in the human species. The size of my classes has ranged from 8 to 35, usually averaging about 23.

The purpose of the course is to help students to be better facilitators by becoming aware of (and perhaps changing) their perspectives of self and others, of learning, of knowledge and of facilitating; becoming aware of their own and others' learning processes; trying out and evaluating procedures to help learners to experience those processes; and putting all of these ideas and skills together in a pattern suitable to them and the context in which they work.

Early in the first phase of my learning about processes, I created a list of processes I was aware learners were experiencing. I had observed them and listened carefully to them.

One version of this list follows, as a further illustration of what I mean by learning processes:

(A) maintaining self-esteem;
(B) becoming increasingly responsible for own learning;
(C) finding own direction for learning;
(D) investing energy, involving and committing oneself;
(E) dealing with personal energy ebb and flow;
(F) relating to others;
(G) finding personal meaning in content and experiences;
(H) noticing, clarifying, consolidating, synthesizing new learning;
(I) testing new ideas, skills, behaviour, ways of being;
(J) asking for, using feedback;
(K) planning the uses of new learning in other situations;
(L) finding and accepting satisfactions, joys, excitement in learning.

Characteristics of processes

The following are characteristics I use in defining a process:

(1) It is a verb. It denotes action.

(2) The action is within the learner. A learning process is a happening within the learner.

(3) A process happens over time. Insights or intuitions may seem to occur instantaneously, but they too take time. They take time for preparing yourself for the insight or intuition to occur. Examination of the above list will reveal that the wording of each process allows for development over time. In past courses, we discovered that the time within a course when a process became relevant to learners varied greatly. The length of time any one learner gave attention to any of these processes varied too. I have asked learners to chart the importance of each of these processes for them individually over a 13-week course; this showed that each process was experienced over a period of time. What we could not discover in our charting was a common pattern of which processes emerged, when, and for how long.

I am constantly reminded of the one generalization I could make from these chartings – summed up in a poem by Piet Hein (1966, p 5):

T.T.T.

Put up in a place
Where it's easy to see
the cryptic admonishment
of T.T.T.

When you feel how depressingly
slowly you climb
it's well to remember that
Things Take Time.

(4) Only the learner knows what he is experiencing. An observer cannot know what the learner is experiencing. I am always amazed after leading students in a class's first session of getting acquainted with one another, to hear the variety of processes they have experienced while the entire group has been going through the same activity. The variety often includes getting acquainted with others, building trust, finding a direction for learning, planning for using new learning in other places, learning about themselves as learners (for example, what helps them to be relaxed in a new situation). An observer would think they are all doing the same thing! We have to ask to know what is really going on.

I remember vividly an experience in a class last spring. Three of us were leading a session on the topic of spirituality and adult learning/teaching. After one exercise we suggested individuals sit quietly to reflect. They met in pairs to share insights, and then we met in a total group. There was such a silence during the 'private time' and at the beginning of the 'pairs'; I was afraid the exercise had produced nothing, participants had found it meaningless, or they were bored or lost. When we met in the total group, I learned how wrong I had been: the intense quiet had meant some deep and very significant thinking was occurring! I was relieved to have been wrong.

Advantages of using the learning process idea

In the beginning of working with the idea of a learning process, I thought it would provide a clear path for the teacher to follow in planning a learning event and a clear way to communicate with learners about what the teacher was planning and, therefore, what was expected of the learners.

For example, I tried to begin a course with processes (F) (relating to others) and (A) (maintaining self-esteem). Next came the beginning of process (B) (becoming increasingly responsible for my own learning) which became necessary because of the expectations that each learner work on process (C) (finding own direction for learning).

I am now aware of more significant advantages of the learning process, which are as follows:

(1) The use of the learning process idea enables the learner to feel valued because what he or she is experiencing matters. Very often, adult learners have been asked what they have learned (especially in terms of what the teacher hoped), not what they have experienced while trying to learn it.

(2) It keeps the teacher focused on what the learners are experiencing, more than on what the teacher is doing. For me, this has been a way to make operational a maxim Roby Kidd often repeated in the early days of the life of our department: 'The work of this department is more about learning than it is about teaching.'

(3) It leads to a revelation among learners that not everyone learns the same way. Discussions of the variety of processes experienced for a given activity reveal differences in learning styles and ways other people see the world.

(4) It helps to prevent impatience and expectation of immediate results. If learners or teachers recognize that a particular process has its own developmental flow, then they do not expect it can be accomplished completely within a short time span.

(5) If a learner has become aware of a learning process experienced in one learning event, he or she is likely to transfer that learning process to other learning events when it is appropriate. This transfer can occur, even though the content areas differ in the two learning events. If this can happen, learners have more control over their learning, and can be more effective learners.

Phases I have experienced in my learning

In retrospect, I realize that I have gone through several phases or stages in my understanding or development of my work with the concept of learning processes. I am calling them phases rather than stages, because the dividing lines between them are not sharp; some qualities from phase one still exist in phase three.

Again, I emphasize that only in retrospect do I recognize this emerging story. It was not developed on the basis of any planning. It is more a story of how an idea can grow and develop out of disappointment and doubt. It is a story that has not reached an ending yet. I am trusting that as I learn and grow, and continue to work with the ideas, they will blossom more fully.

Phase one: the compassionate prescriptive phase

In the beginning, I drew on my own experience of listening carefully to students in groups and as individuals as they experienced my courses, emphasizing group and individual decision-making, learning from experience as well as literature in our field. Students had generally found my courses to be a new kind of learning experience (self-directed learning and experiential learning were still relatively unfamiliar in adult education as well as in Canadian universities). So students had many struggles and frustrations to bring to my attention.

From this background, I tried to formulate statements of learning processes that were commonly shared. In the next few courses I taught, I introduced the idea and asked students to tell me other processes they had experienced that were not on my list. I built a more extensive list and tried to plan my courses around these processes which I thought all students should experience. There was compassion present because I knew these experiences on the list were ones that previous students had struggled with and found frustrating, as well as ones they had found useful in relieving or avoiding frustration. I only now see the prescriptiveness of these lists and the way I used them. I innocently told my students that there were probably additional processes they would experience, and then proceeded to explain the agenda for the class in terms of 'my' processes I had planned they would experience that day. I used a number of different written evaluation forms on which they could tell me how far they had moved toward completing these learning processes, and what more they needed to experience. I dreamed of finding commonly experienced processes and a common pattern or sequencing of attention to these processes. I never realized this dream: I attributed this failure to my lack of pushing hard enough to gather data and my inability to detect a pattern from the limited data I had. The data were limited because I sensed that students generally were not excited by the idea of processes, and even though I continued to find new ways to introduce the concept in classes and involve students in reflecting on their processes (that is, my list of them), I lacked sufficient confidence in the idea to make it work. I never considered that the idea was flawed.

Phase two happened because it happened – not because I saw a flaw in the prescriptiveness of phase one. Yet before I move on to phase two, I should mention research that was generated by phase one, and which fed back additional processes into 'my' list. Some students found the concept of learning processes very useful and built their theses around one of the processes in particular, or the general idea of trying to understand learning from the learner's perspective. Some have reported these understandings in terms of learning processes. Many of these theses are reported in this book. (See chapters by Melamed, Denis, Davies, Griffith, Keane, Taylor, and MacLean. Melamed's and Keane's theses were done when I was in phase two.)

Phase two: the loosening and holistic expansion phase

Frustrated by a class group that was reluctant to list the processes they had experienced during the course, even though it had been a very creative and thoughtful group, I decided to work with the processes I had experienced as a learner in the course. I threw out all previous lists, and 'grounded' my list solely on what I had experienced during the previous three months of class sessions. I had a list of processes that was too long and too specific to be useful to anyone else. So I began to group the processes and found that they could be grouped into five categories:

(1) those related to rational thinking;
(2) those related to intuition, the right brain, and the subconscious (what Bob Samples, 1979, calls the metaphoric mind);
(3) those dealing with relationships in the group and learning from and with others;
(4) those related to emotions and using them to generate learning; and
(5) those related to bodily energies, tensions and using those awarenesses to enable learning.

In the next courses, I was told repeatedly that one area was missing – the spiritual. I added that area, and have since spent several years trying to understand what this spiritual area means to adult learners, teachers of adults, and to me – both as a learner and a teacher. These categories, in shorthand usage, are called: (1) rational mind; (2) metaphoric mind; (3) relational; (4) emotional; (5) physical; and (6) spiritual. Because these areas represent clusters of capabilities that we, as humans, have that we can use to help us learn. I have called them 'capabilities' (Griffin, forthcoming). Because they encompass the whole person, I have labelled this phase the holistic expansion phase. I will discuss the second characteristic of this phase, the 'loosening' quality, later in this section.

An early hope I had was that we would be able to develop a list of specific sub-processes for each of the six areas or capabilities. Marge Denis had done that years earlier for one aspect of the metaphoric mind – intuition (see Chapter 2). This seemed too large a project for course work and too difficult to do until we had reached an advanced level of experiencing a particular capability, so we have papers in which individuals have begun explorations of their experiences in emotional, relational, metaphoric and spiritual capabilities. A thesis is under way in which the researcher is exploring relational learning in greater depth. In my teaching, I find that students are much more excited about the possibilities of discovering and using capabilities they were unaware of having, or knew they had but had never used in 'legitimate' learning events or academic courses.

One of my functions in the course is to help students experience use of all of the capabilities as we conduct sessions in the course. We are discovering or creating activities or procedures that stimulate the use of *each* of the capabilities for learning tasks – processes such as 'finding a personal direction for learning'. Each capability, when stimulated, leads to a different and enriched outcome.

For example, students who first identify with their rational mind what they want to work on in the course find that they become clearer and broader in their thinking about that goal, once they have opportunities to talk with other students about it. Opportunities to use their metaphoric mind often leads them to alter their learning goals to include some aspect of personal growth that, ultimately, would help them to be better teachers/facilitators. Eventually, we discuss each of the capabilities we have experienced; the discussion generally leads to observations about how they are overlapping, or are integrated in each method or procedure used in the course.

We are also learning that we have to question our assumptions about the ways learners experience these procedures. For example, the physical capability process of relaxing is an important introduction to many procedures leading to use of the metaphoric mind and spirituality capability. In one guided imagery session in which the guide suggested that participants imagine themselves in a quiet forest or woods (which could be relaxing for most people), we found one participant who said that that kind of suggestion made her very tense; for her, relaxation comes from being on a busy urban street corner. This discovery has led us to allow participants in such relaxation exercises to make their own choice of peaceful, relaxing places to imagine themselves being in. This small example suggests larger assumptions that need to be tested via systematic research: for example, what kind of learning can be helped by relaxation experiences, how deep does the relaxation need to be, and at what point in the learning experience is it most likely to be helpful? And are people with different learning styles affected differently? Even these simple-sounding questions could lead to a dozen research projects. And they only illustrate how complex adult learning is and how little we really know about it.

In this section I have described the holistic expansion aspect of the phase. Now I want to make the loosening characteristic of the phase explicit because it clearly leads into my third phase.

Because the six areas of capabilities opened so many possibilities of processes for people to experience, I loosened completely the idea of prescribing processes they should experience, and have allowed them freedom to choose their own focus for class work and written assignments (after some suggestions from me).

This 'loosening' on my part has resulted, not in less attention to process, but to very rewarding and valuable work on the part of students (far beyond my suggestions!) in naming their own processes experienced, which now brings us to phase three which builds on and includes much of phase two.

Phase three: naming the process

In December of 1984, I asked a class in their final session to create a list naming the learning processes they had experienced. I present the list as examples of what processes learners can name:

- making meaning;
- creating knowledge;
- expanding alertness;

– releasing creativity;
– creating energy;
– learning from other people's stories;
– learning from all six capabilities;
– rewriting the dictionary in adult terms;
– getting acquainted;
– becoming comfortable with each other;
– developing trust – in self, in some others, in the group, in the process;
– watching modelling;
– seeing congruence;
– experiencing interdependence;
– being aware of self as a learner;
– learning with a partner;
– reflecting on self;
– discovering the power of self-reflection;
– validating oneself;
– listening on all levels, to ourselves and as a group;
– unlearning;
– questioning assumptions and ideas;
– thawing and refreezing into another shape;
– reframing with new assumptions;
– developing a preference to work in a large group;
– developing the ability to take risks;
– being able to experience;
– identifying and becoming comfortable with learning style;
– expanding the awareness of learning;
– learning what questions will be useful to us;
– learning the value of metaphor;
– making discoveries about oneself and the way one learns;
– becoming aware of assumptions and deciding what to do;
– changing the past;
– choosing what is important and distinguishing what is important;
– doing some analysis of what is important;
– developing responsibility for one's own learning;
– accepting help;
– developing a greater appreciation of the facilitator's role;
– learning how to let go, facilitating self out of a role.

This list of 40 processes came from a group of 23 people; the list could have been longer, but I stopped the exercise because of time limits. This is not a list of what they learned in the course, but of processes they experienced and recalled on the last day of class (but these processes are bound to reflect some of the learning that occurred). Some of the processes were ones we had talked about or that appeared on my earlier phase lists; most of them, however, were experiences they named in their own way, and thus were their own.

It was no longer important to me that I provide students with a short list of memorable processes in a clever pattern or diagram that would guide them throughout their professional careers (such a pattern, I discovered, would serve only my ego needs). What was important was that they were able to extract from their experiences some short phrases that would remind them of the essence of their experience and could, thereby, use these processes in other learning events in the future.

Important advantages of learners naming the processes

Earlier in this chapter, I listed five advantages of using the concept of processes. I have observed each of these advantages as still evident when learners are naming their own processes. Boyd and Fales, in the work cited earlier, give impressive testimony to the value to learners of naming their own processes. Lee Davies (Chapter 3) mentions the importance of his interviews to learners: '. . . the interview provided the learners with opportunities to reflect on their learning experience. As a result, new insights, new understanding and an ability to make sense of the experience developed . . .' (p 41). Gwyneth Griffith (Chapter 4) points out how empowering it is to name one's gifts and begin to use them. I equate naming one's learning processes with naming one's gifts, and have observed the empowerment that learners experience in this naming. To all of these observations I can add my own experience, which has been powerful to me. The experience to which I refer is that of coming to understand the three phases of my learning about processes as I have described them here. Because I had lived these ten years of effort, one could assume that I knew what my learning was like. But because I chose to write about these phases, I had to find words to describe this experience. And in finding the words I found meanings I had not recognized.

More extensive research is needed on what learners experience when they name their learning processes. There may be significant differences in the value of such experience related to learning styles, kinds of learning and other factors.

Learning the process of naming the process

It is clear to me now that adults are not equally skilful in naming their own learning process. We need to learn the process of naming our processes. Teachers/facilitators can help adults in this learning. Learners need help in developing a vocabulary, or finding the words, to describe their experiences. We have built up an extensive resource file of term papers and other articles. Often, a student has come to me and said, 'I just read ————'s paper. She has put into words exactly what I have been experiencing. It is so nice to know others have felt what I've been feeling, and that there is a name for it. It is so exciting.' Authors of chapters in this book have presented work based on the learning processes of themselves and others. These and similar works need to be available for learners to read to expand their awareness of what is possible, to find suitable words and to have a framework into which to fit these processes. At the same time, they need to know that their own experiences will probably differ in some important ways from anything they read.

This insight was made clear to me by a comment Pat Pender (1984) made in her thesis. She was comparing her experience of mothering a troubled son with the stages in Mezirow's description of perspective transformation (1981). She said, when she read Mezirow's steps in perspective transformation that it made sense to her and that she could see how they applied in the lives of friends, but that her own experience was far more complex – it could not adequately be described by his ten steps.

Another problem which many people have with the expectation of naming their own processes is an issue of timing. If they attempt to name an experience too early, they may miss the fullness and richness of it and thus, having misnamed it, they rob it of its vigour and it dies. If we are pressured to name something before we have had time to reflect on it and let our understanding of it grow, we are apt to give it a superficial name or 'dig in our heels' and resist the expectation. Another aspect of the issue of timing is the difficulty of experiencing something fully, and trying to describe it at the same time. Attempting to do both at once can hinder learning. Naming the processes can best be done if time for reflection is allowed between the experience and the naming. Many individuals need time to reflect alone and to talk with a supportive learning partner (Robinson, *et al.*, 1985). In a course such as those I teach, naming the processes, with prior time for reflection and conversation with a learning partner, can be done at the end of a class session, at the end of the course or several weeks after the course. Some individuals need a year or more to find the meaning of a course for them. Their 'naming' at the end of the course will be quite different from what it will be a year or so later. It is very difficult to describe the processes of a significant life change while we are in the middle of the change. We have to learn to give ourselves permission to say, 'This is where I am now; the transition is not complete yet. In another year or so I may see things quite differently.' I appreciate that time is needed when I think about the ten years I took to reach my current understanding of the concept of learning processes.

A skill that can be learned that will help learners learn to experience the learning activity and 'watch themselves' learning at the same time is called 'detachment' by Laurie and Tucker (1978, pp 43-5). In their training exercise they enable the learner to observe and describe what he is experiencing, but not to judge himself or others. In psychosynthesis, a closely related concept (of stepping outside a sub-personality and observing it) is called 'disidentification' (Ferrucci, 1982, pp 49-50).

Some adults are accustomed to focusing on what is outside themselves, including what they learn. Learning is, to them, finding better ways to manipulate things, people and events outside themselves. Important learning skills are such as those identified by Squires (1982), common in many universities: reading, note-taking, organizing information, essay writing, working alone, memorizing, and working in groups. They deal primarily with what Mezirow calls the instrumental learning domain (Mezirow, 1985), and are impatient with self-awareness and personal growth as learning in their lives. I think people such as these can learn to be aware of their learning processes, but we will have to help them to be aware, using terms that have meaning to them. The examples I have given here and the learning described in this book involve more awareness and acceptance of personal growth. This occurs in a social, economic, political or historical context, which we should not ignore. We need to be challenged to examine the processes we name for ourselves to uncover the assumptions that underlie them, to see how they reflect the limitations of our awareness, our training, our past experience.

We all bring strengths and limitations in our underlying assumptions – whether they are degrees of awareness and appreciation of self, or results of specific training, such as someone who has worked with Gibb (1978) seeing her processes in terms of trust, or someone thoroughly trained in group dynamics seeing her learning processes as group processes.

It is important that we understand our own perspective or the framework in which we place things, so that we can decide if we wish to change some of it. It is difficult to know we have a particular perspective until we meet someone whose perspective is totally different. We are like a fish who has no idea of what water is because it has never known anything else.

Without a new framework or an awareness of our old, assumed, unquestioned framework, we could experience what one student described: '. . . because I lacked a framework within which to place my experience, I ended up with a muddle of acontextual methods and content-less processes. In short, a void.' Because I, too, feel a need for a framework, I continue to use the framework of capabilities that emerged in phase two. But I try to remain open to expanding the elaboration of each of them or to adding new capabilities. I am also open to new discoveries in this third phase of learners naming the processes.

In spite of all the assertions I have made here, based on my observations and experience, there are still many unanswered questions. Can all learners, at all levels of learning, learn to name their learning processes? Will they find it useful to do so? What will it add to their learning and their lives? Are those who write personal journals as effective in doing it as those who talk everything over with learning partners? Is knowing one way of thinking of processes (such as group process) a hindrance or a help in naming learning processes? What other factors are related to differential effects of timing? For example, does an end-of-course naming lead to different types of learning outcomes in courses of different content?

I am happy that I have reached the understanding of learning processes that I have. I do not know where the path will lead in the future. The stance I am taking now is more congruent with my philosophy of facilitating and learning. What processes would I name from my experience? Some of the main ones I see now are persevering with the core of an idea, listening to others' reactions and use of the idea, letting the idea rest until I have developed in other areas of my life, returning to the idea and integrating new life understandings with it. One of my favourite quotes is relevant here: 'We don't think our way into a new kind of living: we live our way into a new kind of thinking.' (Palmer, 1980, p 60.)

For me, this way of living that has led to a new kind of thinking is well described by Hoff as the Pooh Way (Hoff, 1982).

> Things just happen in the right way, at the right time. At least they do when you *let* them, when you work *with* circumstances instead of saying, 'this isn't supposed

to be happening this way', and trying hard to make it happen some other way. If you're in tune with The Way Things Work, then they work the way they need to, no matter what you may think about it at the time. Later on, you can look back and say, 'Oh, now I understand. That had to happen so that *those* could happen, and those had to happen in order for *this* to happen . . .' Then you realize that, even if you'd tried to make it all turn out perfectly, you couldn't have done better, and if you'd *really* tried, you would have made a mess of the whole thing.

References

Boyd, E M and Fales, A W (1983). Reflective learning: key to learning from experience. *Journal of Humanistic Psychology.* Spring, 1983, 23, 2, 99-117.

Ferrucci, P (1982). *What We May Be: Techniques for Psychological and Spiritual Growth Through Psychosynthesis.* Los Angeles: J P Tarcher.

Gibb, J (1978). *Trust: a New View of Personal and Organizational Development.* La Jolla, California: Omicron.

Griffin, V R (forthcoming). Holistic learning/teaching in adult education: would you play a one-string guitar? In: J Draper and T Stein (eds). *The Craft of Teaching Adults.* Toronto: Department of Adult Education, Ontario Institute for Studies in Education.

Hein, P (1966). *Grooks.* Cambridge, Massachusetts: MIT Press.

Hoff, B (1982). *The Tao of Pooh.* New York: E P Dutton.

Laurie, S G and Tucker, M J (1978). *Centering: a Guide to Inner Growth.* New York: Destiny Books.

Mezirow, J (1981). A critical theory of adult learning and education. *Adult Education.* 32, 1, 3-24.

Mezirow, J (1985). A critical theory of self-directed learning. In: S Brookfield (ed). *Self-Directed Learning: from Theory to Practice.* New Directions for Continuing Education No 25. San Francisco: Jossey-Bass, 17-30.

Palmer, P J (1980). *The Promise of Paradox.* Notre Dame, Indiana: Ave Maria Press.

Pender, P A (1984). Transcendent learning as an aspect of the experience of changing: the discovery of the bitch goddess. (Unpublished MA thesis.) Toronto: University of Toronto.

Robinson, J, Saberton, S and Griffin, V R (1985). *Learning Partnerships: Interdependent Learning in Adult Education.* Toronto: Department of Adult Education, OISE.

Samples, R (1979). *The Metaphoric Mind.* Don Mills, Ontario: Addison-Wesley.

Squires, G (1982). *Learning to Learn.* Newland Papers No 6. Department of Adult Education, University of Hull.

Wittrock, M C (1986). Student though processes. In: Wittrock, M C (ed) *Handbook of Research on Teaching.* (Third edition). New York: Macmillan, 297-314.

Chapter 17

A Facilitator's View of Adult Learning

David Boud
University of New South Wales

Introduction

Whenever I have to face a new group of learners or when people ask me to help them with their learning project, I often think, 'What do I have to offer them?' I am presumably helping their learning in some fashion, but what is it that I can effectively do to assist them? If I see myself as a teacher then the question becomes much easier to answer. I can provide information, give reading lists, make plans for their learning tasks, find ways of assessing their learning and generally direct, to a greater or lesser extent, their work. However, if I see myself as a facilitator of learning rather than as a teacher, what does that imply?

For some people there is no difference at all: teachers are or should be facilitators of learning and they should focus on what students need to learn, not what they, the teachers, want to teach. I have no difficulty with accepting this at face value: of course, teachers should be facilitators of learning and they should take account of learners' needs. But I have the uneasy feeling that what these people are saying about the teaching role does not represent the full range of what is possible in the facilitation of learning. Accepting the role of 'teacher' involves accepting a set of values and expectations which constrain as well as give meaning to the teacher's tasks. These values are rooted in a historical and social context of what teaching is and what a teacher does, and all of us from our experiences of schooling carry powerful memories and expectations of what teachers do and how they want us to relate to them. As adult learners these images can readily get in the way of our being able to use teachers effectively for our own learning projects. As facilitators of the learning of adults these same expectations get in the way, and we can easily fall into the trap of modelling ourselves on others who were effective teachers for us at a different time and in different circumstances from those in which we find ourselves at present.

I do not think it is very fruitful to pursue a contrast between teachers and facilitators even though it has been my subjective starting point in thinking about this issue. Like the supposed differences between the learning of adults and children I suspect that differences between teachers and facilitators are proposed more as a rhetorical device to highlight the need to think carefully about the adult learning than a matter which has sufficient import to concern us. There are differences in how I act when I think of myself as a teacher and as a facilitator but this probably owes more to my own socialization than to any intrinsic difference between the two notions.

Before proceeding any further I want to comment on my use of the term 'facilitator'. I realize that some people do not like it: for them it has connotations of therapy or encounter groups or of manipulation; or, for Brookfield (1986), of an over-emphasis on student centredness and democracy! Although I accept that some will be discomforted by my use of this term, I am unable to identify any better one to portray my intentions. To me a facilitator is anyone who helps others to learn: this can be in a formal educational setting or an informal activity between friends and colleagues. It goes beyond the conventional teaching role into the wide and varied contexts in which adult learning takes place. Facilitation implies neither a cosy acceptance of learners' present conceptions of their needs, nor attempts to raise critical consciousness when that is quite clearly not what is desired. It is multi-faceted and flexible, and its nature is dependent on the context in which it occurs.

My task in this chapter is to attempt to map some of the characteristics of facilitating adult learning while keeping in mind the learners' perspective which we have considered throughout the book. Facilitators are adult learners too, and I wish in this chapter to present some of the ideas which have helped me to make sense of my role as a facilitator of learning. Most of my background is in working with teachers in post-secondary education, students (mostly postgraduate), and other people who are involved in adult education in its many forms. I teach courses on adult learning so I feel under an obligation to apply my knowledge of this area to how I treat the students who enrol. This is one particular context, and I am aware that it places constraints on my role as a facilitator which may not be present in other situations. The context always constrains and, at the same time, provides opportunities for learning; for example, the assessment system in any institution provides limits on what can be done by a facilitator who is also a representative of the system, but it also provides opportunities, if properly exploited, for learners to become aware of their learning (*see*, for example, Boud, 1986, on the use of self-assessment).

Conceptions of adult learning

It is difficult to think about facilitation independently of the kind of learning which is being facilitated and of how that learning is conceived by those engaged in it. During my career I have been influenced by four major traditions in adult learning, and I think it is useful to examine these before looking at how these inform facilitation. Although each tradition holds sway over a different domain of adult learning, it can be productive to set these approaches alongside one another to notice both their commonalities and their differences of emphasis.

(1) Training and efficiency in learning

The view of adult learning which probably has the most extensive research base, and which is not represented in this book for this very reason, is that which treats teaching and learning as though they comprised only a technology. Once a learner has decided to study a particular topic or to learn new skills, the aim of practitioners of this approach is to make this task as straightforward as possible and to ensure that all learning is directed efficiently towards this end. It is an approach which has arisen from the earlier approaches of programmed learning and industrial training and draws upon research on learning from a neo-behaviourist or cognitive psychology standpoint.

Assessments of needs are undertaken from the point of view of the tasks learners are expected to perform and the competencies successful learners should exhibit. Tasks are analysed in great detail and the characteristics and prior skills of learners are assessed; programmes are systematically designed to take account of the structure of knowledge and skills in the area and the motivation and conceptual framework of the expected learners. Programmes are tested on individuals representative of the total population of learners, and the results of this developmental testing are fed back into the design to improve its effectiveness. Attempts are made to allow learners as much flexibility as possible within the overall highly structured programme, but constraints of time and cost often limit this. Major figures in this tradition are Mager (1972; 1975), Davies (1971; 1976) and Gagné (1970; 1974). This approach can be characterized as *freedom from distraction in learning*; it is in many ways a highly effective mode of traditional authoritative teaching.

Effective facilitation of learning in this tradition means being able to predict the full range of possible responses of learners and having suitable activities planned in advance for each possibility. Facilitators collect feedback to help modify the programme and respond to any difficulties by helping learners to adapt to what has been provided; they are essentially managers of the programme.

In adult learning this approach is successful when learning goals are clear, when tasks can be readily analysed, and when there is a commitment on the part of both the programme designer and the learner to the learning activities. These factors are most often found in commercial and industrial training contexts, skill development in sports and those areas where tasks are complex and hierarchical. Although criticisms can be made that learners are treated as intelligent machines, there are areas of learning where this approach is appropriate for at least part of the time.

(2) Self-directed learning and the andragogy school

Perhaps the approach which has had the most impact in recent years on the mainstream of adult education is that which has been promoted by Malcolm Knowles (1975; 1980; 1984a; 1984b), using the term 'andragogy': the art and science of teaching adults. This approach places the unique goals of individual learners as central in the learning process and provides a structure to assist learners to achieve their own ends. This structure may have many forms but typically it takes account of both the necessary supportive interpersonal climate for learning and the need for learners to clarify their own goals, plan programmes drawing on the resources that are available, obtain evidence of their achievement and make judgements about the degree of success of their self-directed programme.

The role of the facilitator is to help the learner define his or her own needs and to respond to them. The facilitator is a resource person who can be drawn upon as needed. The facilitator is not primarily a source of knowledge about the learner-defined task, but someone who can provide support and assist learners to find their ways through the learning process. One widely used device which is used to do this is the learning contract (Knowles, 1986). In a learning contract goals and plans are formalized, ways of indicating achievement of the goals are identified in advance of the main learning activities, and the criteria for evaluation of the success of the activity are made explicit. After discussion, the learner and the facilitator agree to a contract in which these aspects are outlined; thereafter both parties conform to whatever obligations they are committed to. Knowles argues that this is not as rigid as it appears as he believes that contracts should in principle be continuously renegotiable (1975).

This approach can be characterized as freedom from the restrictions of teachers or as *freedom as learners.* In many ways this approach derives from a reaction against that traditional teaching which places the learner in the position of responding to what a teacher provides. Knowles's emphasis on learners being proactive places them and their needs in a central position, with 'teachers' reacting to them. However, when learning contracts are used in formal education, facilitators take on some of the evaluative roles of traditional teachers when they give their approval to a contract.

The self-directed learning approach appears to be best suited to situations in which learners are able to identify and articulate their own learning goals and in which they have resources available. The facilitator acts as a resource and guide and provides the learner with a protected environment within which exploration can take place. No emphasis is placed on questioning this environment, and control over the potential excesses of learner ambition is provided by the contractual nature of the exercise. Self-directed learning as exemplified by Knowles and his contractual approaches has therefore proved suitable for use in formal educational settings where the limitations of the model of total control have been recognized and where concerns about full learner control exist. Although Knowles himself stresses the importance of a wide range of approaches to adult learning, it is the learning contract which has received the greatest attention.

(3) Learner-centred education and the humanistic educators

A tradition which has had some influence on Knowles, but which has characteristics of its own, is that exemplified by the work of the humanistic educators of whom the most influential is Carl Rogers (1961; 1970; 1983). Rogers has articulated an approach to learning and its facilitation (derived from his earlier work in client-centred therapy) which focuses on learners' personal needs, but which recognizes that it is often difficult for learners to acknowledge and express their needs. They are frequently constrained by their own early negative experiences of learning and they need the context of a highly supportive and respectful environment to be able to recognize their needs and begin to explore them. This environment can be provided in a group by a non-directive facilitator who exhibits a total acceptance of the learners, showing them what Rogers terms 'unconditional positive regard'. Within this context, each learner will be valued, will respect his or her own thinking and will be able to draw upon others for assistance in learning tasks. The same principles also hold true in one-to-one situations.

Rogers is adamant about the need to be totally non-directive. However, other practitioners in the human growth movement use a variety of specific techniques and strategies designed to help learners become aware of their own internal constraints and the sources of their perceptions of their limitations (for example, Brown, 1976; Heron, 1973; Perls, 1969; Schutz, 1975). They usually share a commitment to the need to be non-directive about what learners choose to examine and they also emphasize the necessity for the facilitator to behave authentically, but they may be more interventionist about the process which they use to bring learners to an awareness of their own potential and capabilities.

Exemplars of this tradition also place great importance on responding to the full range of attitudes, values, emotions and generally the non-cognitive aspects of individuals' behaviour. They believe that learning must involve the whole person, not just the intellect, and they emphasize affective goals. They recognize that emotions and feelings can severely inhibit learning of all kinds and they aim to liberate learners from their own inner compulsions and inappropriate behaviour. They allow them, in Rogers's famous phrase, *freedom to learn.*

In the adult education context Brockett (1983) believes that the practices of facilitators of this persuasion who emphasize interpersonal relating skills should be used in the facilitation of *all* forms of self-directed learning. He has outlined the roles and skills of practitioners of this approach, drawing extensively on Egan's (1975) model for helping skills training where 'an initial emphasis on development of the helper-client relationship eventually shifts towards taking action to resolve the "problem" '. The skills he identifies as essential for facilitators are those of being able to give one's full attention to the learner, responding in a way that helps the learner explore his or her behaviour, and helping the learner to understand his or her 'problem'. Key attributes of facilitators are empathy, respect for learners, genuineness and concreteness. While this sounds very mechanistic, in practice it is not intended to be, and learners should emerge with a much greater appreciation of what they need to do.

The strengths of approaches in this tradition are the recognition of the importance of understanding and appreciating individuals and assisting them to find their own way through their learning problems. It differs from the andragogy school as articulated by Knowles in the emphasis which is placed on individuals' internal barriers to learning.

(4) Critical pedagogy and social action

The three traditions discussed above treat learning as an individual phenomenon: the view is taken that while the social and physical environment can constrain learning, it is ultimately up to individuals to overcome adversity for themselves and arrive at a better understanding of the world and their place in it. Proponents of critical pedagogy would claim that theirs is not just another perspective on adult learning, but a shift in ideology away from one based on functionalism and the importance of the individual to one based on dialectics and collective action. In this view learning is embedded in a historical, social and material context. Learners must seek to understand this and transcend the constraints it places on them in order to create an understanding which liberates both themselves and their fellow learners. Learning can never be value-free: it must either work towards supporting the status quo or undermining it and replacing it with something which represents a better form of society.

Most proponents of this view have based their views on analyses of learning in societies with great inequalities between classes where it is impossible to adopt a neutral stance: indeed they would reject the notion of neutrality. They claim that learning always serves either to limit people to their current function in society or to lead them to change it: learners must be led to this recognition as an integral part of any educational process. Facilitators need to understand this basic premise and begin their task by assisting learners to appreciate their position in society and how this constrains their goals and the ways in which they learn.

According to Paulo Freire (1972; 1973; 1985), facilitators need to enter into dialogue with learners and promote dialogue amongst them. Dialogue involves more than simply listening to each other; it involves checking of understanding, allowing one's ideas to be criticized by others, exploring one's appreciation of the limitations placed on one's consciousness by historical and social circumstances and being prepared to change one's approach as such awareness creates a new framework within which to act. Advocates of critical pedagogy argue that much more is involved than simply raising consciousness: perspectives must be transformed and action must result. Learning is not solely an individual intellectual process – it should lead to social and political change to transform society.

This is a radical and profoundly disturbing perspective for those who hold positions of power and influence in our existing educational systems. These people tend to try to strip critical pedagogy of its ideology and treat it as just another strategy with its own strengths and weaknesses which may have value under certain circumstances (preferably in another country at another time). The development of critical consciousness is fine so long as it does not lead to radical action. To the proponents this is a contradiction in terms. Critical consciousness is created by an interplay of theory and practice; learning takes place through developing a theoretical understanding which is then tested through practical action, which leads to a fuller understanding and further action. If the humanistic educators are leading us towards freeing ourselves from our self-imposed oppressions, those in the critical tradition are leading us away from the oppression of our history and social context; they are pursuing *freedom through learning.*

Drawing from different traditions

Although I have portrayed forms representing distinct traditions, in practice a given facilitator in a given type of programme might draw on aspects of more than one. For example, as part of a learning contract a student might incorporate a structured learning package as well as a more wide ranging series of activities; or a facilitator in the critical pedagogy tradition might establish relationships with a new group through adopting approaches typical of the humanistic educators. This does not imply that the four approaches are in any sense equivalent or interchangeable, but that each may be a valid response to a given adult learning need. They have strengths in different domains and they each have weaknesses. For example, the efficiency approach, which is based upon assumptions of common priorities among learners, is not as suited to addressing unique learning needs of individuals which cannot be predicted. It can also be questioned whether 'training' should ever occur entirely in the absence of elements of one of the other traditions.

While it is not possible to treat these four positions in the same terms – they hold differing assumptions about individuals and their place in society – it is possible to note a common theme which is expressed in each in rather different ways. It is that of respect for learners and their experience. All require that facilitators respond to learners and take account of their experience, their backgrounds and the influences on them. They also acknowledge that learning must begin with the learner's present understanding, and this must be explored carefully and sympathetically. It is this characteristic which perhaps identifies the facilitator's role: facilitators begin, not with their own knowledge, but with the learners'.

My own educational practices range over these four traditions though I am more at home with some than others. My educational career started in programmed learning. It is a functional view of education and I have a respect for it and an awareness of its inherent limitations. Over the years I have incorporated much from the second and third approaches and I try to promote self-directed and interdependent learning within a group setting with the students with whom I work. My experience with the fourth is more limited and I am yet to feel comfortable with its implications: perhaps this is of its nature or maybe I do not want to address these issues. I can accept intellectually the historical and social constraints on learning and notice that they distort and limit our behaviour, but I resist the follow-through to action. It is one thing to encourage others to be self-critical, but quite another to apply it to one's own situation, as Freire and proponents of the critical tradition would demand.

Elements of facilitation

One's view of the facilitation of learning is obviously a function of the values one holds and the goals one wishes to pursue. I find it helpful in my own practice as a facilitator to think about three main aspects of my role and realize that I need to make decisions about each in any situation. These elements are firstly, the purposes of the activity or project – what the learner does and what role the facilitator plays is crucially dependent on the nature of the goals being pursued; secondly, the forms of intervention that the facilitator makes in the learning process – once the type of goals are determined the facilitator has continual decisions to make about when and how to intervene in the learning process; and thirdly, the role of reflection and evaluation – the importance of reflecting upon and evaluating learning experiences and how facilitators can help in this are being increasingly recognized. These are elements which I believe are of importance irrespective of the tradition upon which one draws.

Purposes

The kinds of learning in which adults engage are a function of their goals and interests. On many occasions, though, these will not have been articulated clearly and learners may not yet be in a position to be able to state them at all in terms that others can readily appreciate. Often goals will emerge only after periods of long exploration, and these goals may change as a result of the continuing events that learners experience.

The kinds of facilitation which are appropriate will vary depending on the learners and the nature of the tasks in which they are engaged. For example, adults returning to study after a period in the workforce or after raising a family may initially be seeking to prove to themselves that they have the capacity to study again. This goal might take on much greater prominence than anything to do with the ostensible content of the courses they are studying. Once self-confidence has been regained then the learner may be in the position of making much greater demands on the subject expertise of the facilitator than on the facilitator's skills of study counselling.

While I have suggested that there is a basic core of facilitator behaviour which involves listening to learners and respecting their needs and interests, the ways in which this will manifest itself will vary. Most people will not like being treated as if they were in need of counselling; they may want to react to proposals made by the facilitator or they may want to try out ideas or test new behaviours as a starting point to their learning projects. They may want and expect quite specific information and guidance from the facilitator, but this always needs to be given in the supportive context and with an eye open for what the learners' underlying needs appear to be. Facilitators must be flexible, reacting to particular needs at any time as they change.

How the facilitators operate also depends on the types of knowledge outcome which are required of a learning activity. Mezirow, drawing on Habermas (1971), differentiates between three interrelated but distinct functions of adult learning. The role and approach of the facilitator is likely to differ in each.

The first kind, instrumental learning, is task-oriented problem-solving relevant for controlling the environment or other people:

> This kind of learning always involves a prediction about observable things or events that can be proved correct or incorrect . . . Learning is directed towards determination of cause-effect relationships. The knowledge gained is prescriptive. Action is instrumental in nature, involving attempts to increase one's control in order to increase one's success in performance . . . Instrumental learning is learning how to; it does not deal with why. *(Mezirow, 1985, p 18)*

Instrumental learning dominates most educational institutions. Although it clearly occurs in the learning of mathematics and in training for games and sports, instrumental learning is often found in areas concerning interpersonal relations where it may be less appropriate and may make unwarranted assumptions about how human beings should relate to one another. Mezirow believes the assumption that all adult learning proceeds as instrumental learning causes a severe distortion of the kinds of activities which are found in continuing education. The training and efficiency tradition is an example of instrumental learning par excellance.

Facilitation for instrumental learning seeks to enable learners to take control of their environment and the events which occur in it so that they can operate more effectively within it. It should help them construct models of their world and assist them to make predictions about what will occur within it. The kinds of activities facilitators are concerned with in instrumental learning are monitoring the constructs held by learners, guiding them towards more effective ones by giving them precise and detailed feedback on their performance. Often facilitation which itself takes an instrumental approach will be used for instrumental learning, but this need not necessarily be the case. A learner could acquire instrumental knowledge with the help of a facilitator who adopted a person-centred approach.

The second kind of learning identified by Mezirow (1985) is what he terms 'dialogic learning'. Most of the significant learning in adulthood is not of a type that allows us to control things or people; it involves moral issues, ideals, values, abstract social, political concepts, and feelings. We attempt to learn what others mean when they communicate with us. We must interpret what they mean without the benefit of any simple yardsticks for judging whether what they say is right or wrong. In our daily lives we all have to assess evidence by relying on as broad a consensus as possible of those whom we accept as informed, objective and rational. New information, which will lead us to revise our judgements, could emerge; therefore, the validity of our views arrived at through dialogue is always provisional.

> The purpose of dialogic learning is not to establish cause-effect relationships but to increase insight and understanding through symbolic interaction . . . The learner draws on his or her experience to explain, and that process suggests what to look for next. (p 20)

Facilitation in the realm of dialogic learning involves assisting learners to appreciate the difference between this form of learning and instrumental learning and trust their own assessments of situations which fall within this domain. They need to understand that for many areas of knowledge there are no correct answers, but different views which must be considered and their validity in any given situation determined by the learner. The importance of self-esteem and openness to consider the views of others cannot be underestimated. Facilitation may involve assisting learners to establish situations where they can share their ideas, values and feelings with others, and engage in mutual exploration. The tradition of the humanistic educators, particularly those aspects which involve small group learning, is a useful one on which to draw here.

The third area is that of self-reflective learning. In Mezirow's view this focuses on 'gaining a clearer understanding of oneself by identifying dependency-producing psychological assumptions acquired earlier in life that have become dysfunctional in adulthood'. We all experience events in our childhood which inhibit us and distort our lives. We may have been told to 'keep quiet', 'don't express your feelings' or, 'you are not going to succeed'; all of us receive persistent messages about how we should be in the world. Also we have usually had traumatic experiences which provoke fears and anxieties with which we are unable to deal at the time. All these experiences remain with us and they surface on particular occasions and powerfully influence our behaviour and our learning as adults.

Mezirow argues that adult educators need to be able to facilitate this important learning function; they need to increase their sophistication in the dynamics of psycho-educational practice. He mentions situations such as common life transitions: the death of a mate or child, divorce, change in job status or being passed over for promotion, retirement, mid-career burnout and others.

> The learner is presented with an alternative way of interpreting feelings and patterns of action; the old meaning or perspective is reorganized to incorporate new insights; we come to see our reality more inclusively, to understand it more clearly, and to integrate our experience better. Only the individual involved can determine the validity of the reorganized meaning scheme or perspective. *(p 21)*

The kinds of facilitation required may take this form, which draws on psychoanalytical therapy. Co-counselling (*see* Heron, 1973) and other methods adopt a more humanistic perspective; they may be more effective in my view.

An important dimension within the category of selt-reflective learning is often omitted by North American writers, although Mezirow does refer to it. Not all distortions of experience can be traced back to traumatic childhood events; many are socially and politically determined and persist through our lives. They are not necessarily amenable to the individual-centred approaches of the psychotherapist or humanistic educator. Individuals are continually oppressed by virtue of their class, race, sex, religion and many other factors. Such oppression needs to be dealt with on a societal scale through social and political action, and there are substantial adult learning tasks involved in removing these oppressive forces. Dealing with the individual alone may help some people to adjust more satisfactorily to their circumstances, but it will not change the factors which fuel the problem. Facilitation is required in this area to assist people to recognize the factors which limit them and to develop a critical consciousness. It is this area in which those of the critical pedagogy school operate and it is to this group that we need to look for some of the strategies which are required.

Whatever the kind of learning being pursued, the desires of learners should always influence the strategies and behaviour of facilitators. However, facilitators may not always judge it prudent to do exactly what is asked of them; as educators they must stand for certain values themselves. For any given domain of knowledge there are a variety of ways of approaching learning tasks. For example, even with an apparently simple task in the technical domain, greater or lesser degrees of learner autonomy can be promoted; Mager and Clark (1963) demonstrated that adult students were more effective in learning electronics when they controlled what they learned than they were when instructed by experienced trainers. Different learners need to be treated differently, and usually they are better judges of what they need to do than are facilitators.

This should not undermine the facilitators' role, but it should caution them to pay sufficient attention to the individuals and the group they are faced with if they are to be fully responsive to their needs.

Forms of intervention

Facilitators will normally be influenced by their own values, the purposes of the activity with which they are associated, and particularly by the kind of learning they are involved in assisting. However, they still have considerable room for manoeuvre and many decisions to take about the approach they will adopt. Heron (1977) has proposed six dimensions of facilitator style which represent the main options that are open to a facilitator of a group. These parallel an analysis he undertook of the dimensions of facilitator interventions in a one-to-one situation (Heron, 1975) which Reason and Marshall discuss in their chapter. While Heron makes no claim for these representing the dimensions of facilitation in all adult learning contexts, his views are helpful in considering the range of things a facilitator might legitimately do. The dimensions are:

Directive-nondirective: the facilitator takes responsibility for deciding what the group does; or delegates this responsibility to the group.

Interpretive-noninterpretive: the facilitator conceptualizes and gives meaning to what is going on in the group; or at most indicates behavioural phenomena in the group and leaves conceptualizing them open to the group.

Confronting-nonconfronting: the facilitator supportively but directly challenges defensive and distorted behaviour in the group; or creates a climate in which the participant confronts him/herself from within.

Cathartic-noncathartic: the facilitator actively elicits cathartic release in the group through laughter, sobbing, trembling, storming; or creates a climate of tension-reduction without catharsis.

Structuring-unstructuring: the facilitator structures the group process in one or more of a variety of ways in order to provide specific types of experiential learning and self-discovery; or provides the type of experiential learning that is consequent of no such structuring.

Disclosing-nondisclosing: the facilitator shares her own feelings, thoughts and responses with the group; or is present to the group in silent ways.

Heron considers but rejects a seventh dimension – political-nonpolitical – concerning explicit connection to or transfer from what is going on in the group to political and social change and action outside the group. He considers that drawing out the political implications of group work can be done by being directive, being interpretive, being confronting and being structuring.

For each of these dimensions Heron considers the type of behaviour which can be facilitative, gives examples of each, discusses how facilitators can gain feedback on their own styles and generally how skills in these areas can be developed. He argues that facilitators can be more effective by developing their capabilities in aspects of the dimensions in which they are weak, and by developing the ability to range widely and freely over the dimensions according to the purpose of the learning activity and the needs of the learners. In workshops using this type of framework, I have found such an analysis of my own approaches very illuminating and I have been unable to identify any other approach which has been quite as effective in enabling me to pinpoint specific areas in which I need to develop my own skills and sensitivities.

Time and timing are other important considerations when deciding on forms of intervention because learning projects extend over time, relationships change and the nature of facilitation may vary depending on the stage an individual has reached in his or her own exploration. At an early stage encouragement and acceptance may be useful; later, challenge and the presentation of other perspectives; later still, evaluation and testing of ideas; later yet, further encouragement and acceptance to see the task through to completion. The nature of the interventions a facilitator makes changes through the cycle of learning.

Reflection

Although Mezirow (1985) talks about self-reflective learning as a particular function of adult learning, reflection is a key element in *any* learning from experience. Human learning is a complex process which is not fully understood. However, it is clear that much of the learning in which adults engage requires considerable effort on the part of learners, not just in receiving new ideas but in assimilating them, adjusting their behaviour in the light of them and taking action of many different kinds. Of great importance in this is the ways in which learners process the experiences they have: the ways in which they reflect on them.

Reflection has usually been assumed to take place automatically, or if conscious effort is required this has normally been regarded as entirely in the province of the individual learner. The learner may want to keep notes, write a diary of personal experiences or talk through his or her activities with others, but that is the business of the individual learner. It is activities of this kind that are effective in helping people learn from their experiences and they do not necessarily occur without prompting. It is important for learners to understand reflection and how they might engage in it, and for facilitators to know how to promote it.

Some colleagues and I have developed a simple schema which focuses on the stages that people reflecting on their learning might proceed through (Boud, Keogh and Walker, 1985). This identifies the main areas in which learners may need to make decisions about the kinds of reflection in which they might engage. This model suggests that the first step might be to *return to the experience*, for participants to recall in detail exactly what happened: who they met, who said what, how each person reacted, what they felt at each point in time, what occupied their attention, what else was going on. The idea is to recapture, in as much detail as possible, the full experience of the event and the reactions of all those associated with it. An individual may do this alone and unaided, but it is helpful to write it down, or recount it to another person, or report it to the group. The facilitator can help in this by prompting learners to describe as objectively as possible what has happened and helping them to avoid interpretations and analysis.

The second step which is useful in reflection is *attending to feelings.* Some aspects of an event provoke stronger feelings than others. These feelings may be experienced as positive, feeling good, negative, feeling bad, frustrated, upset or worried. Sometimes these will be quite simple and participants may have expressed themselves at the time saying what they felt to others. More commonly there will be other occasions when they could recall their feelings but they, quite appropriately, expressed nothing at the time. These times can often have significance for learning, but in formal educational settings these are suppressed as feelings have often not been regarded as legitimate matters on which to focus. Learners can be helped by being encouraged and supported in becoming aware of their feelings and provided with options for how they might work with them.

Sometimes it may be sufficient for them to acknowledge their feelings, just to savour the good ones and pass over the others, but at other times it will be useful for them to express the unexpressed. Not only do the feelings need to be identified, but often the learner needs to work with them to understand their significance and to find ways of discharging, transforming or celebrating them. Heron (1977) discusses some of the approaches which might be used for this in his cathartic-noncathartic dimension. Again, they can attend to their feelings and express them by themselves or on paper, but for this aspect it is often more useful to have another person to listen and be supportive.

The third step, *re-evaluating the experience*, logically occurs after the others, but aspects of it take place in parallel with the first two. This is the stage where new experiences can be related to prior experiences and new knowledge can be fitted into one's existing way of looking at the world. This step is termed *re*-evaluating the experience because evaluation occurs throughout: most people make judgements about events as they occur, but these immediate, unconsidered assessments may not be an adequate foundation on which to rest learning. It is often necessary to re-evaluate, to turn again (and again) to our experience, to examine what it tells us. It can be useful to think of the separate elements of this step, but many of these can occur in parallel with one another and the particular order may vary. The components of the re-evaluation stage are:

Association: the connecting of the ideas and feelings which are a part of the original experience, and those which have occurred during reflection, with existing knowledge and attitudes. Some of the techniques which can be used for this are: free association, allowing oneself to suspend judgement and note whatever comes to mind; or brainstorming of ideas, a form of group association where ideas are initially collected without evaluation. Some people find it useful, depending on what has taken place, to construct diagrams or lists or note analogies. Facilitators can assist by making suggestions about options and by organizing structured activities such as brainstorming sessions.

Integration: processing the associations to examine whether they are meaningful and useful. This may involve looking at patterns in associations, grouping them together, drawing simple maps of linkages, relating the ideas generated to others. In the example this could occur by taking the list of implications and looking for common themes or links between the ideas expressed, by elaborating some and rejecting others. Facilitators can introduce strategies to promote integration.

Validation: subjecting the ideas and feelings which have started to be integrated to what might be called 'reality tests', such as looking for internal consistency between new appreciations and existing knowledge and beliefs, for consistency between these and parallel data from others, or trying out new perceptions in new situations. A facilitator might, for example, help a group to examine how they might take the ideas which they have generated and explore how they might be used in a practical situation through role play, or by checking these ideas out against each individual's experience.

Appropriation: making new knowledge an integral part of how we act and how we feel. This is an element of the process which people may or may not experience once they have worked on a particular event thoroughly. This may occur in our example through one or more people having an insight into how they conduct themselves with others which might affect all their subsequent interactions with others, such as in realizing the off-putting effect that one of their favourite conversational openings has and finding an effective alternative.

In any given situation it may be appropriate for learners to work through these stages systematically using some of the approaches suggested. On other occasions it might be best to concentrate on one aspect in the group and encourage other components to take place outside the group or to plan a separate activity which involves a mixture of group and individual activities. Individuals can facilitate these processes for themselves through keeping diaries and journals and working systematically on them using devices such as those discussed by Rainer (1980).

The kind of reflection in which learners engage may not be critical in the sense used by Freire and Mezirow. Learners will be re-evaluating what they do and arriving at new understandings, but they may not be questioning their taken-for-granted assumptions or becoming aware of how they have been shaped by their environment. Kemmis (1985) and Brookfield (1986) would probably argue that it is necessary to go further than the Boud, Keogh and Walker model. Facilitators need to intervene more actively; as Brookfield puts it:

> . . . the task of the teacher of adults is to help [learners] to realize that the bodies of knowledge, accepted truths, commonly held values, and customary behaviours comprising their worlds are contextually and culturally constructed . . . As teachers, we are charged with not always accepting definitions of felt needs as our operating criteria. We are also charged with the imperative of assisting adults to contemplate alternatives, to come to see the world as malleable, to be critically reflective, and to perceive themselves as proactive beings. *(p 125)*

This view is not inconsistent with the reflective schema above, but it does emphasize a particular role for the facilitator.

However, we should be cautious about accepting any imperative for the role of teacher or facilitator of adult learning. Brookfield writes with a particular view of the mission of adult educators: not all of those who seek to assist others in their learning would identify with this. Facilitators need to be any or all of the following, depending on the situation in which they operate and the learners with whom they are working:

- presenter of expertise;
- democrat and student-centred guide
- provider of access to personal and material resources;
- supporter and encourager;
- critical friend and stimulator of critical reflection; and
- challenger of taken-for-granted assumptions.

The challenging of beliefs and behaviours is not invariably the role of the facilitator any more than is being the presenter of information. In any context at any particular time, one or other of the roles will predominate.

What is important for facilitators of adult learning is that they are able, as circumstances indicate, to deploy themselves with appropriate emphasis on any aspect of their potential roles and that they have facility in doing so. To adopt the 'critical' role too enthusiastically is just as limiting as uncritically accepting learners' initial definitions of their needs. In any situation there will be at least an implied contract between facilitator and learner which, while not specifying fully the range of permissible and legitimate interventions by the facilitator into the world of the learner, will suggest boundaries which the facilitator should consider transgressing only with great care and with a high level of self-awareness. To promote actively critical reflection at any opportunity can be to take an important learning experience of the facilitator and to project it on to the learner. Reflection used in the sense of the processing of experiences supported by others and critical reflection in the sense of the active questioning of experience typically prompted by others are both equally important and complementary aspects of the facilitator's role.

Directions for facilitation

The preceding ideas were ones which had influenced me before the commencement of this book and, to a greater or lesser extent, I have been able to apply them and allow them to influence what I do as a facilitator. Having now read the earlier chapters I have a wealth of other ideas to consider. I have not had a chance to assimilate them all yet, but already I can pick out themes which I wish to ponder further to examine the impact which they might make on my practice. Some are articulations of notions which I had recognized previously but which had not entered my consciousness as a facilitator; others have given me food for thought as I grapple with their implications. Different readers will identify different themes, but for me the following are the most important questions for my practice as a facilitator of learning. Adult learning is becoming better understood, but there are many questions which still need to be addressed. (The chapters which prompted the thoughts are indicated in brackets.)

> How can I deal with the deadening effects of excessive seriousness in what I do? How can I inject a sense of playfulness without it degenerating into flippancy or apparent irrelevance to those with whom I am working? *(Melamed)*

> How can I respect the intuitive dimension and accommodate it in rational plans for programmes? I can accept the importance of the intuitive, but how should a recognition of the non-linearity of people's thinking influence my designs for learning and my interactions with learners? *(Denis and Richter)*

> Energy in groups and learners is an intuitively appealing concept and at one level I realize I act differently when I see a group exhibiting high or low energy, but how do I explain it in a way that communicates it clearly: the more closely defined, the more elusive it becomes? *(Davies)*

Dependence, independence and interdependence are all stages through which learners may progress and facilitators can enhance or inhibit this movement through their attitudes and actions. How can I do more to empower learners to take responsibility for their learning without it leaving me disempowered? *(Griffith)*

What role do I have in facilitating significant personal learning? Is there any role between that of friend and professional which is sustainable? *(Brookfield)*

Can I encourage those learning with me to explore in those areas where I fear to venture myself? Is it responsible for me to let my resistances block my explorations while expecting others not to be constrained? *(Robertson)*

It is easy to underestimate the doubts which learners face and fail to recognize that these doubts are present in almost every learning situation. How can I more effectively acknowledge these doubts and help learners realize their self-worth and self-confidence? *(Keane)*

Promoting horizontal changes in consciousness sounds ambitious enough; what can I do to foster Weiser's vertical integration? *(Weiser)*

Research is one of the great forms of collective learning but its value as a form of personal learning does not have to be obscured by the legitimate demands of public knowledge. How can I satisfy both myself and the research community? *(Reason and Marshall)*

While learning can be thought of as a kind of personal research, the ability to conduct research which respects people's experience requires a sensitivity to how people learn. How can I assist the research students that I supervise to develop the sensitivity and acquire the necessary skills? *(Maclean)*

Facilitation involves more than what teachers do: administrative and organizational arrangements can be just as important in promoting learning. *(Apps)*

Not only those designated as facilitators, but all co-learners can help and hinder learning. How can I effectively share the facilitator role with others? In formal courses, how can I ensure that my responsibility for student assessment does not undermine my ability to foster learning? *(Hodgson) and Reynolds)*

What unexamined assumptions am I bringing to my role as facilitator? Can my strategies and interventions be justified with respect to learning? How am I constrained by my ideology of teaching or facilitation? *(Candy)*

The role of the facilitator changes over time, and the types and nature of interventions change similarly. Groups have a life of their own: do I have 'sufficient humility about the limits of my influence'? *(Taylor)*

My perceptions of what learning involves have gone through substantial shifts similar to those described by Lynn Davie; no doubt there will be further changes in my outlook. Some ways of looking at learning and assessment will endure, but others will be seen to be simply a reflection of the concerns of the times. What will I continue to accept and what will I need to reject of my present perceptions? *(Davie)*

Naming the process is an empowering activity: it can lead to greater confidence in learning and respect for one's own experience. However, any form of labelling has limitations, so under what circumstances is naming the process valuable and when is it not? *(Griffin)*

These questions occur to me when I think of myself as a facilitator, but of course they are central to me as a learner as I come to understand my own learning. After completing this book I am only too aware of vital issues which we have not addressed: for example, the influence of sexism, classism and racism in learning, the power of the institutional context – the list can go on. We have to stop somewhere and let others continue the exploration. Appreciating adults learning is a continuing process.

References

Boud, D J (1986). *Implementing Student Self-Assessment.* Sydney: Higher Education Research and Development Society of Australasia.

Boud, D J, Keogh, R and Walker, D (1985). Promoting reflection in learning: a model. In: D J Boud, R Keogh and D Walker (eds). *Reflection: Turning Experience into Learning.* London: Kogan Page, 18-40.

Brockett, R (1983). Facilitator roles and skills. *Lifelong Learning: the Adult Years.* 6, 7-9.

Brookfield, S D (1986) *Understanding and Facilitating Adult Learning.* Milton Keynes: Open University Press.

Brown, G I (1976). *The Live Classroom: Innovation Through Confluent Education and Gestalt.* New York: Penguin.

Davies, I K (1971). *The Management of Learning.* London: McGraw-Hill.

Davies, I K (1976). *Objectives in Curriculum Design.* London: McGraw-Hill.

Egan, G (1975). *The Skilled Helper: a Model for Systematic Helping and Interpersonal Relating.* Monterey, California: Brooks Cole.

Friere, P (1972). *The Pedagogy of the Oppressed.* Harmondsworth: Penguin.

Freire, P (1973). *Education for Critical Consciousness.* London: Sheed and Ward.

Freire, P (1985). *The Politics of Education.* South Hadley, Massachusetts: Bergin and Garvey.

Gagné, R M (1970). *The Conditions of Learning.* (Second edition) New York: Holt, Rinehart and Winston.

Gagné, R M (1974). *Essentials of Learning for Instruction.* Hinsdale, Illinois: Dryden Press.

Habermas, J (1971). *Knowledge and Human Interest.* Boston: Beacon Press.

Heron, J (1973). Re-evaluation counselling: personal growth through mutual aid. *British Journal of Guidance and Counselling.* 1, 2, 26-36.

Heron, J (1975). *Six Category Intervention Analysis.* Guildford, Surrey: Human Potential Research Project, University of Surrey.

Heron, J (1976). A six-category intervention analysis. *British Journal of Guidance and Counselling.* 4, 2, 143-55.

Heron, J (1977). *Dimensions of Facilitator Style.* Guildford, Surrey: Human Potential Research Project, University of Surrey.

Kemmis, S (1986). Action research and the politics of reflection. In: D J Boud, R Keogh and D Walker (eds). *Reflection: Turning Experience into Learning.* London: Kogan Page, 139-63.

Knowles, M S (1975). *Self-Directed Learning: a Guide for Learners and Teachers.* Chicago: Follet.

Knowles, M S (1980). *The Modern Practice of Adult Education: From Pedagogy to Andragogy.* (Second edition) New York: Cambridge Books.

Knowles, M S (1984a). *The Adult Learner: a Neglected Species.* Houston, Texas: Gulf.

Knowles, M S and Associates (1984b). *Andragogy in Action: Applying Modern Principles of Adult Learning.* San Francisco: Jossey-Bass.

Knowles, M S (1986). *Using Learning Contracts.* San Francisco: Jossey-Bass.

Mager, R F (1972). *Goal Analysis.* Belmont, California: Fearon.

Mager, R F (1975). *Preparing Instructional Objectives.* (Second edition) Belmont, California: Fearon.

Mager, R F and Clark, C (1963). Explorations in student controlled instruction. *Psychological Reports.* 13, 71-6.

Mezirow, J (1985). A critical theory of self-directed learning. In: S Brookfield (ed). *Self-Directed Learning: From Theory to Practice. New Directions for Continuing Education No. 25.* San Francisco: Jossey-Bass, 17-30.

Perls, F S (1969). *Gestalt Therapy Verbatim.* Moab, Utah: Real People Press.

Rainer, T (1980). *The New Diary.* London: Angus and Robertson.

Rogers, C R (1961). *On Becoming a Person.* Boston: Houghton Mifflin.

Rogers, C R (1970). *Carl Rogers on Encounter Groups.* New York: Harper and Row.

Rogers, C R (1983). *Freedom to Learn for the 80s.* Columbus, Ohio: Charles E Merrill.

Schutz, W C (1975). *Elements of Encounter.* New York: Bantam.

Index